The
Economist
as Preacher
and Other Essays

Mar. $85 $ 5. 95   gift of Helen Carmley

George J. Stigler, 1911

The
Economist
as Preacher
and Other Essays

The University of Chicago Press

George J. Stigler is the Charles R. Walgreen Distinguished Service Professor Emeritus in the Department of Economics and in the Graduate School of Business at the University of Chicago. He is also the director of the Center for the Study of the Economy and the State and the editor of the *Journal of Political Economy*.

THE UNIVERSITY OF CHICAGO PRESS, CHICAGO 60637
BASIL BLACKWELL PUBLISHER, OXFORD OX4 1JF
© 1982 by The University of Chicago
All rights reserved. Published 1982
Printed in the United States of America
89 88 87 86 85 84 83   2 3 4 5

Library of Congress Cataloging in Publication Data

Stigler, George Joseph, 1911–
 The economist as preacher, and other essays.

 Bibliography: p. 255.
 Includes index.
 1. Economics—Addresses, essays, lectures.
 2. Economics—Moral and ethical aspects—Addresses, essays, lectures. 3. Economics—History—Addresses, essays, lectures. I. Title.
 HB71.S83   330   82-4807
 ISBN 0-226-77430-9   AACR2

Contents

Preface   vii

Part I: Economics or Ethics?
1. The Economist as Preacher   3
2. The Ethics of Competition: The Friendly Economists   14
3. The Ethics of Competition: The Unfriendly Critics   27
4. The Economists and the Problem of Monopoly   38

Part II: The Sociology of the History of Science
5. Do Economists Matter?   57
6. Textual Exegesis as a Scientific Problem   68
7. The Adoption of the Marginal Utility Theory   72
8. The Scientific Uses of Scientific Biography, with Special Reference to J. S. Mill   86
9. Merton on Multiples, Denied and Affirmed   98

Part III: History of Economic Thought
10. Does Economics Have a Useful Past?   107
11. The Economist and the State   119
12. Smith's Travels on the Ship of State   136
13. The Successes and Failures of Professor Smith   146
14. Mill on Economics and Society   160
15. Henry Calvert Simons   166

Part IV: Quantitative Studies
16. The Pattern of Citation Practices in Economics   *with Claire Friedland*   173
17. The Citation Practices of Doctorates in Economics   *with Claire Friedland*   192
18. The Literature of Economics: The Case of the Kinked Oligopoly Demand Curve   223

Bibliography of Works by George J. Stigler   245

Index   255

Preface

Almost all of the essays in this volume are concerned with questions of intellectual influence. What are the influences that determine which problems the members of a science work on, and how they will deal with them? How do the work and views of scientists influence their societies? My scientists are naturally all economists, but the questions are pervasive.

I cannot promise that the reader will find direct, let alone complete, answers to these questions; for intellectual and political influences are extraordinarily subtle and difficult to trace or measure. A scholar seeking the most candid replies from himself about the major influences on his own ideas and work will testify to the complexity of the relationships. Still, I nibble away at the problems in a variety of ways which I hope will interest others and lead them to improve upon my efforts.

I am happy to acknowledge *some* influence upon me by my conversations with Aaron Director, Gary Becker, Milton Friedman, and other friends. Claire Friedland was indispensable in making the quantitative studies in part 4. I wish also to express my thanks for permissions to reprint the indicated essays to the American Economic Association, for "The Economist and the State" and "The Economists and the Problem of Monopoly"; Duke University Press, for "Does Economics Have a Useful Past?" "Smith's Travels on the Ship of State," "The Adoption of the Marginal Utility Theory," and "The Pattern of Citation Practices in Economics"; *Economica*, for "Textual Exegesis as a Scientific Problem"; New York Academy of Science, for "Merton on Multiples, Denied and Affirmed"; *Southern Economic Journal*, for "Do Economists Matter?"; University of Toronto Press, for "Mill on Economics and Society" and "The Scientific Uses of Scientific Biography, with Special Reference to J. S. Mill"; Western Economic Association, for "The Literature of Economics: The Case of the Kinked Oligopoly Demand Curve."

Finally, the three initial essays were delivered as the Tanner Lectures on Human Values at Harvard University, April 24, 25, and 28, 1980, and originally published in *The Tanner Lectures on Human Values*, volume 2, by the University of Utah Press and Cambridge University Press, 1981. They are reprinted with the permission of The Tanner Lectures on Human Values, a corporation.

Part One   Economics or Ethics?

1

The Economist as Preacher

Economists seldom address ethical questions as they impinge on economic theory or economic behavior. They (and I) find this subject complex and elusive in comparison with the relative precision and objectivity of economic analysis. Of course the ethical questions are inescapable: one must have goals in judging policies, and these goals will certainly have ethical content, however well concealed it may be. These lectures will explore some of the problems raised by ethical questions, using the history of economics as an important vehicle in the exploration.

In this first lecture I propose to discuss how economists—primarily great English economists in the main line of development of economics—have advised men and societies on proper conduct. My interest on this occasion is not so much in the advice they have given as in the ethical basis on which this advice has been grounded. Economists have no special professional knowledge of that which is virtuous or just, and the question naturally arises as to how they are able to deliver confident and distinctive advice to a society that is already well supplied with that commodity.

1. How Much Preaching?

The first, probably the most important, and possibly the most surprising thing to say about the economist-preachers is that they have done very little preaching. I suppose that it is essential to state what I mean by preaching. I mean simply a clear and reasoned recommendation (or, more often, denunciation) of a policy or form of behavior by men or societies of men. It is hardly desirable to label every non-neutral word as preaching—indeed our language is rather short of words that cannot be used in such a way as to hint of approval or disapproval. During a recent war one economist remarked that he was against "business as usual," and a second was moved to ask whether the speaker was against "business, comma, as usual."

Reprinted from *The Tanner Lectures on Human Values*, vol. 2 (Salt Lake City: University of Utah Press; Cambridge: Cambridge University Press, 1981).

I wish to express my gratitude to Gary Becker, Richard Posner, and Stephen Stigler for important assistance, and acknowledge my immense debt to Aaron Director for discussions of these issues both during the preparation of the lectures and in the many years of our friendship. Most of the writing was done while I was a visiting scholar at the Hoover Institution at Stanford University, and I thank Glenn Campbell for providing this attractive setting.

I shall illustrate my loose definition of preaching and many subsequent points by quotations from famous economists, and I digress for a moment to explain their authority to any non-economists who are present. All but one of the economists I quote were highly intelligent, disciplined men whose views on subjects related to economics deserve your attention and thoughtful consideration, but no more. One, Adam Smith, is differently placed: if on first hearing a passage of his you are inclined to disagree, you are reacting inefficiently; the correct response is to say to yourself: I wonder where I went amiss?

When Adam Smith speaks of the debasement of the currency—which of course proceeds at a much more rapid pace today than it did during his lifetime—he says, "By means of those operations the princes and sovereign states which performed them were enabled, in appearance, to pay their debts and to fulfill their engagements with a smaller quantity of silver than would otherwise have been requisite. It was indeed in appearance only; for their creditors were really defrauded of a part of what was due to them."[1] I consider this to be preaching since "fraud" is not merely a descriptive word. On this mild and I hope reasonable definition of a moral judgment, I have just quoted the only clear example of preaching in the first hundred pages of the *Wealth of Nations*. The preaching becomes more frequent in Smith's latter pages, but it is almost nonexistent in Ricardo's *Principles*, quite sparse in Mill's *Principles*, and virtually nonexistent in Marshall's *Principles*. Of course these admirable men expressed approval or disapproval of many things with every degree of literary subtlety. It would be easy to compile many remarks like Jevons's that the Morrill Tariff Act of 1861 was "the most retrograde piece of legislation that this [nineteenth] century has witnessed," in which disapproval is at least hinted at.[2] But these dicta are noteworthy for their scarcity rather than their frequency in the professional works of the economists.

The proposition that economists are not addicted to taking frequent and disputatious policy positions will appear incredible to most non-economists, and implausible to many economists. The reason, I believe, for this opinion is that in talking to a non-economist, there is hardly anything in economics except policy for the economist to talk about. The layman is unequipped to discuss with an economist the problems that concern professional economics at any time: he would find that in their professional writing the well-known columnists of *Newsweek* are quite incomprehensible. The typical article in a professional journal is unrelated to public policy—and often apparently unrelated to this world.

1. *The Wealth of Nations*, Glasgow ed. (Oxford: Clarendon Press, 1976), I, 43–44.
2. *The Coal Question* (London: Macmillan, 1865), p. 326.

Whether the amount of policy-advising activity of economists is rising or falling I do not know, but it is not what professional economics is about.

The great economists, then, have not been preoccupied with preaching. Indeed, none has become great because of his preaching—but perhaps I should make an exception for Marx, whom some people rank as a great economist and I rank as an immensely influential one. The fact that the world at large thinks of us as ardent enthusiasts for a hundred policies is not pure error, but it tells more about what the world likes to talk about than what economics is about. The main task of economics has always been to explain real economic phenomena in general terms, and throughout the last two centuries we have adhered to this task with considerable faithfulness, if not always with considerable success.

2. Preaching to Whom?

It is my impression that the clergy of former times devoted their finest efforts to mending the behavior of individuals, but that in recent times they have sought rather to mend social policy. Whether this impression be right or wrong, economists have seldom spent much time exhorting individuals to higher motives or more exemplary conduct.

Again I return to Mr. Smith. The servants of great joint stock companies such as the East India Company, Smith avers, were concerned only with their own personal fortunes.

> Nothing could be more compleatly foolish than to expect that the clerks of a great counting-house at ten thousand miles distance, and consequently almost quite out of sight, should, upon a simple order from their masters, give up at once doing any sort of business upon their own account, abandon for ever all hopes of making a fortune, of which they have the means in their hands, and content themselves with the moderate salaries which those masters allow them, and which, moderate as they are, can seldom be augmented, being commonly as large as the real profits of the company trade can afford. . . . They will employ the whole authority of government, and pervert the administration of justice, in order to harass and ruin those who interfere with them in any branch of commerce which, by means of agents, either concealed, or at least not publickly avowed, they may publickly chuse to carry on.[3]

After having described these wretchedly venal servants, who exploit both their masters and their victims, Smith hurries on to say, "I mean not, however, by any thing which I have here said, to throw any odious

3. *Wealth of Nations*, II, 638–39.

imputation upon the general character of the servants of the East India Company, and much less upon that of any particular persons. It is the system of government, the situation in which they are placed, that I mean to censure; not the character of those who have acted in it."[4] So it is social institutions that one should castigate: men respond to these situations in predictable, and probably unchangeable, ways. This is not to approve or disapprove of the principle of self-interest that guides men, although Smith might well have agreed with the remark of Frank H. Knight, whom we shall later meet more intimately, that anything which is inevitable is ideal!

Smith's general practice of addressing little preaching to individuals in their private behavior has continued to this day to be the practice of economists. Of course mortal man cannot wholly abstain from all instruction to the young, the inferior, and the great, and an enumeration of these acts would be amusing to you and embarrassing to me. Malthus complained that the lower classes were excessively attentive to what he termed "the passion between the sexes," and even John Stuart Mill shared with him a propensity to propose Draconian methods of dealing with the popular implementation of this passion. Alfred Marshall pointed out the unwisdom of gambling with the aid of the law of diminishing marginal utility, but later, fortunately, Milton Friedman and Jimmie Savage were able to excuse this activity with the aid of a law of increasing marginal utility. A vast number of economists have believed that the sin of myopia with respect to future needs is pervasive. We were once told that a corporation has no soul to damn or body to kick—a statement that has been emphatically and prosperously refuted by many politicians to this day. Yet surely a devil embodied in a person is a much more satisfying object of dislike and disapproval than some impersonal institution. These lapses of economists from concern with social rather than individual behavior are forgivable—a concession to their membership in the human race.

But the lapses are not defensible. Social policies and institutions, not individual behavior, are the proper object of the economist-preacher's solicitude. This orientation is demanded by the very logic of economic theory: we deal with people who maximize their utility, and it would be both inconsistent and idle for us to urge people not to do so. If we could persuade a monopolist not to maximize profits, then other reformers could persuade resources not to flow to their most remunerative uses, and our theory would become irrelevant.

3. Preaching Efficiency

In the economists' sermons the dominant theme has been that good policy favors, and bad policy interferes with, the maximizing of income of

4. Ibid., II, 641.

a society. We shall find other themes, but over the last two hundred years efficiency in the sense of fuller achievement of uncontroversial goals has been the main prescription of normative economists. Let us first look at a major example before turning to an examination of the content and authority of this primary rule of good conduct.

The most sustained application of this principle by Adam Smith was in the attack on interferences with free trade and on mercantilism generally; he devoted one-fourth of his large treatise to this cause. Smith thus asserted that:

> The natural effort of every individual to better his own condition, when suffered to exert itself with freedom and security, is so powerful a principle, that it is alone, and without any assistance, not only capable of carrying on the society to wealth and prosperity, but of surmounting a hundred impertinent obstructions with which the folly of human laws too often incumbers its operations; though the effect of these obstructions is always more or less either to encroach upon its freedom, or to diminish its security.[5]

The argument for free trade was deepened some forty years later by the theory of comparative costs, but the central policy conclusion remained, in Ricardo's words, that "under a system of perfectly free commerce, each country naturally devotes its capital and labour to such employments as are most beneficial to each."[6] This position has been almost universally accepted by economists to this day.

Many other examples, but none more important, of the economists' use of efficiency as the criterion for desirable economic policy could be given. The central element of the criticism of monopoly is that it reduces the efficiency of the use of resources. The central element of the criticism of labor market interferences, such as minimum wage laws or barriers to geographical or occupational mobility, has been their effect on the allocation of resources. An economist is a person who, reading of the confinement of Edmond Dantès in a small cell, laments his lost alternative product.

In Smith's time and for a few decades thereafter the argument for efficiency was embellished with a rhetoric of sacred and inviolable rights of natural liberty. But if the concern with natural liberty was ever strong,[7] it had disappeared by the mid-Victorian age.

---

5. Ibid., I, 540.
6. David Ricardo, *Principles of Political Economy and Taxation*, P. Sraffa ed. (Cambridge: Cambridge University Press, 1951), p. 133.
7. Of which I have some doubts. Thus Smith declares that prohibiting banks from issuing small bank notes is of course a violation of natural liberty, and yet it should be undertaken for the greater good of society; see *Wealth of Nations*, I, 324.

The attack on the efficiency of public policies will only be appropriate and convincing when achievement of the goals and costs of the policies are undisputed. If one policy will achieve more of a given goal than a second policy with the same cost in resources, the former policy is clearly superior, and there is no room for argument over ethics. This has indeed been the essential nature of the great majority of the economists' preachings on public policy.

On this reading, the economist-preacher has simply helped to straighten out the issues for a frequently muddled nation. John Stuart Mill explained the misunderstandings that supported mercantilism with his customary lucidity: how common discourse confused money and wealth; how a trader does not consider his venture successful until he has converted his goods into money; how money is *par excellence* the command over goods in general, ready on the instant to serve any desire as no other commodity can; how the state "derives comparatively little advantage from taxes unless it can collect them in money," and so on.

> "All these causes conspire to make both individuals and government, in estimating their means, attach almost exclusive importance to money. . . . "

But mark well the conclusion:

> "An absurdity, however, does not cease to be an absurdity when we have discovered what are the appearances which made it plausible. . . ."[8]

And there we have the answer to the question of how the economist can operate so extensively and so easily as a critic of policy when he is not in possession of a persuasive ethical system. The answer is that he needs no ethical system to criticize error: he is simply a well-trained political arithmetician. He lives in a world of social *mistakes*, ancient and modern, subtle and simple, and since he is simply pointing out to the society that what it seeks, it is seeking inefficiently, he need not quarrel with what it seeks.

A world full of mistakes, and capable of producing new mistakes quite as rapidly as the economists can correct the old mistakes! Such well-meaning, incompetent societies need their economic efficiency experts, and we are their self-chosen saviors.

Take away the linen of sophistication in which economists are nowadays dressed, and I believe that this is still the fundamental belief that underlies the large majority of the policy recommendations of our profession. There have indeed been grave income redistribution questions which are receiving increasing attention, but day in and day out for the

---

8. *Principles of Political Economy* (Toronto: University of Toronto Press, 1965), I, 67.

economist the society's problems are usually problems of efficiency. We live in a mistake-prone world.

I believe that this view of society as a community with acceptable, if not always admirable, goals but possessing only a feeble understanding of efficient methods of achieving them was and is profoundly mistaken.

The mistake in this view should have been evident simply because throughout the period I am discussing there were vigorous controversies over the goals of policy. Indeed, in every literate society, even the most dictatorial, there are critics of the goals of the society. In Ricardo's day, for example, Godwin forcefully argued that the institutions of government and property were among the main causes of social misery. Perhaps Godwin is not an apposite illustration; I suppose that an anarchist is a free trader. Consider, then, Malthus, the first professor of political economy in the history of England, who was a supporter of the very protection of agriculture which was the target of Ricardo's attack.

Malthus argued that a nation specializing in manufactures and trade could easily find that its advantages were eroded by foreign or domestic competition, and in any event could be strongly dependent upon the prosperity of its trading partners. An exclusively agricultural nation could find itself locked into a stagnant feudal social system, or alternatively it could find itself unable to employ capital efficiently once its agricultural plant ceased to grow. Hence Malthus wished a mixed agricultural-commercial system.

I shall not conceal my doubt that Malthus actually demonstrated the superiority of this mixed agricultural-commercial system, but it is surely true that he raised a cloud of complications which were only slowly dealt with by later generations of free traders. Some of these complications concern the determinants of the long-term growth and stability of economies, on which to this day economists have not found confident understanding.

There is a second, and even stronger, reason why the economist—of all people—should be reluctant to characterize a large fraction of political activity as mistaken. The discipline that assumes man to be a reasonably efficient utility maximizer is singularly ill-suited to assuming that the political activity of men bears little relationship to their desires. I have argued the theme of intelligent political behavior often enough that I must here limit myself to the barest of remarks.[9] The failure to analyze the political process—to leave it as a curious mixture of benevolent public interest and unintentional blunders—is most unsatisfactory.

9. See, however, "Smith's Travels on the Ship of State," *History of Political Economy* 3, no. 2 (Fall 1971) [chap. 12, below], and "The Theory of Economic Regulation," *The Bell Journal of Economics and Management Science* 2, no. 1 (Spring 1971), as well as the underlying literature of Anthony Downs, James Buchanan, and Gordon Tullock, and the public choice field.

Whether one accepts or rejects the high hopes that some of us now entertain for the economic theory of politics, the assumption that public policy has often been inefficient because it was based upon mistaken views has little to commend it. To believe, year after year, decade after decade, that the protective tariffs or usury laws to be found in most lands are due to confusion rather than purposeful action is singularly obfuscatory. Mistakes are indeed made by the best of men and the best of nations, but after a century are we not entitled to question whether the so-called "mistakes" produce only unintended results?

Alternatively stated, a theory that says that a large set of persistent policies are mistaken is profoundly anti-intellectual unless it is joined to a theory of mistakes. It is the most vacuous of "explanatory" principles to dismiss inexplicable phenomena as mistakes—everything under the sun, or above the sun, can be disposed of with this label, without yielding an atom of understanding.

We economists have traditionally made innumerable criticisms of the inefficiency of various policies, criticisms which have often been to their own (and my own) utter satisfaction. The meager success of these criticisms in changing these policies, I am convinced, stems from the fact that more than narrow efficiency has been involved in almost every case—that inexplicit or incomprehensible goals were served by these policies and served tolerably efficiently. Tariffs were redistributing income to groups with substantial political power, not simply expressing the deficient public understanding of the theory of comparative costs. We live in a world that is full of mistaken policies, but they are not mistaken for their supporters.

I wish to recur for a moment to the policy of mercantilism, which Smith attributed to the clever machinations of the merchants and traders against the simple, honorable landowners who still constituted the governing class of Great Britain in his time. Smith and his followers should have asked themselves whether simple error could persist, to the large and centuries-long cost of a class intelligent enough to hire the likes of Edmund Burke. I say, with great fear and trembling, that it is more probable that Smith, not the nobility of England, was mistaken as to the cost and benefits of the mercantile system. I say this for his sake: a world of great and permanent error would be a poor place for economics to live.

4. Preaching Equity

There is one large set of policies which cannot easily be judged merely as to efficiency in reaching widely accepted, comparatively uncontroversial goals: I refer to those which seek to redistribute income. If Nelson and Jones have equal incomes, and a policy takes half of Nelson's income and gives it to Jones, a question of equity will inevitably arise in the minds of everyone except Jones.

10

For the century from Smith to Jevons, economists were correspondingly discreet in their discussions of income distribution. It may be supposed that Smith thought income distribution was a matter for markets to determine when he said, "To hurt in any degree the interest of any one order of citizens, for no other purpose but to promote that of some other, is evidently contrary to that justice and equality of treatment which the sovereign owes to all the different orders of his subjects."[10] I am inclined to accept this view even though one can find occasional departures such as his proposal to tax the "indolence and vanity of the rich" by having disproportionately heavy tolls on carriages of luxury (II, 246), for these departures are few and casual.[11]

The classical school did not depart far from Smith's practice. The evil effects of equality were held to be two: a decrease in incentives to thrift and work; and an increase in the population on Malthus' principles. Ricardo would deny the suffrage to those who would not respect the rights of property.[12] Mill, although he was the author of the comforting thesis that the distribution of wealth, unlike its production, was socially malleable, was unprepared to support a progressive income tax—in his case, because of a fear of the effects of leveling income upon the growth of population as well as because such a tax would be insufferably inquisitorial in administration. Bentham's flirtation with notions of equality flowing from the utilitarian calculus left no imprint on friends, disciples, or tenants.

There was one interesting near-exception to this rule of near-silence on the redistribution of income. The rent of land, the payment for the use of its "original and indestructible" properties, was by definition a nonfunctional income, so that social control over rent would not affect the use of land. Hence Mill was the ardent supporter of the nationalization of future

---

10. *Wealth of Nations*, II, 654.

11. We find complaints at window taxes as being regressive (II, 373) and at tithes for not being proportional to rents (II, 358).

12. "So essential does it appear to me, to the cause of good government, that the rights of property should be held sacred, that I would agree to deprive those of the elective franchise against whom it could justly be alleged that they considered it their own interest to invade them. But in fact it can be only amongst the most needy in the community that such an opinion can be entertained. The man of a small income must be aware how little his share would be if all the large fortunes in the kingdom were equally divided among the people. He must know that the little he would obtain by such a division could be no adequate compensation for the overturning of a principle which renders the produce of his industry secure. . . . The quantity of employment in the country must depend, not only on the quantity of capital, but upon its advantageous distribution, and above all, on the conviction of each capitalist that he will be allowed to enjoy unmolested the fruits of his capital, his skill, and his enterprise. To take from him this conviction is at once to annihilate half the productive industry of the country. . . ." *Observations on Parliamentary Reform*, in *Works and Correspondence*, 500–1.

increments of land values. But even here Mill wished to compensate present landowners fully.[13]

All this was to change when, but not because, the theory of utility became a centerpiece of economics. In 1881 Edgeworth published *Mathematical Psychics*, in which the utilitarian calculus was presented with magnificent subtlety, imagery, and fruitfulness. A marriage was performed between utility and natural selection, culminating in proposals such as that people below a certain level of capacity should not be allowed to have children,[14] and that the possible correlation of capacity to produce with capacity to enjoy might lead even to the superiority of aristocracy. This effusion was in due time replaced by the classic formulation of the utilitarian rule of taxation, minimum sacrifice. The state should tax the rich *before* the poor, not simply more heavily than the poor, subject to the unexplored dangers of the effects of aggressively progressive taxation on production.[15] Progression followed from the twin assumptions that the marginal utility of income falls as income rises, and that there is no systematic relationship between the amount of income a person possesses and his efficiency in converting income into utility.

By 1912 Pigou was prepared to assert as an axiom of welfare economics that "economic welfare is likely to be augmented by anything that, leaving other things unaltered, renders the distribution of the national dividend less unequal".[16] He was still reluctant to engage in extensive direct redistribution, on the ground—so characteristic of this eccentric man—that the poor would not use the funds intelligently: "Women, who cook badly or feed their children on pickles, are not bankrupted out of the profession of motherhood; fathers who invest their sons' activities unremuneratively are not expelled from fatherhood. . . . What has been said, however, . . . should suffice to establish the thesis . . . that the poor, as entrepreneurs of investment in themselves and their children, are abnormally incompetent."[17] Fortunately the intelligence of the poor was rising at a powerful rate, so a few years later Pigou was able to write that "To charge the whole body of the poorer classes with ignorance and lack of capacity for management would, indeed, be to utter a gross libel."[18] Or was Pigou getting in step with society?

13. Mill was mistaken only in believing that present values did not include unbiased estimates of future increments in rents. A similar problem lurks behind his support of progressive taxation of estates. The posthumous *Chapters on Socialism* pays no attention to inequality (aside from that implicit in the discussion of poverty), even in discussing Blanc, Fourier, and Owen.

14. Those denied "a share of domestic pleasures" might be consoled by emigration!

15. See Francis Edgeworth, "The Pure Theory of Taxation," in *Collected Works Relating to Political Economy* (London: Macmillan, 1925), I, 111–42.

16. *Wealth and Welfare* (London: Macmillan, 1912), p. 24.

17. Ibid., pp. 356–57, 358.

18. *Economics of Welfare* (London: Macmillan, 1924), p. 709.

I shall assert what I believe I could document, a steadily rising concern with the distribution of income among economist-preachers during the last one hundred years. Today the consequences of any policy on the distribution of income is the early subject of every appraisal, and egalitarianism is an almost uncontroverted goal of social policy. Two broad statements can be made about the ascendancy of income distribution as the subject of ethical judgments on economic policy.

The first is that the expanding concern of economists with income distribution did not come from within economics. Until recently, the professional literature on income distribution has been sparse, relatively iconoclastic (especially with reference to the possibility of interpersonal comparisons of utility), and noncumulative. It cannot be doubted that the economists have imported egalitarian values into economics from the prevailing ethos of the societies in which they live, and they have not been important contributors to the formation of that ethos. In the English tradition from which I have been drawing my examples, the Fabian socialists were immensely more influential and outspoken supporters of egalitarianism than the neoclassical economists.

The second generalization is that the wide acceptance of the ethical desirability of extensive income redistribution has inhibited the development of a positive theory of income distribution. Such a positive theory would explain how the size distribution of income affected, and was affected by, developments such as rising wealth and education, the roles of taxation and other forms of political action, the institutions of inheritance, and the changing nature of the family. Just such a positive theory is beginning to emerge, and I predict that it will have important effects upon the attitudes of economists toward policies of redistribution. The remarkable circumstance, however, that professional study of income distribution up to recent times was small and noncumulative is attributable to the fact that economists viewed the subject as primarily ethical.

5. Conclusion

I must bring this sermon on economic sermons to a close. The main lesson I draw from our experience as preachers is that we are well received in the measure that we preach what the society wishes to hear. Perhaps all preachers achieve popularity by this route.

The degree of popularity of a preacher does not necessarily measure his influence as a preacher, let alone as a scholar. In fact one could perhaps argue that unpopular sermons are the more influential—certainly if the opposite is true, and preachers simply confirm their listeners' beliefs, pulpits should be at the rear of congregations, to make clearer who is leading. Whether economic preachers lead or follow, they need an ethical system to guide their recommendations. I shall address the nature and sources of their ethics in the next lecture.

2 The Ethics of Competition: The Friendly Economists

The system of organization of an economy by private decisions on the allocation of resources and the private determination of the composition and distribution of final outputs is variously known as the market system, the enterprise system, competition, laissez-faire, and by the Marxian word, monopoly-capitalism. This system has been the main method of control of economic life in the last two hundred years in the Western world, but the extent of governmental intervention has increased enormously in both its scope and depth of detail.

In this lecture I plan first to discuss the attitudes of the mainstream of English economists toward this system—the measure and content of their approval and disapproval of the enterprise system. I shall dwell only briefly on the pre-modern evolution of their attitudes and treat primarily with the modern attitudes toward the market. Thereafter, I shall address the questions of where the economists get their ethics and the effects of these ethical values on their work.

1. To 1900: The Growth of Caution in the Economists' Defense

Until the mid-nineteenth century, the virtues of the enterprise system were as widely accepted as the belief in its efficiency. Private property turned sand into gold, and no one complained at the loss of the sand or the presence of gold. The "natural system of liberty" was extended widely. It is true that considerable lists have been compiled of the public tasks which the classical economists assigned to the state to correct or reinforce private actions, but they were not widespread or systematic *programs*, rather a spattering of Band-Aids to be put on the body economic. Malthus denounced systems of equality as part of his population essay and Ricardo ridiculed Robert Owen's parallelograms.[1]

John Stuart Mill was much more ambivalent on the comparative merits of private enterprise and various forms of socialism. The ambivalence

Reprinted from *The Tanner Lectures on Human Values*, vol. 2 (Salt Lake City: University of Utah Press; Cambridge: Cambridge University Press, 1981).

1. For those who are more familiar with the parallelograms of Euclid than those of Owen, the latter proposed a utopia composed of communities of 500 to 2,000 people, each located in a village "arranged in the form of a large Square, or Parallelogram," with a balanced agricultural and manufacturing economy in which "a full and complete equality will prevail"; see "Constitution, Laws, and Regulations of a Community," in *A New View of Society*, 1st American ed. (New York: Bliss and White, 1825), pp. 162–63.

14

was attributable to three sources: his remarkable propensity to understand and state fairly almost any view; the influence of Harriet, the *femme fatale* of the history of economics; and the astonishing and absurd deficiencies which he assigned to private enterprise. He asserted that perhaps nine-tenths of the labor force had compensation which at best was loosely related to exertion and achievement—indeed so loosely that he expressed indignation that the "produce of labour should be apportioned as we now see it, almost in an inverse ratio to the labour."[2] He felt able to assert that a competitive market could not achieve a shortening of hours of work, even if all the laborers wished it.[3] It has been said that only a highly educated man can be highly mistaken. Mill is no refutation.

Nevertheless, while stating in explicit and implicit ways that political economy did not imply laissez-faire, he initiated a practice that was soon to become widely imitated. After listing several reasons for preferring laissez-faire—chiefly grounded on a desire for individual freedom and development, but grounded also on efficiency—Mill concludes, "few will dispute the more than sufficiency of these reasons, to throw, in every instance, the burthen of making out a strong case, not on those who resist, but on those who recommend, government interference. *Laissez-faire*, in short, should be the general practice: every departure from it, unless required by some great good, a certain evil."[4] The practice of denying laissez-faire as a theorem but asserting its expediency as a general rule soon became, and to this day (I shall later argue) has remained, the set-lecture of the economist. Soon Cairnes, Jevons, Sidgwick, Marshall, and J. N. Keynes confirmed the tradition.[5] Monopoly, externalities, ignorance, and other reasons for departing from laissez-faire accumulated, but as individual exceptions to a general rule.

This compromise, in which Pure Science was silent but Heavy Presumption favored laissez-faire, troubles me more than it has most economists. A science is successful in the measure that it explains in general terms the behavior of the phenomena within its self-imposed boundaries. Let me give an example: the science should be able to tell us the effects of a minimum wage law on the employment and compensation of all workers, the effects on consumers through price changes, and so on. The

---

2. *Principles of Political Economy* (Toronto: University of Toronto Press, 1965), I, 207.
3. Ibid., II, 956–57.
4. Ibid., II, 944–45. The argument is presented fully in book V, chapter XI.
5. J. E. Cairnes, "Political Economy and Laissez-Faire," in *Essays in Political Economy* (London: Macmillan, 1873): "Economic science has no more connection with our present industrial system than the science of mechanics has with our present system of railways" (p. 257); W. S. Jevons, *The State in Relation to Labour* (London: Macmillan, 1882); H. Sidgwick, *Principles of Political Economy*, 3d ed. (London: Macmillan, 1901), bk. III, ch. II; A. Marshall, "Social Possibilities of Economic Chivalry," in *Memorials of Alfred Marshall*, ed. A. C. Pigou (London: Macmillan, 1925); and J. N. Keynes, *Scope and Method of Political Economy*, 4th ed. (London: Macmillan, 1930), ch. II.

standard analysis, to be specific, predicts that a minimum wage law reduces the incomes of the least capable workers and of the community at large, and various other effects.

One could say that the theory does not lead to an unambiguous rejection of minimum wage laws because of limitations imposed by the economist's framework: for example, monopsony in the labor market or ignorance of workers leads to inefficient market results. Then, however, the economist should analyze the effects reached under (say) minimum wage laws and laissez-faire with monopsony, and reach a definite result or no result. In either event, no *presumption* is established.

Alternatively, the theory may be deemed inconclusive for reasons lying outside the economists' domain; in particular, social values not recognized by the theory may reverse the conclusion.[6] For example, a desired income redistribution (or some other social value) may be achieved by the minimum wage law. Thus the apparent beneficiaries of a minimum wage law are the workers above the minimum wage, and indeed that is the reason the AFL-CIO supports the law. Or the workers in a high-wage area may be protected from the competition of a low-wage area, preserving a desired distribution of population.

Very well, let these or other reasons be sufficient to explain the informed passage and continuance of the minimum wage law by the community. Is it not then a fair request of economic theory that it include these results in its study of the minimum wage law? Why shouldn't the full range of consequences important to the society be important to the economist? Unless we invoke consequences outside the scope of rational inquiry—say, that the law favors believers in the true God, without further identification—it is not easy to live with both a pure science of economic phenomena and a set of nonderivative presumptions about practice. Of course the neglect of values other than efficiency may be defended on grounds of scientific division of labor, even though no other science seems inclined to study the neglected share. In any event, one wonders again where the presumption comes from.

I suspect the answer to these questions is that the economists have decided, possibly implicitly and silently, that the other values that might overcome the efficiency presumption are usually weak or conflicting, or even reinforce the conclusion based upon the studied effects. I am in no position to quarrel with this as a working philosophy: no matter how full the explanation of why we have minimum wages—and it is a study we should broaden—I predict that we economists will not like the law. But the working philosophy should not parade as science.

---

6. In Mill's view, the freedom from compulsion was the chief value justifying the presumption of laissez-faire; book V, chapter XI of the *Principles* is a preview of *On Liberty*.

2. Marginal Productivity Ethics

The decline in open, unconditional praise of the enterprise system by economists suffered one important interruption at the end of the nineteenth century. The occasion was the discovery and widespread adoption of the marginal productivity theory.

The marginal productivity theory states that in competitive equilibrium each productive factor receives a rate of compensation equal to the value of its marginal or additional contribution to the enterprise that employs it. If the productive factor is a laborer, and he works as (say) a service worker with negligible capital equipment, in equilibrium his wage will equal simply the amount of revenue his services add to the enterprise. If, as is usually the case, the product of all factors is commingled, the marginal product may be manifested as a slightly larger crop or a more reliable machine or some other salable attribute.

If you declare to a layman that a certain individual is paid his marginal product, after explaining perhaps more clearly than I have what a marginal product is, and then add, "Isn't that simply outrageous?," I predict that this layman will be amazed by your comment. In any event, several economists who were among the founders and disseminators of the marginal productivity theory did take exactly the view that the value of the marginal product of a person was the just rate of his remuneration.

The most famous exponent of this view was John Bates Clark. In his magnum opus, *The Distribution of Wealth* (1899), he stated:

> The welfare of the laboring classes depends on whether they get much or little; but their attitude toward other classes—and therefore the stability of the social state—depends chiefly on the question, whether the amount they get, be it large or small, is what they produce. If they create a small amount of wealth and get the whole of it, they may not seek to revolutionize society; but if it were to appear that they produce an ample amount and get only a part of it, many of them would become revolutionists, and all would have the right to do so. . . .
> Having first tested the honesty of the social state, by determining whether it gives to every man his own [product], we have next to test its beneficence, by ascertaining whether that which is his own is becoming greater or smaller.[7]

T. N. Carver of Harvard was also an exponent of productivity ethics:

> But if the number of a particular kind of laborers is so small and the other factors are so abundant that one more laborer of this particular kind would add greatly to the product of the combination, then it is not inaccurate to say that

7. (New York: Macmillan Co., 1899), pp. 4–5.

17

his physical product is very high. That being the case, his value is very high. This, therefore, is the principle which determines how much a man is worth, and consequently, according to our criterion of justice, how much he ought to have as a reward for his work.[8]

I have not sought to discover how many economists joined in this ethical justification of competition. I believe that many economists did so, not so often by explicit avowal as by the implicit acceptance of the propriety of marginal productivity as the basis for remuneration. Pigou, for example, wished to define an exploitive wage, and he chose as his definition a wage which fell below the value of the marginal product of the worker.[9]

This literature is usually referred to as "naïve productivity ethics," with the adjective serving not to distinguish it from some other more sophisticated ethical system but to express disapproval. The classic statement of this disapproval is the famous essay by Frank Knight, "The Ethics of Competition" (1923).[10] Four charges are made against the claims of the competitive system to be just:

1. An economic system molds the tastes of its members, so the system cannot be defended on the ground that it satisfies demands efficiently.[11]
2. The economic system is not *perfectly* efficient: there are indivisibilities, imperfect knowledge, monopoly, externalities, etc.[12]
3. The paramount defect of the competitive system is that it distributes income largely on the basis of inheritance and luck (with some minor influence of effort). The inequality of income increases cumulatively under competition.[13]
4. Viewed (alternatively) as a game, competition is poorly fashioned to meet acceptable standards of fairness, such as giving everyone an even start and allowing a diversity of types of rivalries.

When I first read this essay a vast number of years ago, as a student writing his dissertation under Professor Knight's supervision, you should

8. *Essays in Social Justice* (Cambridge: Harvard University Press, 1915), p. 201.

9. *The Economics of Welfare*, 2d ed. (London: Macmillan, 1924), p. 754.

10. *Quarterly Journal of Economics*; reprinted in *The Ethics of Competition* (Chicago: University of Chicago Press, 1976).

11. " . . . the social order largely forms as well as gratifies the wants of its members, and the natural consequence [is] that it must be judged ethically rather by the wants which it generates . . . " (ibid., p. 51).

12. Hence, "in conditions of real life no possible social order based upon a *laissez-faire* policy can justify the familiar ethical conclusions of apologetic economics" (ibid., p. 49).

13. "The ownership of personal or material productive capacity is based upon a complex mixture of inheritance, luck, and effort, probably in that order of relative importance" (ibid., p. 56). "The luck element is so large . . . that capacity and effort may count for nothing [in business]. And this luck element works cumulatively, as in gambling games generally" (ibid., p. 64).

not be surprised to hear that I thought his was a conclusive refutation of "productivity ethics." When I reread it a year or so ago, I was shocked by the argumentation. Knight made a series of the most sweeping and confident empirical judgments (such as those underlying the first and third charges) for which he could not have even a cupful of supporting evidence. Moreover, why was it even relevant, with respect to his second charge, that real-world markets are not perfectly competitive in his special sense: one can define a perfect standard to judge imperfect performance, and assuredly real-world performance under any form of economic organization will be less than perfect by any general criterion. Knight kept referring to the objections to competitive results under any "acceptable ethical system" but never told us what such a system contained in the way of ethical content. His own specific judgments do not seem compelling, as when he asserted that "no one contends that a bottle of old wine is ethically worth as much as a barrel of flour." Dear Professor Knight, please forgive your renegade student, but I do so contend, if it was a splendid year for claret.

I shall have more to say about acceptable ethical positions shortly, but for the moment I wish only to assert that the appeal of productivity ethics for income distribution commands wide support not only from the public but also from the economists when they are watching their sentiments rather than their words. Ethical values cannot be counted by a secret ballot referendum, but the support for a productivity ethic is indeed widespread. Even Marx, like Pigou, defined surplus value as the part of a worker's product that he was not paid. The fact that more than skill and effort go into remuneration—that in Knight's example bearded women get good circus jobs simply by not shaving—is not enough to dismiss productivity ethics.

3. The Ethics of Economists

I have postponed as long as possible the question: where do economists get their ethical systems? My answer is: wherever they can find them.

One occasional source has been a widely acceptable philosophical system. The most important such system in the history of economics has been utilitarianism, which was strongly influential on Bentham's circle, Sidgwick, Marshall, Pigou, and above all Edgeworth. I have already referred to Edgeworth's *Mathematical Psychics* (1881), which is in good part a reproduction of his earlier monograph, *New and Old Methods of Ethics* (1877). Edgeworth presents the utilitarian ethic in full grandeur:

> 'Mécanique Sociale' may one day take her place along with
> 'Mécanique Celeste,' throned each upon the double-sided
> height of one maximum principle, the supreme pinnacle of
> moral as of physical science. As the movements of each parti-
> cle, constrained or loose, in a material cosmos are continually

subordinated to one maximum sum-total of accumulated energy, so the movements of each soul, whether selfishly isolated or linked sympathetically, may continually be realizing the maximum energy of pleasure, the Divine love of the universe.[14]

Edgeworth's calculus and Sidgwick's *Methods of Ethics* represent the high point of the utilitarian ethics in neoclassical economics.

It proved to be a major obstacle to the explicit use of the utilitarian ethic that it required additional information, particularly about the efficiency of different persons in producing utility, that admitted of no objective determination. Recall that Edgeworth was led to recognize the possibility that an aristocracy might be the best of all societies.

Even when the difficulty of comparing utilities could be overcome, and it was generally overcome by consensus rather than by argument or evidence, the systematic ethic led to an embarrassing consequence. Let me explain by example.

When one traces out the applications of a general ethical system one encounters problems such as one that Alfred Marshall faced. He examined the properties of good excise taxes in a chapter suitably entitled "Theories of Changes in Normal Demand and Supply in Relation to the Doctrine of Maximum Satisfaction."[15] According to the utilitarian theory, it is more desirable, Marshall stated, to tax necessaries rather than luxuries because the demand for necessaries is less elastic and therefore an excise tax will occasion a smaller loss of consumer utility (surplus).[16] Of course he rejected this recommendation of regressive taxation because it ignored ability to pay taxes.

It might be argued that if Marshall had properly weighted the marginal utility of income of the poor as greater than that of the rich, he would be freed of embarrassment. Possibly, although he would then have needed to compare the magnitudes of utilities with taxation of luxuries and taxation of necessities. In any event, other embarrassing implications are readily found, for example, that the utilitarian goal would imply cosmopolitan income redistribution.

And that is the trouble with a comprehensive ethical system: it leads to conclusions which are unpopular with the community and therefore unpopular with the economists. I believe, although I have not undertaken the substantial task of verifying, the proposition that wherever an ethical system has clashed with widespread social values, the economists have abandoned the implications of the ethical system. If that is indeed the case, it strongly argues for the acceptance of the community's values with whatever inconsistencies they contain.

14. *Mathematical Psychics*, p. 12.
15. *Principles of Economics* (1920), bk. V, ch. XIII.
16. Ibid., p. 467 n.

John Rawls once proposed a way out of this impasse—a method of deriving general ethical values that were both inductive and capable of consistent application. His proposal was as follows. Select a set of competent judges and ask them to decide many and varied specific conflicts that arise between individuals in the society. Given their decisions, seek an explication or principle that correctly predicts these decisions on average and call that principle the ethical principle. Any implicit ethical principles that had been followed by the competent judges would be recovered by this procedure. One might complain at the elitist nature of the procedure, and a fundamental question is of course whether any principles would be found to exist.[17] Rawls's later and influential presentation of a modified utilitarian theory of justice has no such inductive basis, which suggests that he also found an inductive ethics difficult to systematize, and possibly difficult to accept.[18]

If economists have been content to base their goals upon the ruling views of the educated classes, as I believe to be the case, that is not quite the same thing as saying that they have simply taken an implicit opinion poll on ethical values and either accepted the majority view or distributed themselves in proportion to the frequencies of views held by these classes. Their own discipline has had its own influence.

Members of other social sciences often remark, in fact I must say complain, at the peculiar fascination that the logic of rational decision-making exerts upon economists. It is such an interesting logic: it has answers to so many and varied questions, often answers that are simultaneously reasonable to economists and absurd to others. The paradoxes are not diminished by the delight with which economists present them. How pleased Longfield must have been when he showed that if, in periods of acute shortage, the rich bought grain and sold it at half price to the poor, the poor were not helped. How annoyed the ecclesiastical readers of Smith must have been to learn that the heavy subsidization of clerical training served only to lower the income of curates. How outraged even some economists are with Becker's "rotten kid theorem," which demonstrates that altruistic treatment of a selfish person forces him to behave as an unselfish person would.

Economic logic centers on utility-maximizing behavior by individuals. Such behavior may be found in every area of human behavior—and my just-mentioned colleague, Gary Becker, has analyzed it with striking results in areas such as crime, marriage and divorce, fertility, and altruistic behavior—but the central application of economic theory has been in explicit markets. The power of self-interest, and its almost unbelievable delicacy and subtlety in complex decision areas, has led economists to

17. See "Outline of a Decision Procedure for Ethics," *The Philosophical Review* 60 (1951): 177–97.
18. See *A Theory of Justice* (Cambridge: Harvard University Press, 1971).

12422

seek a large role for explicit or implicit prices in the solution of many social problems.

As a result, in a period of rapid and extensive movement away from reliance on competitive markets to allocate resources and to distribute income, economists have not led the trend but rather followed it at substantial distance. They have sought persistently to employ prices to abate pollution or to ration energy or to incite safety conditions. They have been at the forefront of what presently appears to be a modest policy of deregulation of certain areas of economic behavior.

It would take a wiser person than I to determine which shares of this market orientation of economists are due to professional training, to attachment to a demonstrably efficient machinery for allocating resources that is largely (but not completely) independent of the goals being sought, and to ethical values in the market organization of economic activity. But this last component, the ethical attractiveness of voluntary exchange, plays at least some part in our attitudes, and I shall give an example of its role.

Market transactions are voluntary and repetitive. These traits are much less marked in political transactions, or military transactions, although perhaps not in religious transactions. Because the market transactions are voluntary, they must benefit at least one party and not injure the other. Because they are repetitive, they (usually) make deceit and nonfulfillment of promises unprofitable. A reputation for candor and responsibility is a commercial asset—on the enterprise's balance sheet it may be called goodwill.

Nothing in rational behavior precludes the formation of habits which economize on decision-making costs. One such habit according to Marshall is probity: "The opportunities for knavery are certainly more numerous than they were; but there is no reason for thinking that men avail themselves of a larger proportion of such opportunities than they used to do. On the contrary, modern methods of trade imply habits of trustfulness on the one side and power of resisting temptation to dishonesty on the other, which do not exist among a backward people.[19] A still stronger, and much earlier, extension of the same argument was made by Smith:

> Whenever commerce is introduced into any country, probity and punctuality always accompany it. These virtues in a rude and barbarous country are almost unknown. Of all the nations in Europe, the Dutch, the most commercial, are the most faithful to their word. The English are more so than the Scotch, but much inferiour to the Dutch, and in the remote parts of this country they (are) far less so than in the com-

19. *Principles of Economics*, 8th ed. (London: Macmillan, 1920), p. 7.

mercial parts of it. This is not at all to be imputed to national character, as some pretend. There is no natural reason why an Englishman or a Scotchman should not be as punctual in performing agreements as a Dutchman. It is far more reduceable to self interest, that general principle which regulates the actions of every man, and which leads men to act in a certain manner from views of advantage, and is as deeply implanted in an Englishman as a Dutchman. A dealer is afraid of losing his character, and is scrupulous in observing every engagement. When a person makes perhaps 20 contracts in a day, he cannot gain so much by endeavouring to impose on his neighbours, as the very appearance of a cheat would make him lose. Where people seldom deal with one another, we find that they are somewhat disposed to cheat, because they can gain more by a smart trick than they can lose by the injury which it does their character. They whom we call politicians are not the most remarkable men in the world for probity and punctuality. Ambassadors from different nations are still less so: they are praised for any little advantage they can take, and pique themselves a good deal on this degree of refinement. The reason of this is that nations treat with one another not above twice or thrice in a century, and they may gain more by one piece of fraud than (lose) by having a bad character. France has had this character with us ever since the reign of Lewis XIVth, yet it has never in the least hurt either its interest or splendour.[20]

I do not know whether in actual fact the participants in economic transactions behave more honestly than those in diplomatic exchanges or in primitive barter, and I am reasonably confident that Marshall and Smith also did not know when they wrote these passages, whatever they have learned since. But I do believe that they, and most modern economists, accept the substance of their position on commercial morality.

This belief is based not upon some poll of opinion but on our daily practice. Modern economists almost invariably postulate transactions free of fraud or coercion. This postulate is partially presented in mathematical versions as the budget equation, which states that for each economic agent the sum of values received equals the sum of values given up. No transaction therefore leaves anyone worse off, ex ante, than he was before he entered it—almost a definition of a noncoercive transaction.

There is no inherent reason for us to make this assumption, and two good reasons for not doing so. The first reason for including fraud and

20. *Lectures on Jurisprudence* (Cambridge: Cambridge University Press, 1978), pp. 538–39.

coercion in economics is that they are probably impossible to distinguish from honorable dealing. Assume that I take a shortcut home through a park each night, and once a week on average I am robbed of my trousers—I have learned not to carry money. Is this not a voluntary transaction in which I pay a toll of one-fifth of a pair of trousers per day for access to the shortcut? Assume that I sell to you a plot of land which you erroneously believe to cover an oil pool, and I know the truth. Am I being fraudulent? If so, modify the circumstances so that you know there is oil and I don't. Clearly we can find situations in which the presence of fraud is rejected by half the population.

Second, even when fraud or coercion is unambiguous in the eyes of the society, that is no reason to believe that ordinary economic analysis is inapplicable. Fraudulent securities will be supplied in such quantity that their marginal costs, including selling costs, equal their marginal revenue. One would not expect criminals to earn more than they could obtain in legitimate callings, proper allowance being made for all costs of doing business. The ordinary propositions of economics hold for crime.

I conclude that we economists have customarily excluded fraud and coercion because we have thought that they are not empirically significant elements in the ordinary economic transactions of an enterprise economy.

Although economists have displayed a larger affection for the system of private enterprise than has the remainder of the educated public, this is not to say that prevalent social views have no influence on technical economic writing. Consider the enormous attention that is devoted to monopoly in modern economic theory, an attention so vast that it has virtually taken possession of the literature on industrial organization. The evidence that monopoly is important is negligible, and the evidence that it is a quite minor influence on the workings of the economy is large. I have slowly been approaching the view of Schumpeter, that the eminent role of monopoly in economic literature is due to the influence of general social views.[21]

4. What Is Ethics?

Economists, I have just said, believe that economic transactions are usually conducted on a high level of candor and responsibility, because it is in the interest of the parties to behave honorably in repetitive transactions. Hence honesty pays.

Against this view we may set that of Archbishop Richard Whately, himself something of an economist as well as a noted logician and divine. The man who acts on the principle that honesty is the best policy, said his

---

21. The recent attention economists have paid to conservation of resources and to all varieties of pollution also represents a response to popular discussion of these matters rather than the result of autonomous professional economic research.

Grace, is a man who is not honest.[22] He did not elaborate, but the meaning is clear: he who behaves honestly because it is remunerative is simply an amoral calculator; an honest man is one whose principles of right conduct are adopted independently of their consequences for him.

If every person in a society shared the utilitarian goal of maximum utility for the society, all would presumably behave honestly because there is a large deadweight loss to society in erecting defenses against dishonesty and punishing its manifestations. If even one person did not share this ethic, it might well pay him to engage in acts of dishonesty—indeed it would hardly pay the society to take defensive steps against him or her. One may therefore conclude that honesty would be a utilitarian ethic for the society as a whole, even though honesty did not pay (was not utilitarian) for an individual.

Do people possess ethical beliefs which influence their behavior in ways not dictated by, and hence in conflict with, their own long-run utility-maximizing behavior? This question is not free of ambiguity: if we allow unlimited altruism in the individual's utility function, we are back to social utilitarianism. Less to avoid this result than to attain a position that seems empirically defensible, I shall assume that the altruism is strong within the family and toward close friends and diminishes with the social distance of the person—very much the position Adam Smith advanced in his *Moral Sentiments*.[23] This interpretation does not determine the answer to the question whether people act on ethical principles. Indeed it eliminates the easy answer, "of course, they give to charity."

The question of the existence of effective ethical values is of course an empirical question, and in principle it should be directly testable. I recall reading of an experiment in which stamped and addressed but unsealed envelopes with small sums of money were scattered in the streets, and records were compiled of which envelopes were mailed to the designated recipient. My faint recollection is that more envelopes were mailed when the designated recipient was a charity, but that most sums were appropriated by the finders.

One could quarrel at the design of this test, as I recall it, for it gave no information on the finders: perhaps those who were conversing with their clergymen when the envelope was found behaved differently from those who were conversing with their bookies. Still, it is an interesting line of inquiry, one that would be a better employment of the recent doctorates in philosophy than the employments which are reported.

Let me predict the outcome of the systematic and comprehensive testing of behavior in situations where self-interest and ethical values with

22. Nassau W. Senior, *Journals, Conversations and Essays Relating to Ireland* (London: Longmans Green, 1868), II, 271.
23. See Ronald H. Coase, "Adam Smith's View of Man," *Journal of Law and Economics* 19 (1976): 529–46.

wide verbal allegiance are in conflict. Much of the time, most of the time in fact, the self-interest theory (as I interpreted it on Smithian lines) will win. In a set of cases that is not negligible and perhaps not random with respect to social characteristics of the actors, the self-interest hypothesis will fail—at least without a subtle and unpredictable interpretation of self-interest.

I predict this result because it is the prevalent one found by economists not only within a wide variety of economic phenomena, but in their investigations of marital, child-bearing, criminal, religious, and other social behavior as well. We believe that man is a utility-maximizing animal—apparently pigeons and rats are also—and to date we have not found it informative to carve out a section of his life in which he invokes a different goal of behavior. In fact, the test I have just proposed has very little potential scope, I shall argue, because most ethical values do not conflict with individual utility-maximizing behavior.

I pursue this dangerous line of thought in my final lecture.

3

The Ethics of Competition:
The Unfriendly Critics

In the century following the appearance of the *Wealth of Nations*, the pace of economic progress accelerated to levels never before achieved on so continuous and comprehensive a scale. The technology, the economy, the lives, and even the politics of the Western world underwent profound and lasting changes. The standard of living reached continually higher levels, longevity increased, and education spread over the entire society.

It was to be expected that the radical changes accompanying this astonishing economic development would arouse deep opposition and bitter criticism from some groups. Important figures in the cultural circles of Great Britain were soon nostalgic for a romantic past. Robert Southey, the poet laureate, viewed the earlier cottage system and the factory system through bifocal spectacles with rose and black tints, respectively:

> . . . we remained awhile in silence, looking upon the assemblage of dwellings below. Here, and in the adjoining hamlet of Millbeck, the effects of manufactures and of agriculture may be seen and compared. The old cottages are such as the poet and the painter equally delight in beholding. Substantially built of the native stone without mortar, dirtied with no white-lime, and their long low roofs covered with slate, if they had been raised by the magic of some indigenous Amphion's music, the materials could not have adjusted themselves more beautifully in accord with the surrounding scene; and time has still further harmonized them with weather-stains, lichens and moss, short grasses and short fern, and stone-plants of various kinds. The ornamented chimneys, round or square, less adorned than those which, like little turrets, crest the houses of the Portuguese peasantry; and yet not less happily suited to their place, the hedge of clipt box beneath the windows, the rose bushes beside the door, the little patch of flower ground, with its tall holly-hocks in front; the garden beside, the beehives, and the orchard with its bank of daffodils and snowdrops (the earliest and the profusest in these parts), indicate in the owners some portion of ease and leisure, some regard to neatness and comfort, some sense of natural and innocent and healthful

Reprinted from The Tanner Lectures on Human Values, vol. 2 (Salt Lake City: University of Utah Press; Cambridge: Cambridge University Press, 1981).

enjoyment. The new cottages of the manufacturers are . . . upon the manufacturing pattern . . . naked, and in a row.

How is it, said I, that everything which is connected with manufactures presents such features of unqualified deformity? From the largest of Mammon's temples down to the poorest hovel in which his helotry are stalled, these edifices have all one character. Time cannot mellow them; nature will neither clothe nor conceal them; and they remain always as offensive to the eye as to the mind![1]

Of the innumerable voices that joined in this swelling chorus, I shall briefly notice two.

Thomas Carlyle, who gave the dismal science this name, wrote with his customary passion:

> And yet I will venture to believe that in no time, since the beginnings of Society, was the lot of those same dumb millions of toilers so entirely unbearable as it is even in the days now passing over us. It is not to die, or even to die of hunger, that makes a man wretched; many men have died; all men must die—the last exit of us all is in a Fire-Chariot of Pain. But it is to live miserable we know not why; to work sore and yet gain nothing; to be heartworn, weary, yet isolated, unrelated, girt in with a cold universal Laissez-faire: it is to die slowly all our life long, imprisoned in a deaf, dead, Infinite Injustice, as in the accursed iron belly of a Phalaris' Bull! This is and remains forever intolerable to all men whom God has made. Do we wonder at French Revolutions, Chartisms, Revolts of Three Days? The Times, if we will consider them, are really unexampled.[2]

Finally, John Ruskin's immense Victorian audience was repeatedly instructed in the vices of industrialism. He was prepared to sum up his entire message in the declaration: "Government and co-operation are in all things the Laws of Life; Anarchy and competition the Laws of Death."[3] A more explicit version runs: "It being the privilege of the fishes as it is of rats and wolves, to live by the laws of demand and supply; but the distinction of humanity, to live by those of right."[4]

A full tour through the modern critics of the competitive organization of society would be a truly exhausting trip. It would include the drama, the novel, the churches, the academies, the lesser intellectual establishments, the socialists and communists and Fabians and a swarm of other

1. *Sir Thomas More; Or Colloquies on the Progress and Prospects of Society* (London: John Murray, 1829), I, 173–74.

2. *Past and Present* (Chicago: Henneberry, n.d.), p. 296.

3. *The Complete Works of John Ruskin* (New York: Thomas Crowell, n.d.).

4. *The Communism of John Ruskin* (New York: Humboldt, 1891), edited by W. P. B. Bliss, p. 52n.

dissenters. One is reminded of Schumpeter's remark that the Japanese earthquake of 1924 had a remarkable aspect: it was not blamed on capitalism. Suddenly one realizes how impoverished our society would be in its indignation, as well as in its food, without capitalism.

It is no part of my present purpose to sketch this opposition, and still less to attempt to refute it. Many excellent replies have been penned: Southey's passage with which I began called forth the full scorn—and that is truly a vast scorn—of Macaulay:

> Mr. Southey has found out a way, he tells us, in which the effects of manufactures and agriculture may be compared. And what is this way? To stand on a hill, to look at a cottage and a factory, and to see which is the prettier. Does Mr. Southey think that the body of the English peasantry live, or ever lived, in substantial or ornamented cottages, with box-hedges, flower-gardens, beehives, and orchards? If not, what is his parallel worth? We despise those mock philosophers who think that they serve the cause of science by depreciating literature and the fine arts. But if anything could excuse their narrowness of mind, it would be such a book as this.[5]

Macaulay in fact would give Southey credit for only "two faculties which were never, we believe, vouchsafed in measure so copious to any human being—the faculty of believing without a reason, and the faculty of hating without a provocation."[6]

Later, and usually lesser, defenders of laissez-faire have proved that the critics behaved as critics usually do: inventing some abuses in the system they attacked; denouncing some of its virtues as abuses; exaggerating the real shortcomings; and being singularly blind to the difficulties of any alternative economic system, when they faced this problem at all. But these characteristics are not unique to the critics of private enterprise and may well be inherent in criticisms of any existing order.

I begin with this smattering of early critics only to suggest that important leaders of public opinion have long been opposed to a competitive economic system. There is a natural temptation to credit to them and their numerous present-day progeny the decline that has occurred in the public esteem for private enterprise and the large expansion of state control over economic life. I urge you to resist that temptation. After a preliminary look at the so-called followers of opinion, I shall return to the leaders and seek to explain their attitudes and to question their importance. If my interpretation is correct, it raises interesting questions on the future of private enterprise.

5. "Southey's Colloquies on Society," in Thomas Babington Macaulay, *Critical, Historical, and Miscellaneous Essays* (New York: Mason, Baker & Pratt, 1873), II, 148–49.
6. Ibid., p. 132.

1. Have Attitudes Changed?:
The Lower Classes

History is written by and for the educated classes. We know more about the thoughts and actions of an eighteenth-century lord than about 100,000 members of the classes which were at or near the bottom of the income and educational scales. No one can deduce, from documentary evidence, the attitudes of these lower classes toward economic philosophies, whereas the noble lord's words are enshrined in Hansard and several fat volumes of published correspondence. Hence we cannot determine from direct documentary sources what the attitudes toward laissez-faire of these lower classes have been.

totally not true

Nevertheless, it is an hypothesis that is plausible to me and I hope tenable to you that these lower classes—who have increased immensely in wealth and formal education in the last several hundred years—have been strongly attracted to the economic regime of laissez-faire capitalism. One highly persuasive evidence of this is the major spontaneous migrations of modern history: the armies of Europeans that came to the United States, until barriers were created at both ends; the millions of Chinese who have sought entrance to Hong Kong, Shanghai, and other open Asian economies; the millions of Mexicans who these days defy American laws designed to keep them home. These have not been simply migrations from poorer to richer societies, although even that would carry its message, but primarily migrations of lower classes of the home populations. An open, decentralized economy is still the land of opportunity for the lower classes.

The stake of the lower classes in the system of competition is based upon the fact that a competitive productive system is remarkably indifferent to status. An employer finds two unskilled workers receiving $3.00 per hour an excellent substitute for a semiskilled worker receiving $8.00 per hour. A merchant finds ten one-dollar purchases by the poor more profitable than a seven-dollar purchase by a prosperous buyer. This merchant is much less interested in the color of a customer than in the color of his money.

If it is true that a large share of the population of modern societies (and many other societies as well) eagerly migrates to competitive economies when given the opportunity, why have these people supported the vast expansion of governmental controls over economic life in the many democratic societies in which they constitute an important part of the electorate?

I shall postulate now, and argue the case later, that the lower classes have not supported regulatory policies and socialism because they were duped or led by intellectuals with different goals. Instead, these classes have shared the general propensity to vote their own interests. Once the unskilled workers enter an open society, they will oppose further free

30

immigration. The most poorly paid workers are aware of the adverse effects of minimum wage laws, and their representatives vote against such laws.[7] It would be feasible to devise numerous tests of this rational interpretation of lower-class political behavior: as examples, have they been supporters of heavy governmental expenditures on higher education, or of the pollution control programs?

Studies such as I call for will demonstrate, I believe, that the lower classes have been quite selective and parsimonious in their desired interventions in the workings of the competitive economy, simply because not many regulatory policies work to their benefit. These classes will seek and accept all the transfer payments the political system allows, but they have little to gain from regulatory policies that reduce the income of society.

But these lower classes do not dominate our political system. In the long run they have more votes in the marketplace than they have at the ballot box, despite appearances to the contrary. They do not have in full measure the necessary or useful attributes of successful political coalitions, such as common economic and social origins and interests, nor are they localized in space or cohesive in age and social background. They have access to the press or the electromagnetic spectrum only as receivers. They do not directly control the flow of information. These characteristics do not imply that they are the victims of some conspiracy or that they have no influence on political events. It does mean that the marketplace measures their preferences more finely and more promptly than the literature or the politics of the society, even if that society is as democratic as Great Britain or the United States.

This premium placed by politics on certain educational and social characteristics of the voting population is, I believe, the first of two reasons for the failure of the lower classes to play a larger role in modern regulatory policy. The second and more fundamental reason is that the lower classes are by no means a majority: the very efficiency of the competitive economic system has depleted the ranks of the poor and the ill-educated! The productivity of the economy has moved the children of immigrants or poor farm families into the middle classes. A fair fraction of the best economists in the United States are one or two generations away from the garment trades.

When private enterprise elevates many of its lower-class supporters to the middle classes, they find a much larger agenda of desirable state action. The restrictions on entrance into skilled crafts and learned occupations will serve as an important example of the large number of profitable uses of political power that are open to the various groups in the middle classes. If Groucho Marx would not join a country club that

7. See J. B. Kau and P. H. Rubin, "Voting on Minimum Wages: A Time-Series Analysis," *Journal of Political Economy* 86 (1978): 337–42.

would admit the likes of him, private enterprise has reversed the paradox and expells those who learned to play the game well.

2. Have Attitudes Changed?:
The Intellectuals

The intellectual has been contemptuous of commercial activity for several thousand years, so it is not surprising that he has made no exception for the competitive economy. Yet the larger part of the present-day class that lives by words and ideas rather than by commodity processing owes its existence to the productiveness of modern economic systems. Only economies that are highly productive by historical standards can send their populations to schools for twelve to eighteen years, thus providing employment to a large class of educators. Only such a rich society can have a vast communications industry and pervasive social services—other large areas of employment of the intellectual classes. So it is at least a superficial puzzle why these intellectuals maintain much of the traditional hostility of their class to business enterprise—contemptuous of its motives, critical of its achievements, supportive at least of extensive regulation and often of outright socialization.

An answer that many will give is that the competitiveness of economic relationships, the emphasis on profit as a measure of achievement, the difficulties encountered by those cultural activities that do not meet the market test—are precisely the source of opposition: materialism is hostile to the ethical values cherished by the intellectual classes.

A second, and almost opposite, explanation is that these upper classes find their chief patrons and their main employment in government and its activities. Even though the growth of government relative to private economic activity is conditional on the productivity of the private economy, the self-interest of the intellectual is in the expansion of the government economy.

I believe that this is true in the short run, and the short run is at least a generation or two. The extensive regulatory activities of the modern state are, both directly and in their influence on the private sector, the source of much of the large demand for the intellectual classes. For example, if higher education in America were private, so its costs were paid directly by students rather than so largely by public subventions, the education sector would shrink substantially, not because of increases in efficiency, although such increases would surely occur, but because for large numbers of older students, school attendance would no longer be a sensible investment of their time. The state has greatly reduced the relative cost of higher education for the individual student, although it has raised the relative cost for society. Similarly, the immense panoply of regulatory policies has generated a public employment of perhaps half a million persons, with an even larger number of people occupied in complying with or evading the policies the first group are prescribing.

In short, the intellectuals are the beneficiaries of the expansion of the economic role of government. Their support is, on this reading, available to the highest bidder, just as other resources in our society are allocated. Have not the intellectuals always been respectful of their patrons?

I am not striving for paradox or righteousness, so I would emphasize, like Adam Smith, that no insinuations are intended as to the deficient integrity of the intellectuals, which I naturally believe to be as high as the market in ideas allows. No large number of intellectuals change positions after wetting a finger and holding it in the wind: they cultivate those of their ideas which find a market. Ideas without demands are simply as hard to sell as other products without demands. If anyone in this audience wishes to become an apostle of the single tax after the scripture of Henry George, for example, I recommend that he or she acquire and cherish a wealthy, indulgent spouse.

3. Ideology and the Intellectuals

A self-interest theory of the support for and opposition to private enter-prise will shock many people, and not simply because the theory I propose is so elementary and undeveloped (although these are admitted defects). Many and perhaps most intellectuals will assert that the opposi-tion of intellectuals to private enterprise is based upon ethical and cul-tural values divorced from self-interest, and that the intellectuals' opposi-tion has played an important leader role in forming the critical attitude of the society as a whole.

An invariably interesting scholar who urged the powerful influence of the intellectuals on social trends was Joseph Schumpeter. Schumpeter's full argument for the prospective collapse of capitalism contains an elusive metaphysical view of the need for legitimacy of a social system, and a charismatic role for its leading classes, that was, he felt, incompati-ble with the rational calculus of the capitalist mind. The intellectuals were playing their customary role of critics of social order:

> On the one hand, freedom of public discussion involving freedom to nibble at the foundations of capitalist society is inevitable in the long run. On the other hand, the intellectual group cannot help nibbling, because it lives on criticism and its whole position depends on criticism that stings; and criti-cism of persons and of current events will, in a situation in which nothing is sacrosanct, fatally issue in criticism of classes and institutions.[8]

8. *Capitalism, Socialism and Democracy*, 3d ed. (New York: Harper Torchbooks, 1950), p. 151.

The intellectuals are credited in particular with radicalizing the labor movement.

That intellectuals should believe that intellectuals are important in determining the course of history is not difficult to understand. The position is less easy for even an intellectual economist to understand since it sets one class of laborers aside and attributes special motives to them. On the traditional economic theory of occupational choice, intellectuals distribute themselves among occupations and among artistic, ethical, cultural, and political positions in such numbers as to maximize their incomes, where incomes include amenities such as prestige and apparent influence. On the traditional economic view, a Galbraith could not do better working for Ronald Reagan and a Friedman could not do better working for Carter or Kennedy, and I could not do better telling you that intellectuals are terribly important.[9] It is worth noticing that Schumpeter partially accepted this position in pointing out that the declining market prospects of the intellectual class were one basis for its criticism of the market.[10]

Please do not read into my low valuation of the importance of professional preaching a similarly low valuation of scientific work. Once a general relationship in economic phenomena is discovered and verified, it becomes a part of the working knowledge of everyone. A newly established scientific relationship shifts the arena of discourse and is fully adopted by all informed parties, whatever their policy stands. Whether a person likes the price system or dislikes it and prefers a form of non-price rationing of some good, he must accept the fact of a negatively sloping demand curve and take account of its workings. The most influential economist, even in the area of public policy, is the economist who makes the most important scientific contributions.

On the self-interest theory, applied not only to intellectuals but to all of the society, we should look for all to support rationally the positions that are compatible with their long-run interests. Often these interests are subtle or remote, and often the policies that advance these interests are complex and even experimental. For example, it would require a deeper and more comprehensive analysis than has yet been made of the effects of the vast paraphernalia of recent regulation of the energy field to identify and measure the costs and benefits of these policies. But at least in principle, and to a growing degree in practice, we can determine the effects of public policies and therefore whose interests they serve.

The case is rather different with respect to the role of ideology, if that

9. Please recall the statement that concludes the last section, that the allocation system works, usually *not* by individuals choosing merchantable ideas, but by only certain of their ideas finding markets.

10. *Capitalism, Socialism and Democracy*, pp. 152–53.

ambiguous word is appropriated to denote a set of beliefs which are not directed to an enlarged, long-run view of self-interest. If an anti-market ideology is postulated, and postulated to be independent of self-interest, then what is its origin and what is its content? Do we not face an inherently arbitrary choice if we follow this route?: anti-market values are then some humanistic instinct for personal solidarity rather than arms-length dealings, or a search for simplicity and stability in a world where competitive technology is the sorcerer's apprentice, or a wish for a deliberately inefficient egalitarianism, or something else. Choices in this direction are surely as numerous and arbitrary as choices of ethical systems, and indeed that is what they are. Perhaps no one, and certainly no economist, has the right to disparage such nonutility-maximizing systems, but even an economist is entitled to express skepticism about the coherence and content, and above all the actual acceptance on a wide scale, of any such ideology.

In the event, ideology is beginning to make fugitive appearances in the quantitative studies of the origins of public policies. Thus, if one wishes to know why some states lean to income taxes and others to sales taxes, the most popular measure of the higher values (or of intellectual confusion?) entertained by a state is the percentage of its vote cast for McGovern in 1972! At this level, ideology is only a name for a bundle of undefined notions one refuses to discuss.

The simplest way to test the role of ideology as a nonutility-maximizing goal is to ascertain whether the supporters of such an ideology incur costs in supporting it. If on average and over substantial periods of time we find (say) that the proponents of "small is beautiful" earn less than comparable talents devoted to urging the National Association of Manufacturers to new glories, I will accept the evidence. But first let us see it.

4. The Calculus of Morals

I arrive by the devious route you observe at the thesis that flows naturally and even irresistibly from the theory of economics. Man is eternally a utility-maximizer, in his home, in his office—be it public or private—in his church, in his scientific work, in short, everywhere. He can and often does err: perhaps the calculation is too difficult, but more often his information is incomplete. He learns to correct these errors, although sometimes at heavy cost.

What we call ethics, on this approach, is a set of rules with respect to dealings with other persons, rules which in general prohibit behavior which is only myopically self-serving, or which imposes large costs on others with small gains to oneself. General observance of these rules makes not only for long-term gains to the actor but also yields some outside benefits ("externalities"), and the social approval of the ethics is a mild form of enforcement of the rules to achieve the general benefits.[11] Of course some people will gain by violating the rules. More precisely, everyone violates some rule or other occasionally, and a few people violate important rules often.

Two difficulties with enlarging and elaborating this approach to ethical codes are worth mentioning. The first is the constant temptation to define the utility of the individual in such a way that the hypothesis is tautological. That difficulty is serious because there is no accepted content to the utility function—I gave my interpretation at the end of the second lecture, and it made a person's utility depend upon the welfare of the actor, his family, plus a narrow circle of associates. Still, the difficulties in using utility theory can be exaggerated. A rational person learns from experience, so it is a contradiction of the utility-maximizing hypothesis if we observe systematically biased error in predictions: thus one cannot surreptitiously introduce the theory of mistakes. The development of a content-rich theory of utility-maximizing is a never-ending task.

A second difficulty with the utility-maximizing hypothesis is that it is difficult to test, less because of its own ambiguities than because there is no accepted body of ethical beliefs which can be tested for consistency with the hypothesis. In the absence of such a well-defined set of beliefs, any ad hoc ethical value can be presented, and of course no respectable theory can cope with this degree of arbitrariness of test.

In particular, a system of ethics of individual behavior is all that one can ask a theory of individual utility-maximizing behavior to explain. Political values—values that the society compels its members to observe by recourse to political sanctions—include such popular contemporary policies as income redistribution and prohibition of the use of characteristics such as race and age and sex in certain areas of behavior (but not yet in other areas such as marriage). It requires a political theory rather than an individualistic ethical theory to account for policies and goals whose chief commendation to a substantial minority of people is that their acceptance spares them a term in jail.

With these disclaimers, I believe that it is a feasible and even an orthodox scientific problem to ascertain a set of widely and anciently accepted precepts of ethical personal behavior, and to test their concordance with utility-maximizing behavior for the preponderance of individuals. In fact Rawls's proposal of a method of constructing an inductive ethical system, which I briefly described earlier, is exactly the procedure that would show that the ethical system was based on utility-maximizing behavior. My confidence that the test would yield this result will be

---

11. The expression of this social approval by an individual is itself enforced by the approval of other individuals and therefore constitutes a system of informal law. Clearly this line of argument takes us (as Michael McPherson pointed out) into political (i.e., not purely individualistic) theory.

disputed by many people of distinction, and that argues all the more for making the test.

5. Conclusion

I have presented the hypothesis that we live in a world of reasonably well-informed people acting intelligently in pursuit of their self-interests. In this world leaders play only a modest role, acting much more as agents than as instructors or guides of the classes they appear to lead.

The main aspects of social development all have discoverable purposes and should run predictable courses. It is precisely the great virtue—and the great vulnerability—of a comprehensive theory of human behavior that it should account for all persistent and widespread phenomena within its wide domain.

If the hypothesis proves to be as fertile and prescient in political and social affairs as it has been in economic affairs, we can look forward to major advances in our understanding of issues as grave as the kinds of economic and political systems toward which we are evolving. Even if it does not achieve this imperial status, I am wholly confident that it will become a powerful theme guiding much work in the social sciences in the next generation. I would give much to learn what it will teach us of the prospects of my friend, the competitive economy.

4

The Economists and the Problem of Monopoly

For much too long a time, students of the history of the American antitrust policy have been at least mildly perplexed by the coolness with which American economists greeted the Sherman Act. Was not the nineteenth century the period in which the benevolent effects of competition were most widely extolled? Should not a profession praise a Congress which seeks to legislate its textbook assumptions into universal practice? And with even modest foresight, should not the economists have seen that the Sherman Act would put more into economists' purses than perhaps any other law ever passed?

Of course there were partial explanations. The coolness of the economists sometimes rested more on disbelief in the efficacy of the Sherman Act than on hostility to its purpose. The route of regulation was preferred—although this preference hardly restores the reputations of those economists as prophets. One might even point out that there were not many good American economists at the time, although an undeniable giant such as Irving Fisher shared the common view.

I intend on this occasion to review the attitudes of economists toward monopoly as a problem in public policy. My subject, however, is a good deal broader than the Sherman Act and its reception: the last two centuries of the economic writings on monopoly policy, particularly in England and the United States, will be surveyed. Thereafter I shall examine the reciprocal effects of economics and antitrust policy upon each other.

1. From Smith to Sherman

Adam Smith, that great manufacturer of traditions, did not fail us in the area of monopoly, for he created or rendered authoritative three traditions that were faithfully followed in English economics for almost one hundred years. The first tradition was to pay no attention to the formal theory of monopoly, a tradition first challenged in 1850 by Dionysius

This essay was delivered as the Ely Lecture before the American Economic Association in Washington, D. C., December 28, 1981, and appeared in the *American Economic Review*, May, 1982.

An equally appropriate title, which I would have chosen if speaking to the American Monopolists' Association, is "Monopoly and the Problem of Economists." I wish to thank Aaron Director and Stephen Stigler for helpful comments, and William Baxter, Bruce Snapp, and John Peterman for the data in the tables.

Lardner in dealing with railway rates.[1] How fortunate was Smith: even by neglect of a subject he could create a tradition! It is the one area where many of us, however, are his equal or superior.

The second tradition was to identify the serious monopolies of his time with the grants of exclusive power by the state. For Smith the two leading instances were the guild corporations and the great joint stock trading companies.[2] He could not have been unmindful of the existence of many other examples—one would be the highland village which could support only one or two enterprises in one trade. But almost by definition they were of small importance: economic mosquitos collecting their drop of blood from the body economic.[3]

His third tradition-setting view was that nothing could be done about the instances of monopoly and collusion of small numbers of rivals. Actual prohibition of collusive meetings could not be achieved by "any law which either could be executed, or would be consistent with liberty and justice."[4] Those meetings of businessmen which he made famous would seldom create "merriment," of course, if they left profits where they found them.

I shall be brief in dealing with the later bearers of these traditions. Let me only notice in passing that Ricardo called a price a monopoly price only if cost of production had no influence on its level,[5]—an adequate proof of the low state of monopoly theory. He would demand, however, that I record the statement attributed to him by Hansard: "Mr. Ricardo . . . [had] never given a vote in favor of monopoly in his life."[6]

John Stuart Mill recognized the baneful effect of small numbers on the vigor of competition: "Where competitors are so few, they always end up agreeing not to compete."[7] In such industries as water supply, therefore, although the state must control entry to prevent waste, it must also sooner or later regulate and possibly operate such enterprises. In keeping with custom, Mill saw no way for the state to support competition other than by failing to create monopolies.

We have one early antimonopoly policy on which to test the attitudes of the classical economists. A host of earlier laws were codified into the

1. *Railway Economy* (New York: Harper and Bros., 1850), ch. XIII.
2. *The Wealth of Nations* Glasgow ed. 1976 (Oxford: Clarendon Press, 1976) passages on apprenticeship and joint stock companies.
3. The only large markets in which Smith expected important economies of scale, and hence small numbers, were banking, insurance, canals, and waterworks (ibid., II, 281).
4. Ibid., I, 144.
5. *Principles of Political Economy and Taxation* (Cambridge: Cambridge University Press, 1951) pp. 249–50; also *Works and Correspondence* (Cambridge: Cambridge University Press, 1951–55), II, 260, IX, 97–98. In extenuation, he should be credited with an early recognition of Mr. Harberger's triangle, II, 409.
6. Ibid., V, 301.
7. *Principles of Political Economy* (Toronto: University of Toronto Press, 1965), I, 142.

Combination Acts of 1799 and 1800, which forbade either employers or employees to join to influence the wage bargain. The passage of those acts did not attract the attention of any economists (who were few indeed in those years) but their repeal in 1824, which was engineered by Francis Place, did receive modest attention.[8] That McCulloch wrote strongly in support of the repeal of the acts is a plain expression of the remoteness from the economists' thoughts of an active antimonopoly program.[9] This well-informed writer ("We should never have done were we to attempt to lay before our readers a tithe of the information of which we are possessed"), in the course of a discussion marvelous for its insights as well as its inconsistencies, remarks,

> The merest tyro in economical science would not hesitate to ridicule all apprehension of famine, or even of a stinted supply of the market, from a combination of corn dealers, or of bakers, to raise the price of corn or bread: For we would feel assured, that there were a hundred chances to one that no such combination would ever be generally entered into; and that supposing it were, the moment prices had been raised ever so little above their natural rate, it would become the interest of a large body of combiners to secede from the combination, and to throw their stock on the market.[10]

The weakness of collusion continued to be a widely accepted belief of economists.

The views of the community at large, as well as those of economists, are well-expressed in the admirable article on monopoly in the *Penny Cyclopedia* (1839). I quote two passages.

> It seems then that the word monopoly was never used in English law, except when there was a royal grant authorizing some one or more persons only to deal in or sell a certain commodity or article.

> If a number of individuals were to unite for the purpose of producing any particular article or commodity, and if they should succeed in selling such article very extensively, and

---

8. A comprehensive survey is made by William D. Grampp in "The Economists and the Combination Laws," *Quarterly Journal of Economics*, November 1979; see also the famous discussion by A. V. Dicey, in *Law and Opinion in the Nineteenth Century* (London: Macmillan, 1905). The effects of the early acts on unions deserve study. Grampp finds the laws "unworkable" and failing to prevent combinations from forming, but also quotes with approval the view that the repeal was "the starting point of a great new development in the history of English trade-unionism" (*op. cit.*, pp. 515, 522).

9. "Draft of proposed Bill . . . Relating to Combinations of Workmen, etc.," *Edinburgh Review* 39 no. 77 (January 1824).

10. Ibid., pp. 320–21.

almost solely, such individuals in popular language would be said to have a monopoly. Now, as these individuals have no advantages given them by the law over other persons, it is clear they can only sell more of their commodity than other persons by producing the commodity cheaper and better. (15:341.)

On this view, laissez-faire served the ends of an antitrust policy.

The omission of a theory of monopoly and oligopoly began to be remedied in the last third of the century. The remarkable work of Cournot and Dupuit began to enter English economics, in particular through Edgeworth, Sidgwick, and Marshall.[11] Putting aside the intractable problem of oligopoly, substantial advances were made in the theory of monopoly and price discrimination. So ended the first Smith tradition.

The second tradition—that all important monopolies were created by the state—began to be eroded in the nineteenth century with the development of railroads and other large-scale utilities, as Mill's practice has already told us. We now had a class of monopolies which might, and usually did, get grants of power (eminent domain) and more merchandisable assets from the state, but whose existence rested chiefly on important economies of scale. The recommendation, first of publicity of accounts, and then regulation or public ownership, became general. By 1890, Britain and the United States were the only important nations in the world with privately owned railroads. Before that date little attention was paid in the English or American economics to monopoly in the manufacturing or trading sectors. So Smith's second tradition had bifurcated into state-created monopolies and those created by economies of scale, and the latter constituted the public utility sector of the period.

Smith's third tradition, that the state should only refrain from creating monopolies, was thus amended to assign responsibility to the state also for the control and perhaps operation of railroads and similar utilities. A careful student of the history of economics would have searched long and hard, on the unseasonably cool day of July 2 of 1890, the day the Sherman Act was signed by President Harrison, for any economist who had ever recommended the policy of actively combatting collusion or monopolization in the economy at large.

2. Since Sherman

The historians of American antitrust policy have emphasized the lack of enthusiasm, and often the downright hostility, with which economists

---

11. I am coming to admire Henry Sidgwick almost as much as the other two. His *Principles of Political Economy* (1883; 3rd ed., London: Macmillan, 1901) has two chapters (bk. II, ch. IX and X) which are among the best in the history of microeconomics, dealing with the theories of human capital and noncompetitive behavior.

greeted the Sherman Act.[12] Jeremiah W. Jenks, author of a standard work, *The Trust Problem*, offered this appraisal a decade after the passage of the law:

Twenty-seven States and Territories have passed laws intended to destroy such industrial combinations as now exist, and to prevent the formation of others. Fifteen States have similar provisions in their constitutions, . . . Besides this legislation on the part of our States, we have a Federal Anti-Trust Act. . . . A study of these statutes and of the decisions of our courts of last resort which have been made under them, will show that they have had comparatively little, practically no effect, as regards the trend of our industrial development.[13]

This scepticism was shared by probably a majority of economists of the period, in England as well as here. Thus, D. H. Macgregor, Marshall's premier student of market organization, observed that leading economists believed that the development of large-scale enterprise represented a powerful historical force:

If this is so, the State places itself in an altogether untenable position by the enactment of laws against combinations as such—laws, for instance, so general in their terms as the Sherman Act of 1890. . . . If there are economic tendencies, the State cannot prevent, although it can harass them; and the belief of economists in the possibilities of combination appears justified by the utter failure of the American laws to stop the development, although these laws now fill a bulky volume. More than this, even if there were a greater divergence of expert opinion than there is, it would not be the function of the state to prejudge the question, and to set up a standard of economic orthodoxy. The position is an intolerable one when the course of industrial development stultifies the statute-book, monopolistic associations flourish in the face of the law, and anti-Trust proposals have exhausted their function when an electoral campaign is over.[14]

Two influential economists were somewhat more sympathetic to limited antitrust policies. J. B. Clark believed that large enterprises were inevitable, but that they would be deprived of monopoly power by the

12. See H. Thorelli, *Federal Antitrust Policy* (Baltimore: Johns Hopkins University Press, 1955), pp. 311 ff.; John D. Clark, *The Federal Trust Policy* (Baltimore: Johns Hopkins University Press, 1931), ch. V.

13. *The Trust Problem* (New York: McClure, Phillips, 1900), pp. 217–18. Richard T. Ely was no less emphatic: "If there is any serious student of our economic life who believes that anything substantial has been gained by all the laws passed against trusts. . . . this authority has yet to be heard from" (*Monopolies and Trusts* [New York: Macmillan, 1906], p. 243).

14. *Industrial Combination* (London: George Bell, 1906), pp. 231–32.

threat of potential entry, provided these great enterprises were denied the use of predatory policies such as local price cutting.[15] Marshall viewed the Federal Trade Commission as primarily a research arm of policy, able to collect facts and submit them to "long-continued, organic and scientific study," and therefore become competent to distinguish the effects of socially desirable and undesirable economic practices.[16] I am not prepared to ridicule this vision, and indeed the commission viewed itself partly in that light in its first days. Nevertheless, it would have been helpful if Marshall, or some of his lesser contemporaries, had explained the nature and workings of their sovereign regulatory tool, publicity. How and where publicity (after all, a policy akin to legal blackmail) could control undesirable behavior was never spelled out.[17]

In the decades that immediately followed, it would be more accurate to say that tolerance of antitrust policy grew, than to say that it became a popular cause among economists. As late as 1932 Arthur R. Burns characterized the antitrust laws as "a notable failure,"[18] but friends of the policy had begun to appear. Henry C. Simons, in his celebrated *Positive Program for Laissez-Faire*,[19] demanded that

> There must be outright dismantling of our gigantic corporations, and persistent prosecution of producers who organize, by whatever methods, for price maintenance or output limitation. There must be explicit and unqualified repudiation of the so-called "rule of reason." . . . In short, restraint of trade must be treated as a major crime. . . .

No doubt my memory exaggerates the influence of this voice, which sounded so clear and brave when I listened to it in a Chicago classroom.

In any event, I believe that a census of economists' attitudes would show a steady rise in the popularity of antitrust policy in the 1950s and 1960s. One telling indication of the present state of professional opinion is that Professor Galbraith, who attacks only popular views, has repeatedly delighted in disparaging the effectiveness of our antitrust policy, or denying its consistency with other policies.

This rapid sketch of the evolution of economists' attitudes toward antitrust policy poses many questions, of which I shall discuss three with merciful brevity:

15. *The Control of Trusts* (New York: Macmillan, 1901). The role for legislation is much larger in the second edition, where he asked for prohibitions on interlocking directorates, requirements, and unfair methods of competition. See J. B. and J. M. Clark, *The Control of Trusts*, 2d ed. (New York: Macmillan, 1912), pp. 104 ff., ch. VII.

16. *Industry and Trade*, 1st ed. (London: Macmillan, 1919), pp. 516–18.

17. For an example of the bold claims for publicity, see Hadley, *Railroad Transportation* (New York: G. P. Putnam's and Sons, 1893), p. 137.

18. *The Decline of Competition* (New York: McGraw-Hill, 1932), p. 523.

19. *Positive Program for Laissez-Faire* (University of Chicago Press, 1934).

1. Why did the economists' attitudes change?
2. What effect has economics had on antitrust policy?
3. What effect has antitrust policy had on economics?

3. The Causes for the Change of Opinion

The surprise often expressed at the early indifference or opposition to antitrust policy by economists stemmed from the traditional praise of competitive organization of markets and industries in our literature. Free trade is a sort of international antimonopoly program in itself: the markets of our nation should be open to producers in other nations. So vast a majority of economists had vigorously supported free international trade for the century before the Sherman Act that it was not a bizarre expectation that intranational competition should be favored as much as international competition. But we know that this was not the case, and we shall shortly propose a reason for this difference.

It would be gratifying to me if I could report that our profession's changing view was based upon the systematic study by economists of the effects of the policy, in short, that hard evidence carried the day. Unfortunately, there have been no persuasive studies of the effects of the Sherman and Clayton Acts throughout this century. Simon Whitney's two-volume survey reaches a favorable verdict on the antitrust laws,[20] but his chapter surveys of industries and cases are joined to his conclusions by leaps of Olympic grandeur. My attempt in 1967 at measurement of the effects of the antitrust laws was able to dismiss nonsense such as the prohibition of interlocking directorates, but reached only feebly favorable presumptions on sections 1 and 2 of the Sherman Act.[21] James Ellert's more recent comprehensive analysis of the influence of antitrust actions on stock prices of defendant companies finds only small effects at best, except when triple damage suits follow.[22]

Indeed, the early scepticism of the effectiveness of the laws has even received some recent confirmation. The dissolutions of the American Tobacco Company and especially of the Standard Oil Company were at the time widely viewed with scepticism. In a measure these doubts were recently confirmed when Malcolm Burns showed that the stock market soon set the relevant future effects of these dissolutions at naught.[23] There are numerous scraps of evidence on the issue, but they are by no means single-minded in their tendencies, so we must look further.

20. *Antitrust Policies* (New York: Twentieth Century Fund, 1958).
21. "The Economic Effects of the Antitrust Laws," *Journal of Law and Economics* 9 (1967): 225–58.
22. "Antitrust Enforcement and the Behavior of Stock Prices," Ph.D. dissertation, University of Chicago, 1975.
23. "The Competitive Effects of Trust-Busting: A Portfolio Analysis," *Journal of Political Economy* 85(1977): 717–39.

I would propose as a first main explanation for the change of opinion a simple, and yet I believe an important, point. In the first decades of the Sherman Act, *all*—literally all—the attention of economists and public was focused on combination and explicit cooperative arrangements (now labeled cartels) with monopoly power. Everyone knew that the first section of the Sherman Act concerned collusion, and the Addyston Pipe case was duly observed, but informal collusion seemed a peripheral target of the law. J. B. Clark was explicit:

> So long as mere pools or contracts to control prices were depended on they were not as menacing as the later forms of union [of firms] became; and they did at least allay a warfare that involved much evil. In doing this they made their contribution to general prosperity, and the modest price of this was something to which the public reconciled itself, though it did not make the payment altogether willingly. It was the appearance of consolidations that were firmer and more complete that caused the menacing shadow of general monopoly to deepen.[24]

The Sherman law was primarily a law against trusts. The Clayton Act did not even concern itself with conspiracies, with the exception of the prohibition of interlocking directorates.

Gradually the emphasis of the enforcement of the laws shifted toward the conspiracies in restraint of trade. In historical retrospect there have been many conspiracy cases for every attempt to prevent or dissolve a monopoly. That shift in focus had an important consequence for professional opinion.

Collusion cases do not raise the question of economies of scale, at least in any easy or explicit way. All the fears that dissolution of large firms would lead to great inefficiencies seem to fall by the side in collusion cases. The defender of antitrust policy as it was practiced need not offer defences against a charge of economic inefficiency or obstruction of great historical forces. As the main content of the effective definition of monopoly changed, it became easier to oppose monopoly.

There is and was no tradition of affection for cartel organizations in the Anglo-Saxon literature: indeed the words cartel and guild are frequently used to anathematize an industry or practice. Standard theory associates cartels with less efficient uses of resources than with monopoly proper, and with much less technological progress. Cartels belong in the class of indefensible institutions, and it would more appropriately express American economists' attitudes if cartellizing had been labelled industrial incest.

24. Clark and Clark, *The Control of Trusts* (1912), p. 4.

Let me consider more briefly a second possible explanation for the growth of professional liking for antitrust policy, in addition to the shift in policy emphasis to collusion that I have just described. The main methods of controlling economic activity alternative to the market are public regulation and ownership. It would be very easy to say that growing disenchantment with political controls of economic activity has increased the desire of economists for market solutions. The reputations of the NRA, incomes policies, and general price controls—to say nothing of the post office—are not of the best. The reputation of industry regulation of transportation and agriculture is no better. Yet I am unwilling to press this case: for every criticism of the failures of political controls, I suspect that I can still find two or three allegations of market failure.

Finally, let me propose one further explanation, one that economists are very good at understanding. After many years of abstention, I have recently been a participant in several antitrust cases. From these cases I have learned three things:

1. It was not exactly news, but it was impressed upon me that justice does not always prevail, and it is fortunate that Justice does not always prevail.
2. The number of economists, ranging from Nobel prize winners to graduate students no better known than the Unknown Soldier, who are employed in antitrust actions is large, running into the many hundreds.
3. The rate of compensation for economists in this activity is not in violation of the federal minimum wage law.

I simply record that antitrust testimony is probably one of the three or four major sources of income of economists, well below teaching and research but possibly equal to that earned from writing, lecturing, and televising the mother science, or from making macroeconomic predictions.

If you are unsatisfied with the adequacy of these explanations for the rise in favor among economists of the antitrust policy, you share that feeling with me.

4. The Economists' Influence on Policy

When a set of recommendations is made at one time by a prominent economist and soon followed by the passage of laws consistent with those recommendations, it is possible to believe that the recommendations were being followed. This sequence can be observed with respect to J. B. Clark's detailed pronouncements against predatory competition and the antitrust laws of 1914.

Yet I am unwilling to believe that economists in general, or Professor Clark in particular, had any appreciable influence on antitrust legislation. It would be possible to mention many other people who were making similar recommendations, but that merely complicates the chain of causation. The real reason for doubt is that no economist had any professional knowledge on which to base recommendations that should carry weight with a sceptical legislator. Consider two important examples. First, the major role of predatory competition in obstructing and suppressing the competitors of a trust was based upon anecdotal hearsay, primarily of the muckrakers. Here is a sample from J. B. Clark:

> A producer . . . once called on the manager of the trust that was driving him to the wall, and was received with the brusque admonition that he had "better get out of the business." "But do you not see," said the independent producer, "that, in my territory, I can produce more cheaply than you can?" "Do you not see," was the reply, "that if we lose money in the twenty cities where you are operating, and make money in the two hundred other cities where we are operating, we come out ahead?"[25]

Candor forces me to state my belief that the distinguished Columbia professor invented this dialogue, but even if he had a recording of it, it is no evidence for an economist. Modern scholarship, I may observe, has raised strong doubts about the frequency of use of predatory competition, and has by no means resolved the theory of its operations.[26]

Second, the view that the watering of stock and the fleecing of investors was one main purpose of the formation of trusts rested, so far as I can tell, on the fact that some mergers were extremely profitable to promoters—with scarcely a glance at the effects upon investors. If J. P. Morgan's yacht was a powerful argument, it should still not have come from professors of economics. We shall return again to this problem of established economic knowledge.

The active participation of economists in antitrust policy has of course grown immensely. The first economist in the Antitrust Division may have been Corwin Edwards, in the regime of Thurman Arnold.[27] The number of economists has now risen to about forty-five, and the Federal Trade Commission has twice as many (see table 1). The commission, indeed, was assigned large tasks of economic research by its enabling statute, and in its first fifteen years the number of economists rose to forty-four (in

---

25. Ibid., pp. 34–35.
26. John S. McGee, "Predatory Price Cutting: The Standard Oil (N.J.) Case," *Journal of Law and Economics* 1 (1958); L.G. Telser, "Cutthroat Competition and the Long Purse," *Journal of Law and Economics* (1966); and for references to the substantial literature, J. S. McGee, "Predatory Competition Revisited," *Journal of Law and Economics* 23 (1980).
27. He provides a characteristically noneconomic account of Arnold in "Thurman Arnold and the Antitrust Laws," *Political Science Quarterly* 58 (1943): 338–55.

Table 1. *Economists in the Antitrust Agencies, 1913–81*

Year	Dept. of Justice[1]	FTC[2]
1913	n.a.	n.a.
1923	n.a.	30
1930	n.a.	44
1951	n.a.	18
1955	n.a.	26
1971	n.a.	47
1972	21	53
1973	26	56
1974	24	66
1975	36	67
1976	43	73
1977	40	73
1978	44	81
1979	45	78
1980	45	80
1981	n.a.	92

[1]Data provided by William Baxter and Bruce R. Snapp, of the Antitrust Division.
[2]Data provided by John Peterman of the FTC.

1930),[28] only to fall by more than half in the next two decades. The wonder, of course, is that any large number of economists ever survive in a law enforcement agency. To these public servants we must add the number of economists employed by private parties, which has been possibly twenty times as large. But unless one believes in a labor theory of value, the magnitude of economists' influence remains uncertain. Even on the labor theory of value, our socially necessary amount of labor is a tiny part of antitrust product value.

Those who are sceptical of our influence will find support in Suzanne Weaver's interviews in the Antitrust Division, where the tension between economists and lawyers is emphasized.[29] The powerful resentment of the lawyers to Donald Turner's economic orientation is well known. A parallel study of the FTC by R. A. Katzmann finds economists achieving a position of some power after 1970, which suggests that someone's learning curve is rather flat.[30] Knowledgeable economists have proposed much more favorable verdicts on our influence, but they do not offer evidence of a specificity or power such as we normally require in professional work.[31]

28. It is not apparent that these economists had a large influence on the commission's work; they are studiously ignored by G. C. Henderson, *The Federal Trade Commission* (New Haven: Yale University Press, 1924).

29. *Decision to Prosecute* (Cambridge: MIT Press, 1977), esp. pp. 120–36.

30. *Regulatory Bureaucracy* (Cambridge: MIT Press, 1980), ch. IV.

31. See Oliver Williamson's commentary in R. D. Tollison, *The Political Economy of Antitrust* (Lexington, Mass.: D. C. Heath, 1979), pp. 84–90.

Economists have their glories, but I do not believe that the body of American antitrust law is one of them. I rest my fundamental doubts about our influence on antitrust policy on the fact that we have provided precious little tested economic knowledge to guide policy. No one can believe that we have established a precise relationship between concentration and market power. Doctrines such as "shared monopoly," "preemptive product differentiation," and price fixing by interviews with the trade press have all been proposed by economists and antitrust agencies in the past decade. None is even agreed to generally by economists, let alone tested empirically. The prosecution and defense both find economists to their liking, but that hardly establishes the direction of causation. Some cases seem sophisticated and sensible (e.g., the widely acclaimed Sylvania decision), but shouldn't this happen with random fluctuation?

If law is efficient—as my colleague (now Judge) Richard Posner has argued with great learning and ingenuity—we should expect it to incorporate tested knowledge, and for the rest to respond to the effective political forces impinging upon policy formation. It would be remarkably vain to believe that today's industrial organization economics supports much specific policy. I freely grant that our economic analysis is better than J. B. Clark's. I hope Professor Clark agrees. If we have improved, our influence should be somewhat greater than it once was but that does not mean that it should be large. We need to be humble in a day when the greatest function of the antitrust laws appears to be to arm the defenses of the corporate officials who, when a takeover proposal is made, seek to maintain their tenure against the avarice of their stockholders.

5. The Influence of
Monopoly Policy on Economics

Let us now turn the question around and ask what the effect of the antitrust policy has been on economists. We are addressing a special case of the general problem of how a science responds to the interests of its society.

The direct demand for the services of economists in implementing antitrust policy—particularly in litigation—has already been referred to. No one has repealed the aphorism about pipers and the tunes they play: I would conjecture that the influence of direct employment is neither negligible nor large. I suspect that the large number of economists who are beneficiaries of the Bell system (including its journal) are less prone to criticize that system than they would otherwise be. Again, antitrust experts surely lose one or two degrees of freedom in dealing with the effects of concentration or the definition of a market in each antitrust case in which they appear.

Table 2. *Articles Published on Monopoly and Public Utilities, United Kingdom and United States*

Journals, by Nation	1900–1909	1930–39	1960–65[a]
	1. Monopoly[b]		
1. U.S.: Articles	27	137	206
2. As percentage of estimated total articles*	5.4%	2.6%	2.5%
3. U.K.: Articles	7	16	71
4. As percentage of estimated total articles*	1.3%	1.3%	3.0%
	2. Public Utilities[c]		
5. U.S.: Articles[d]	100	179	195
6. As percentage of estimated total articles*	20.0%	3.8%	2.5%
7. U.K.: Articles	30	35	102
8. As percentage of estimated total articles*	5.5%	2.8%	4.3%

SOURCE: American Economic Association, *Index of Economic Journals* for years indicated.
[a]Recent years of the *Index* are not directly comparable because of the revision of subject codes and the adoption of the deplorable policy of including reprintings of articles.
[b]Subject codes 15.23 through 15.39.
[c]Subject codes 15.6 through 15.99.
[d]Excluding the *Journal of Land and Public Utility Economics*, which had 260 articles (mostly noneconomic in nature) in the second period, and 46 in 1960–65.
*Estimated total articles by nation based on a 50% sample of those in the authors' index for 1900–1909 and a 14% sample for 1930–39 and 1960–65.

Jacob Viner once told me of his experience in testifying for the government in an early basing-point price system case. I may add that his compensation was probably negligible or less.[32] He began, he said, as a detached scholar, but after some hours of sharp cross-examination he found that he had become an aggressive supporter of the government's position. Only the economist who withdraws completely from all policy discussions is insulated from such influences, and insulated also from much of the real world.

A quantitative measure of our profession's changing interest in monopoly and public regulation can be derived from that customary guide, the *Index of Economic Journals*.[33] This source tells us that we fully shared the excitement of the progressive era and the muckrakers

32. I am reminded of the time Viner gave a splendid lecture at the University of Minnesota on the balance of power. The lecture bureau asked him for the customary 15 percent of his fee, which he gleefully reported to be zero.
33. The data are reported in table 2, which I must thank Claire Friedland for compiling. The relative attention to industrial organization in the earlier period is probably underestimated because of the omission of books, which were the major vehicle for publication in that area.

problem of monopoly: fully one-fourth of all articles in America in the first decade of this century were on monopoly and public regulation. Four out of five of these articles were on the panacea of that age, public regulation of utilities. With the passage of time the relative interest in monopoly fell in half, and the interest in public utilities fell by seven-eighths, and now neither subject receives as large a share of economists' attention as in Britain. The absolute level of writing on these subjects has of course risen substantially.

I find this relative decline in the measure of our interest less surprising, and not at all disturbing, compared to the minor influence that our antitrust policy has had upon fundamental economic research. One scholar, Aaron Director, did examine a variety of industrial practices in the course of teaching a famous course on antitrust law with Edward Levi and made fascinating theoretical contributions (virtually all oral) on predatory competition, tie-in sales and other forms of price discrimination, and patent policy. But his work has had few imitators.

Consider the problem of defining a market within which the existence of competition or some form of monopoly is to be determined. The typical antitrust case is an almost impudent exercise in economic gerrymandering. The plaintiff sets the market, at a maximum, as one state in area and including only aperture-priority SLR cameras selling between $200 and $250. This might be called J-Shermanizing the market, after Senator John Sherman. The defendant will in turn insist that the market is worldwide, and includes not only all cameras, but also portrait artists and possibly transportation media because a visit is a substitute for a picture. This might also be called T-Shermanizing the market, this time after the Senator's brother, General William Tecumseh Sherman. Depending on who convinces the judge, the concentration ratios will be awesome or trivial, with a large influence on his verdict. My lament is that this battle on market definitions, which is fought thousands of times what with all the private antitrust suits, has received virtually no attention from us economists. Except for a casual flirtation with cross-elasticities of demand and supply, the determination of markets has remained an undeveloped area of economic research at either the theoretical or empirical level. Other branches of antitrust economics, such as vertical mergers and franchising and leasing, have been almost equally neglected.

It would not be proper to conclude that our antitrust policy has had no effect upon economic research. A literature such as that on workable competition or administered prices—neither an ornament to our science—was created to give advice on monopoly policy. The data supplied to the scholars by litigation have provided a wealth of materials, which have yielded among other good things innumerable dissertations on as many industries. Industrial organization was a much more active field in the United States than elsewhere between the two World Wars, and our antitrust policy was surely the main reason for this difference. Yet this history is an unnecessary reminder that active public policy carries no assurance that fundamental economic research relevant to that policy area will flourish.

6. Conclusion

The only conclusion I shall seek to draw from this survey of the relationship between economics and antitrust policy is that the attitude of economists toward monopoly policy is strongly influenced by the corpus of technical price theory. Our present support for procompetitive policies is due in good part to the strong virtues we attach to competitive markets and industries.

That point is illustrated rather than contradicted by our historical survey. Competition is now much more virgorously supported than it was in 1890 primarily because we understand it much better today. In 1890 competition was a commonsense notion in economics, more a loose description of economic behavior than an analytical concept. In no sense was the supremacy of competition challenged by the then small, emerging literature on monopoly. A concept without enemies, however, is also a concept without informed friends. The content and power of competition have become much better understood after several generations of far-ranging debate about monopolistic and imperfect competition and oligopoly—a word unknown to the profession in 1890. Consider one small example: The earlier literature of predatory competition had the predator cut prices in the vicinity of the prey and raise prices elsewhere to recoup the loss. Today it would be embarrassing to encounter this argument in professional discourse.

I once encountered vigorous criticism when I argued the related thesis that professional economists are more favorable to the use of a price system than other academic people.[34] Even the urbanity of Harvard economists was ruffled at the suggestion that they leaned more than intellectuals generally toward more use of the price system and less use of the political system in dealing with economic problems. Quite independently of the question of how one should lean, I believed then, as I do now, that it is a tribute to the strength of the corpus of knowledge in a discipline if its practitioners accept it even in areas outside their professional work. We have trouble enough showing how economics influences our society, so it is of some consolation to assert that it influences us!

34. See "The Politics of Political Economists," reprinted in my *Essays in the History of Economics* (Chicago: University of Chicago Press, 1965).

References
Burns, Arthur. *The Decline of Competition.* New York: McGraw-Hill, 1932.
Burns, Malcolm. "The Competitive Effects of Trust-Busting: A Portfolio Analysis," *Journal of Political Economy* 85 (1977): 717–39.
Clark, J. B. *The Control of Trusts.* New York: Macmillan, 1901.
_____, and Clark, J. M. *The Control of Trusts.* 2d edition. New York: Macmillan, 1912.
Clark, John D. *The Federal Trust Policy.* Baltimore: Johns Hopkins University Press, 1931.
Dicey, Albert Venn. *Law and Opinion in the Nineteenth Century.* London: Macmillan, 1905.
Ellert, James. "Antitrust Enforcement and the Behavior of Stock Prices." Ph.D. dissertation, University of Chicago, 1975.
Ely, Richard T. *Monopolies and Trusts.* New York: Macmillan, 1906.
Edwards, Corwin. "Thurmon Arnold and the Antitrust Laws." *Political Science Quarterly* 58 (1943): 338–55.
Grampp, William D. "The Economists and the Combination Laws." *Quarterly Journal of Economics* 93 (November 1979): 501–22.
Hadley, George. *Railroad Transportation.* New York: G. P. Putnam's and Sons, 1893.
Henderson, G. C. *The Federal Trade Commission.* New Haven: Yale University Press, 1924.
Jenks, Jeremiah W. *The Trust Problem,* New York: McLure, Phillips, 1900.
Katzmann, R. A. *Regulatory Bureaucracy.* Cambridge: MIT Press, 1980.
Lardner, Dionysius. *Railway Economy.* New York: Harper and Bros., 1850.
McCulloch, J. R. "Draft of proposed Bill . . . Relating to Combination of Workmen, etc." *Edinburgh Review* 39, no. 77 (January 1824).
McGee, John S. "Predatory Price Cutting: The Standard Oil (N.J.) Case." *Journal of Law and Economics* 1 (October 1958): 137–69.
_____. "Predatory Competition Revisited." *Journal of Law and Economics* 23 (October 1980).
Macgregor, D. H. *Industrial Combination.* London: George Bell, 1906.
Marshall, Alfred. *Industry and Trade.* 1st ed. London: Macmillan, 1919.
Mill, J. S. *Principles of Political Economy.* Toronto: University of Toronto Press, 1965.
Ricardo, David. *Principles of Political Economy and Taxation,* edited by P. Sraffa. Vol. 1 of *Works and Correspondence.* Cambridge: Cambridge University Press, 1951.
_____. *Works and Correspondence,* edited by P. Sraffa and M. H. Dobbs. 10 vols. Cambridge: Cambridge University Press, 1951–55.
Sidgwick, Henry. *Principles of Political Economy.* 1883. 3d ed. London: Macmillan, 1901.
Simons, Henry C. *Positive Program for Laissez-Faire.* Chicago: University of Chicago Press, 1934.
Smith, Adam. *The Wealth of Nations.* Glasgow edition. Oxford: Clarendon Press, 1976.
Stigler, George. "The Economic Effects of the Antitrust Laws." *Journal of Law and Economics* 9 (October 1967): 225–58.

_____. "The Politics of Political Economists." In *Essays in the History of Economics*. Chicago: University of Chicago Press, 1965.

Telser, Lester G. "Cutthroat Competition and the Long Purse," *Journal of Law and Economics*, 1966.

Thorelli, H. *Federal Antitrust Policy*. Baltimore: Johns Hopkins University Press, 1955.

Weaver, Suzanne. *Decision to Prosecute*. Cambridge: MIT Press, 1977.

Whitney, Simon. *Antitrust Policies*. New York: Twentieth Century Fund, 1958.

Williamson, Oliver. "Commentary." In *The Political Economy of Antitrust*, edited by R. D. Tollinson. Lexington, Mass.: D. C. Heath, 1979.

Part Two   The Sociology of
the History of Science

5 Do Economists Matter?

A professor of economics is torn between two views of his professional role in this world. At least, *this* professor is.

One view, in which most of us were brought up, is that economists are the expert critics or defenders of any and all economic policies—not the only critics but surely among the more powerful. We study existing and alternative economic arrangements, and we are armed in our study with a theory of substantial power. We may not win all our battles—the persistence and even the upward surge of economic protectionism is a sufficient reminder that we may be more impotent than omnipotent—but we win some battles, and hope and strive to win more.

The contrasting view, to which I am led by this same professional training, is that consumers generally determine what will be produced, and producers make profits by discovering more precisely what consumers want and producing it more cheaply. Some may entertain a tinge of doubt about this proposition, thanks to the energy and skill of Professor Galbraith, but even his large talents hardly raise a faint thought that I live in a house rather than a tent because of the comparative advertising outlays of the two industries. This Cambridge eccentricity aside, then, it is useful to say that consumers direct production—and therefore, do they not direct the production of the words and ideas of intellectuals, rather than, as in the first view, vice versa?

There you have my dilemma and my theme. Now let me back up a little and examine the foundations of the two attitudes toward the intellectual in general, and the economist in particular.

1. The Economist as Friend and Guide to The Public

Why, when the economist gives advice to his society, is he so often and so cooly ignored? He never ceases to preach free trade—although the sermons are getting less frequent—and protectionism is growing in the United States. He deplores the perverse effects of minimum wage laws, and the legal minimum is regularly raised each 3 or 5 years. He brands usury laws as medieval superstition, but no state hurries to repeal its law.

We economists give several explanations for the unwisdom of our society. The first explanation is that the public does not understand our

Reprinted from *Southern Economic Journal* 42 (January 1976).

arguments, and therefore does not understand its self-interest. Tariffs are with us because the theory of comparative cost is beyond the comprehension of ordinary citizens. Consider, let us say, the tired factory hand or physician who has picked up Ricardo, and reads:

"England may be so circumstanced, that to produce the cloth may require the labour of 100 men for one year; and if she attempted to make the wine, it might require the labour of 120 men for the same time. England would therefore find it her interest to import wine, and to purchase it by the exportation of cloth.

To produce the wine in Portugal, might require only the labour of 80 men for one year, and to produce the cloth in the same country, might require the labour of 90 men for the same time. It would therefore be advantageous for her to export wine in exchange for cloth. This exchange might even take place, notwithstanding that the commodity imported by Portugal could be produced there with less labour than in England. Though she could make the cloth with the labour of 90 men, she would import it from a country where it required the labour of 100 men to produce it, because it would be advantageous to her rather to employ her capital in the production of wine, for which she would obtain more cloth from England, than she could produce by diverting a portion of her capital from the cultivation of vines to the manufacture of cloth.

Thus England would give the produce of the labour of 100 men, for the produce of the labour of 80. Such an exchange could not take place between the individuals of the same country. The labour of 100 Englishmen cannot be given for that of 80 Englishmen, but the produce of the labour of 100 Englishmen may be given for the produce of the labour of 80 Portuguese, 60 Russians, or 120 East Indians. The difference in this respect, between a single country and many, is easily accounted for, by considering the difficulty with which capital moves from one country to another, to seek a more profitable employment, and the activity with which it invariably passes from one province to another in the same country."

The import this layman is likely to embrace is not the English theory of free trade but a bottle of Portuguese wine.

The second explanation, which is really an extension of the first, is that self-seeking special interests—protected industries and their camp followers—suborn the political process and muddy the public understanding. No doubt these self-serving factions do all they can to feather their own nests, but they pluck the rest of us to get the feathers so we are back to the first explanation: the public geese can't be persuaded that they are being plucked.

These explanations for social error in economic policy imply a belief, to which I suspect that almost all economists subscribe, that noneconomists are slow and perverse in accepting the reasonably reliable findings of our science. Elsewise would not some of our relatively uncontroversial findings, such as the perversity of minimum wage laws as devices to aid poorly paid workers, long ago have been accepted?

To this belief in the backwardness of public understanding of economics, the tribe of economists generally associate a second belief: that *eventually* this retarded public can be taught at least the elementary lessons of efficient economic life. If the tribe did not temper its scorn for public understanding in this way, we would face the embarrassing question: why bother to try to educate the public? And then at least in the short run *we* economists would become effectively subject to the minimum wage laws, a thought too gruesome to contemplate.

Is it not peculiar, however, that physical scientists do not encounter the difficulties in public adoption of their findings that we economists meet? Theories of physics and chemistry and physiology more complex and abstract than ours, are readily accepted by a public that finances space exploration, swallows antibiotics and contraceptives, and puts its life savings in IBM. Complexity alone cannot explain the economists' comparative failure at persuasion: certainly the public comprehension of the underlying theories of these other sciences is inferior even to its comprehension of economic theory.

One can contrive special replies, such as that economists are less agreed upon their findings, but with little conviction. Even when we are most agreed, our success is often small, as the free trade example illustrates. Contrariwise, where agreement is small—as in the current state of Monetarist vs. Keynesian theories of the level of aggregate activity—a theory (now the monetarists') receives substantial (verbal) acceptance.

In short, the general belief of economists that the public is a slow, uncertain, but not utterly hopeless pupil in the school of economics, does not fit well with the reception of scientific advice in our society. It is a belief not calculated to explain our feeble successes and our mighty failures.

II. The Economist as a Customer's Man

A useful essay could be written on the subject of which phenomena an economist views as economic phenomena, but it would not be a popular essay. Few economists object seriously to treating political phenomena as explicable in terms of rational pursuit of self-interest, but they have qualms at using the same analysis on religion or warfare. They talk freely of the economics of labor, but hesitate at the economics of marriage or human fertility. They permit Dennis Robertson to speak of economizing on love, but do not wish love itself to be explained as utility-maximizing.

In particular, economists do not relish an explanation of their own scientific behavior in ordinary economic terms. To tell an economist that he chooses that type of work and that viewpoint which will maximize his income is, he will hotly say, a studied insult. Such market-oriented behavior will be characterized not with our customary phrases such as consumer sovereignty, but in terms as harsh as "intellectual prostitution." To adapt one's views to one's audience is hardly to be distinguished from the falsification of evidence and other disreputable behavior.

This hostile reaction is unduly hasty. It is possible, and in fact usually the case, that an intellectual can please his customers without recourse to professing beliefs he does not actually hold, or other dishonorable practices. Each economist has a variety of views, and let us assume for a moment that they come directly from heaven or hell. Unless one of us is singularly narrow in his inventory of views, some of the views appeal to some people and some views to others, and the audiences to which they appeal vary widely in size. It would be astonishing if we did not cultivate those views which had the largest audience. Indeed, it would be difficult not to cultivate these views because they are precisely the views that one is asked most often and most remuneratively to expound. I will be asked on occasion to denounce regulatory bodies, which I can do with tolerable knowledge and adequate sincerity, but no one solicits my related views on the methods of granting of degrees by universities.

And of course our views do not come *directly* from heaven or hell: they reach us through conduits with names like family, public press, and school. Most known ideas never reach us, or reach us shaped in caricature and charged with emotion. Our dependence upon the ideas and values of our culture is so complete that the true wonder is that on occasion a man creates a new idea.

One evidence of professional integrity of the economist is the fact that it is *not* possible to enlist good economists to defend protectionist programs or minimum wage laws. The groups who seek such legislation accordingly must seek elsewhere for their spokesmen and theorists—and judging by their success, the *ersatz* economists do their work well.

That intellectuals purvey ideas congenial to their society, however, is due much more to demand than to supply factors. I am prepared to assume that individuals always know their true self-interest, given sufficient time to learn the effects of alternative policies. Each sector of the public will therefore demand services from intellectuals favorable to the interests of that sector. Those whose skill and viewpoint are congenial to the interests of large groups will prosper and become "leaders of opinion" and those lacking either skill or acceptable viewpoint will write letters to provincial newspapers.

Thus the intellectuals find themselves addressing audiences with the messages those audiences desire to hear. This process is often compatible, as I have just argued, with full intellectual integrity. It would be less than candid of us to deny that the accommodation of message to listener is at times eased by the flexibility of conscience of the intellectual. It serves little (but some) purpose to mention this source of intellectual accommodation: we ought occasionally to remind ourselves that there is no presumption that intellectuals possess less or more courage and integrity than the rest of the population.

III. What the Customer Wants

Let me put aside, for the purposes of this paper, the consideration of the most time-consuming function of economists, the teaching of economics. Most economists, including most of the doctorates from premier universities, do little else in economics except teach. In a study Claire Friedland and I recently made of citation practices of doctorates in economics of major universities, we found that in the first fifteen years after receiving the Ph.D., one-third do not publish a single article and the median journal output of those who publish is about 2 articles. For the profession as a whole, the output of articles is probably one per economist per 20 years.

There is no reason to quarrel with society's verdict that teaching is useful and honorable work. Yet it is surely a mediate, not an ultimate, reason for economists—why does society wish economics to be practiced, and therefore taught?

The first and the purest demand of society is for scientific knowledge: knowledge of how the economic system works. Knowledge of the consequences of economic actions. Knowledge of the causes of unemployment, of the effects of various taxes, of the sources of income inequality. Whether one is a conservative or a radical, a protectionist or a free trader, a cosmopolitan or a nationalist, a churchman or a heathen, it is useful to know the causes and consequences of economic phenomena. One can be a more efficient protectionist or a more efficient free trader if one knows the effects of tariffs on factor prices, on the sizes of various industries, on national income.

Such scientific information is value-free in the strictest sense: no matter what one seeks, he will achieve it more efficiently the better his knowledge of the relationship between action and consequences.

I conjecture that a society—all of the society—eventually accepts the demonstrably valid discoveries of the relationships between actions and events. Indeed it would be a truly anti-rational society which refused to accommodate its policies to known characteristics of the world in which it lived. Even if one believes in witches he should take account of the difficulty women have in riding a broom. I conjecture that if we examine tested economic knowledge—for example, the doctrine that demand curves have a negative slope—we will find that a society does not deny or ignore this knowledge, whatever the policy preferences of that society.

The second function of the economist is to propose and to defend the economic policies which favor large or small groups in the community. One group that has been special beneficiary of our favor is the broad class of consumers, and at times we even forget that they are a class, and not the whole society. Economists spend much time and ingenuity in behalf of consumers, or what we call welfare economics, possibly rather more than on the discovery of laws of economic phenomena: for example, the contributions of each Nobel prize winner in economics except Kuznets have been largely in this area. It is not an ignoble function: as my colleague, Ronald Coase, has recently observed, if an economist can delay by a week the adoption of a policy that will decrease national income by a present value of $100 million—and that is such a small policy!—he will have saved society twice his lifetime salary, and his teaching services will have been thrown in for free. To generalize Coase's arithmetic, the United States has perhaps the equivalent of 5,000 full time research economists, costing—with ancillary services—perhaps $250 million per year. If the various special producer interest policies cost the nation $40 billion per year—a wild estimate but one that is not easily refuted!—then we earn our keep if we reduce these exactions of consumers by about one-half of one-percent.

The broad class of consumers is only the largest of many groups whose special interests are urged by economists. There are reasonably well defined economic groups—like the members of American labor unions and the American farmers—and less well defined groups such as the upper and middle and lower income classes, the blacks, the foreign language groups, and the religious groups. These various groups have interests which must be discovered and articulated into coherent and viable political programs. The impact upon the group of new events—an energy crisis or a new tax law—must be explored and publicized. The conflicts of interest within a group must be defined, and somehow reconciled. Natural or temporary allies must be found.

The leaders of opinion for major groups in the society perform useful tasks, and the group necessarily compensates their services. Their books sell well, their lectures are well-attended, their universities receive tangible expressions of gratitude. These leaders seem to be, and are, men of importance. But I must emphasize that their importance is of a different type than that of the scholar who discovers relationships that operate in the real world. The leader of a group exerts a measure of influence on *his* group, whereas the scholar forces all groups to take his findings into account. The one leads a group in active policy formulation, the other changes the platform on which the debates on policy take place.

Income redistribution is the hall-mark of any special interest group: gains in aggregate output will usually be shared with everyone, so the efficient use of political power usually involves income redistribution. Almost all the great policy issues of modern economics are of this sort: progressive taxation, unemployment insurance and social security, public aids to education, and health and welfare programs; each is an example of policies which, whether they increase or decrease national income, effect important redistributions of that income. The lesser policies of our times, ranging from oil depletion to public support of the arts, are equally directed to the redistribution of income, and every party gets its spokesmen.

IV. Problems for the Historians of Economics

If my interpretation of the role of economists is correct, it should be fully applicable to the contemporary scene. Nevertheless it is preferable to test the hypothesis on the influence of economists by examining their role in earlier times. When it was still permissible to joke about women, there was a well-known exchange:

> He: "The trouble with women is that they insist on interpreting abstract propositions in personal terms."
>
> She: "I do not."

But of course we all do.

I shall introduce here one personal note. My friend Robert Fogel has told me that I am a Marxist, perhaps partly because of the role I assign to intellectuals as spokesmen of important groups within the society. My reply is that if I were a Marxist, Karl would not be a very good one. His acid-filled pen was indeed thrown often at the apologists of capitalism and earlier systems. The unrighteous indignation aside, I accept the view that Smith was the honorable spokesman for the agricultural and worker classes of England, as well as the premier economist of all time. But Marx with unbelievable vanity or myopia, excused himself and his doctrines from this description, whereas on my view he was obviously the spokesman for rising industrial proletariat, as well as a premier sociologist. I do not believe that every view of every person is market-oriented—indeed I am not able wholly to explain the views I am presenting here on this basis. And markets for opinions are also provided by non-economic classes, such as religious groups, contrary to Marx's view. If the view that people produce what consumers desire needs a name, that of Smith is more appropriate than that of Marx.

My central thesis is that economists exert a minor and scarcely detectable influence on the societies in which they live. The thesis should of course be tested, and the historians of economics are the most qualified group to undertake the tests. They no doubt have other things to do than test my hypotheses, but I believe that problems of general historical importance are raised by the attempt to assess the effect of economists on their societies.

Example 1: The theory of free trade is commonly credited with the repeal of the Corn Laws in 1846.[1]

The traditional history of the repeal of the Corn Laws is as follows: Ricardo developed with rigor the main economic argument against protection already sketched by Adam Smith, and that codiscoverer of comparative cost theory, Torrens, and disciples such as James and John Mill, McCulloch and General Thompson carried the message to the educated classes. Among these educated men, the powerful orators Cobden and Bright, and lesser figures in the Anti-Corn Law League carried the message to the country,—and eventually also to that great prime minister, Peel. The Irish famine may have triggered the repeal, but that famine could have been dealt with by a temporary suspension of duties. Ultimately sound economic principles achieved what Spain in its greatest hour could not, the conquest of Great Britain. How heartening a tale! Economists turned a great nation from error to truth, from inefficiency to maximum output.

I believe, on the contrary, that if Cobden had spoken only Yiddish, and with a stammer, and Peel had been a narrow, stupid man, England would have moved toward free trade in grain as its agricultural classes declined and its manufacturing and commercial classes grew. Perhaps a few years later, but not many. In 1846 the agricultural classes of England had fallen to about one-fourth of the labor force. (C. R. Fay argued persuasively that the enclosure movement, by eliminating the peasant, had fatally weakened the political support of landlords.) Truly effective import prohibitions would have driven grain to intolerable price levels, and it is a quite general rule that intolerable things are not tolerated.

Hence the repeal of the Corn Laws was the appropriate social response to a shift of political and economic power. This counter-hypothesis to the great-economist theory of history is capable of empirical test. Examine the tariff histories of the nations becoming industrialized at a high rate, and approaching a period of strong demand for imports of food. Estimate the net gains to the nation from the adoption of free trade. Then I predict that when the gains are large relative to national income, that is, where agriculture is fairly large but far from sufficient to feed domestically the next generation, free trade will be approached.

1. The next three paragraphs are largely taken from a paper, "The Intellectual and His Society," given at a conference on Capitalism and Freedom at Charlottesville, Va., Oct. 21, 1972, in honor of Milton Friedman. It has recently appeared in *Capitalism and Freedom: Problems and Prospects*, published by University Press of Virginia, Charlottesville, Virginia.

Or, as an alternative line of argument, consider the association between trade theory and trade policy. The same theory of trade rules in Sweden, England, the United States, Canada, and Australia, and has ruled in them throughout the twentieth century. How do we explain the differences in their policies, or the rising tide of protectionism?

Example 2: Lord Keynes and the theories associated with his name are often credited with the emergence of full employment policies in western lands. The assertion poses an interesting question for the historian of science: how do we determine the prevailing views of a science in a society at any time? Most people, even influential people, do not announce their beliefs on all current questions, and we know that novel ideas do not instantly sweep through a community. Indeed simple economic truths such as that both parties to a voluntary transaction gain from it are widely ignored. The determination of prevailing views is a challenging task for the historians of economics.

In order to test the hypothesis that Keynesian doctrine played a leading, rather than possibly a following, role in the adoption of full employment policies in the western world, we need to devise and to apply concepts of prevalent economic opinion. In one sense it is of course possible, if not easy, to determine which ideas prevail—one simply has to see which policies have prevailed, and by definition the views supporting these policies also prevailed. But the reign of ideas, like that of laws, is partial and limited, and much imaginative research will be necessary to quantify the role of either laws or ideas.

When we have ascertained prevalent professional economic opinion, I predict that the census of Keynesians will be found to be much less helpful in the explanation of full employment policies than factors such as the depressions of the 1930's and the political strength of the industrial working classes. Terence Hutchison's book, *Economics and Economic Policy in Britain, 1946–66*, suggests that economists adapt with substantial speed to the changing economic and political atmosphere.

Example 3: Economists have long written on the proper attributes of a just tax system. In the western world they have usually supported taxes which were progressive with respect to income. Here the direction of causation is fairly clear. Since there are no respectable *scientific* arguments for—or against—income equalization goals, the economists were translating ruling political views into the language and apparatus of their science. My favorite example of this practice is Marshall. He proved that less consumer surplus would be lost if excises were placed upon commodities of inelastic rather than elastic demand; or, as he put it, if the tax were levied on necessaries rather than luxuries. (*Principles*, page 467 n.) But of course he was opposed to such regressive taxation. Since we get our notions of equity from the community, we can hardly play a large role in the community's choice of policies with respect to income distributions.

Example 4: The economic theory of public regulation is equally instructive on the influence of economists. As each area of potential regulation reaches the public favor, the reason for regulation is promptly
restated in the language of economics. If it is land tenure in Victorian
England, the landlord and tenant, we say, do not know how to divide the
costs and benefits of durable investments; if it is pollution today, we say
that there are external diseconomies; if it is railroad rates in the 19th
century, we call it a monopoly problem; if it is workers' injuries in 1910,
we conjecture that it is the failure of workers to charge for risk exposure
or imperfections in the insurance market. But where was a regulatory
policy introduced in response to a problem discovered and popularized
by economists? The Sherman Act, I would remind you, was quite generally opposed by American economists. And where has regulation taken
the form dictated by the theory of optimal prices? Surely concepts like
"historical cost" were not taken from the economists' theory of value.

Although I simply cannot be so fair to views I do not share as John
Stuart Mill was, I try. So I must concede that I am asking for examples of
influences on economic policy demonstrably due to economists. I must
also concede that if economists are being used efficiently, their impact on
policy will be small. Remember my estimate that our research bill in
economics is perhaps one-quarter of a billion dollars, and considerable
parts of this are spent in support of economists with conflicting views.
Those who believe that economists are more important than this meagre
standard by an order of magnitude, must believe that society is seriously
underinvesting in economics. I do not despair of empirical tests of this
optimistic hypothesis.

V. Some Concluding Remarks

A curious tension emerges from the simultaneous workings of two
influences upon us. We wish to be scientists, with sound logic in our
theories, reliable procedures in our empirical applications of those
theories, and objective and fair-minded statements of the limitations of
our knowledge. We wish also to be important—or, in the language of this
day, we wish to do good—much good, and generally recognized as such.

I have already argued that within narrow limits these goals are compatible: the society wants and will benefit from increments of the objective knowledge of economic life. A few men actually adhere only to this
type of work, eschewing all pronouncements on matters of current policy.
(Such pronouncements and participation will inevitably influence their
scientific works, and not simply by being alternative uses of time.) These
near-saints of scholarship are wholly unknown to the public, and not
always well-known within the profession. Frank Knight was an approximate illustration of this rare type.

66

Most of us are more impatient to do good, and probably we are not sanguine about our ability to engage usefully in full time scientific work. Nor, perhaps, are we wholly satisfied with what Samuelson calls our own applause—indeed we cannot be confident that this applause is unaffected by our policy positions. I concede to Samuelson, nevertheless, that to a scientiest educated hands make more melodious applause than ignorant hands, but too often the educated hands seem to be sat upon by educated asses.

On my reading of the nature of the influence of the economist, it presents a paradox. The economist is truly and fundamentally important when he is increasing the knowledge of the workings of economic systems. New knowledge on the workings of economies is almost certainly specialized and technical in its nature, so it will be known first and primarily to one's professional colleagues. Hence the influence of an economist's work and the popular (non-professional) esteem in which he is held are most likely to be *negatively* correlated. This chain of arguments is not inescapable—an Einstein becomes, after due time, a celebrity to the millions who have no concept of his discoveries—but in general one may conclude that wide popularity and major influence, are rivals, not partners.

6

Textual Exegesis as a Scientific Problem

In a recent essay in *Economica*,[1] Professor H. Barkai faces a problem often met in the history of economics: which passage in a man's writings do you accept when several passages are inconsistent? His specific problem is Ricardo's theory of per capita demand for "corn." Ricardo asserted, Barkai correctly notes, two different propositions:

1. That the demand has zero elasticity, in two passages in the *Principles*:

   "With the same population, and no more, there can be no demand for an additional quantity of corn, . . ." (*Works and Correspondence of David Ricardo*, Sraffa ed., vol. I, p. 79; also vol. I, p. 193.)

2. That the demand is inelastic but not zero, in the following passage in *Protection to Agriculture*:

   "The demand for corn, with a given population, must necessarily be limited; and, although it may be, and undoubtedly is, true, that when it is abundant and cheap, the quantity consumed will be increased, yet it is equally certain that its aggregate value will be diminished." (*Ibid.*, vol. IV, pp. 219–20.)

Barkai chooses the latter view as the one Ricardo fundamentally held. The choice is made on two ostensible grounds:

1. Marshall did not assert that Ricardo customarily assumed a zero demand elasticity for corn (nor, I may add, did Marshall assert that Ricardo customarily did not assume a zero elasticity).

2. The existence of the counter-quotation from *Protection to Agriculture*.

The problem of inference which is posed by such an example is more interesting than the example itself.

If a substantive economic relationship were under discussion—say the proposition that the per capita demand for corn has zero elasticity—we would never dream of establishing its validity by citing one or two or three facts (observations on pairs of years, say)—let alone by citing two "facts" against it and one "fact" for it, as Barkai does. We would all agree that

Reprinted from *Economica*, November 1965.
1. "Ricardo's Static Equilibrium," *Economica*, February 1965.

larger, more objectively chosen bodies of evidence should be brought to bear upon the problem.

Why should we allow the hand-picked quotation to carry an interpretation when we would reject the hand-picked fact as an empirical test of a hypothesis? In fact the two problems are basically the same.

The substantive hypothesis seeks to isolate the main variables in the economic phenomena under consideration, and to formulate the major relationships among these variables. A successful hypothesis accounts for the important relationships in the appropriate data, but it need not account for random variation. Similarly, the textual interpretation must uncover the main concepts in the man's work, and the major functional relationships among them. The interpretation need not account for careless writing or unintegrated knowledge.

The processes of testing a quantitative hypothesis and an analytical interpretation differ in details. The basic way of increasing the confidence in the statistical test of a hypothesis is to enlarge the sample; one instance of zero demand elasticity in a sample of two means almost nothing, but only one instance in a sample of a hundred is nearly conclusive evidence of a non-zero demand elasticity. We should not be so literal-minded as to count the passages in a book to decide an author's general position because the passages are not of equal importance. We increase our confidence in the interpretation of an author by increasing the number of his main theoretical conclusions which we can deduce from (our interpretation of) his analytical system.

The test of an interpretation is its consistency with the main analytical conclusions of the system of thought under consideration. If the main conclusions of a man's thought do not survive under one interpretation, and do under another, the latter interpretation must be preferred. (The analogy to maximum likelihood is evident.)

This rule of interpretation is designed to maximize the value of a theory to the science. The man's central theoretical position is isolated and stated in a strong form capable of contradictions by the facts. The net scientific contribution, if any, of the man's work is thus identified, amended if necessary, and rendered capable of evaluation and possible acceptance. This rule of consistency with the main conclusions may be called the principle of scientific exegesis.

Of course men make logical errors or slip into tautologies and otherwise blemish their work. One may seek to determine what the man really believed, although this search has no direct relevance to scientific progress. One will then invoke a different criterion to choose between conflicting passages: that interpretation which fits best the style of the man's thought becomes decisive. This may be called the principle of personal exegesis.

Let us now revert to Ricardo and the per capita demand curve for wheat.

At the level of scientific exegesis, we ask: what happens to Ricardo's general theory if the labourer's demand for food has (1) zero elasticity, and (2) substantial elasticity. (To consider also an "almost" zero elasticity would be to quarrel over a scientific negligibility.) The answer is as follows:

With the growth of population, consequent (I here assume) on an increase in capital, the real price of grain rises under the operation of the law of diminishing returns. The prices of non-food goods may rise because they contain raw materials from the soil but this minor movement is put aside (vol. I, pp. 110, 118, 122). If the demand for food is not zero-elastic, Ricardo must explain how the composition of output varies as population grows. He could assume that the composition of output varies with relative prices (as Barkai believes) or that the composition is given by the fixed-coefficients budget (as I believe).

The fixed-coefficient approach had two obvious analytical merits: it was simpler to use; and it cost nothing—Ricardo had no interest in the compositoin of wages between food and non-food. The fixed-coefficients approach also had a positive advantage: it made rigorous his main theorem on economic progress: "The natural tendency of profits then is to fall; for, in the progress of society and wealth, the additional quantity of food required is obtained by the sacrifice of more and more labour" (vol. I, p. 120). If non-food is substituted for food as the relative price of food rises, the natural tendency of profits to fall is abated (and in the extreme case of perfect substitution between food and non-food, completely thwarted). One of Ricardo's major conclusions would thus be weakened if the demand for wheat were not zero-elastic. Indeed, the main message of Barkai's essay is apparently that Ricardo's system is indeterminate because he did not have a demand function for food.

If we shift to What He Really Meant, or personal exegesis, the same interpretation of Ricardo commends itself. The simplifying assumption was Ricardo's trademark; the assumption of fixed consumption coefficients joins the empirical labour theory of value, the simplified quantity of money theory of inflation, and similar abstractions.

More specifically, Ricardo never discusses the composition of output— and yet the whole purpose of a variable consumption coefficients approach would be to deal with this question. The arithmetic of his distribution theory rests upon the fixed-coefficients approach: the worker's family is given the following demand schedule for wheat (vol. I, pp. 103, 116):

Consumption (Quarters)	Price of Wheat (Per Quarter)
3	41.
3	41., 8s., 8d.
3	41., 10s.
3	41., 16s.
3	51., 2s., 10d.

Of course Ricardo knew that when there is a crop failure the quantity consumed falls—the laws of arithmetic insure this. Appropriate citations could have been given from the *Principles* (thus, vol. I, pp. 217, 385). He was not unusual in knowing things he did not incorporate in his theory.

Let us recognize the fact that the interpretation of a man's position—especially if the man has a complex and subtle mind—is a problem in inference, not to be solved by the choice of quotations.

7

The Adoption of
the Marginal Utility Theory

The utility theory was extensively developed as a theory of human behavior before the end of the Napoleonic Wars. This is a proposition supported in the first section of this paper, although it requires only modest support. The theory of utility was not deployed successfully in economics until after its introduction by Jevons, Menger, and Walras. This is a matter of common knowledge, although the time at which the theory was effectively adopted comes later than common knowledge would have it. The explanation for the retarded adoption and development of utility theory in economics constitutes the central task of this essay.

I. Early and Accessible Utility Theories

Of early statements of utility theory, incomparably the best-known to economists, intimately and not merely by hearsay, is that of Jeremy Bentham. Recall the soaring claims for the principle of utility which introduce *The Principles of Morals and Legislation*:

> Nature has placed mankind under the governance of two sovereign masters, *pain and pleasure*. It is for them alone to point out what we ought to do, as well as to determine what we shall do. On the one hand the standard of right and wrong, on the other the chain of causes and effects, are fastened to their throne. They govern us in all we do, in all we say, in all we think: every effort we can make to throw off our subjection, will serve but to demonstrate and confirm it.[1]

Whatever the role of utility as a moral guide—and I believe it was the intellectual tragedy of Bentham's life that he limited his analysis of utility primarily to this role—it can hardly be disputed that the principle of utility is an all-embracing theory of purposive conduct. When a man acts with a view to anticipated consequences of the act, the desired consequences (pleasures) and undesired consequences (pains) surely govern his choice of action.

Already by Chapter 4 of the *Introduction* Bentham has listed the dimensions of utility (intensity, duration, certainty, propinquity, etc.) and asserted the universality of its domain:

Reprinted from *History of Political Economy*, Fall 1972. © 1972 by Duke University Press, Durham, N.C.

1. J. Bentham, *An Introduction to the Principles of Morals and Legislation*, ed. J. H. Burns and H. L. A. Hart (London, 1970), p. 11.

An article of property, an estate in land, for instance, is valuable, on what account? On account of the pleasures of all kinds which it enables a man to produce, and what comes to the same thing the pains of all kinds which it enables him to avert. But the value of an article of property is universally understood to rise or fall according to the length or shortness of the time which a man has in it: the certainty or uncertainty of its coming into possession: and the nearness or remoteness of the time at which, if at all, it is to come into possession [ibid., pp. 40–41].

Bentham did not perform *all* of the task of developing a utility theory of economic behavior. He did not develop the marginal utility theory of relative prices, and he did offer a variety of opinions which we now believe to be at least obscure.[2] Yet he carried the analysis a good way—well past the point where a Ricardo or a Mill could easily have taken over the baton. The powerful chapter (14) on "The Proportion Between Punishments and Offences" is enough to support this proposition. Consider a few of his Rules:

1. The value of the punishment must not be less in any case than what is sufficient to outweigh that of the profit of the offence.[3]

3. When two offences come in competition, the punishment for the greater offence must be sufficient to induce a man to prefer the less.[4]

5. The punishment ought in no case to be more than what it is necessary to bring it into conformity with the rules here given.[5]

2. "... it is manifest, that there are occasions on which a given sum will be worth infinitely more to a man than the same sum would at another time: where, for example, in a case of extremity, a man stands in need of extraordinary medical assistance" (*Introduction*, p. 59). The need for large medical expenditures may not raise the marginal utility of a *given* number of dollars if the utility of health is reckoned into the total wealth of the individual.

3. Ibid., p. 166. Profit is "not merely the pecuniary profit, but [also] the pleasure" (p. 166 n). One striking passage, never published during Bentham's life, was unusually explicit: "If I having a crown in my pocket, and not being athirst hesitate whether I should buy a bottle of claret with it for my own drinking, or lay it out in providing for a family I see about to perish for want of any assistance, so much the worse for me at the long run: but it is plain that, so long as I continue hesitating, the two pleasures of sensuality in the one case, of sympathy in the other, were exactly worth to me five shillings, to me they were exactly equal.

"I beg a truce here of our man of sentiment and feeling while from necessity, and it is only from necessity, I speak and prompt mankind to speak a mercenary language. The Thermometer is the instrument for measuring the heat of the weather; the Barometer the instrument for measuring the pressure of the Air. Those who are not satisfied with the accuracy of those instruments must find out others that shall be more accurate, or bid adieu to Natural Philosophy. Money is the instrument of measuring the quantity of pain or pleasure." See C. W. Everett, *The Education of Jeremy Bentham* (New York, 1931), pp. 35–36.

4. Bentham, *Introduction*, p. 168.

5. Ibid., p. 169.

7. To enable the value of the punishment to outweigh that of the profit of the offence, it must be increased, in point of magnitude, in proportion as it falls short in point of certainty.[6]

The calculus of pleasure and pain extends throughout all human behavior: "all men calculate. I would not say, that even a madman does not calculate."[7]

Even fuller directions on the calculus of utility were given in the *Theory of Legislation*, synthesized from numerous manuscripts by Bentham's disciple, Dumont—a work well-known to the Benthamites.[8] The master seldom forgot the utility calculus for long, and our final quotation is from his *Rationale of Judicial Evidence*, a work which the young John Stuart Mill prepared with extreme labor and skill from a forest of manuscripts:

> . . . the matter of wealth is of no value, but in proportion to its influence in respect of happiness. Multiply the sum of a man's property by 2, by 10, by 100, by 1000, there is not the smallest reason for supposing that the sum of his happiness is increased in any such proportion, or in any one approaching to it: multiply his property by a thousand, it may still be a matter of doubt, whether, by that vast addition, you add as much to his happiness as you take away from it by dividing his property by 2, by taking from him but the half of it.[9]

A second and independent strand of utility theorizing can be disposed of more briefly: this is the calculus of moral expectation initiated by D. Bernoulli in dealing with the St. Petersburg paradox.[10] That paradox involved the proper price of a gamble in which a fair coin is flipped successively until a heads occurs, with payments to the player:

H	1 ducat
TH	2 ducats
TTH	4 ducats
. . .	. . .
T^nH	2^n ducats

The expected value of the gamble is infinite,[11] and to resolve this paradox Bernoulli postulates that the player seeks to maximize *moral* rather than mathematical expectation. He introduced the assumption that "the util-

6. Ibid., p. 170.
7. Ibid., p. 174.
8. Bentham, *The Theory of Legislation*, trans. Hildreth (London, 1864), esp. pt. 1, chaps. 6, 16.
9. J. Bentham, *Rationale of Judicial Evidence* (London, 1827), 5:656.
10. See D. Bernoulli, "Exposition of a New Theory on the Measurement of Risk," *Econometrica*, 1954; it first appeared in 1738. Also my *Essays in the History of Economics*, pp. 108 ff.
11. Since the probabilities of these outcomes are

ity resulting from any small increase in wealth will be inversely proportionate to the quantity of goods previously possessed."[12] Using the law of utility,

$$du = \frac{bdw}{w}$$

where w is wealth, u is utility, and b is a constant, a finite value will be found for the gamble, and one dependent upon the individual's initial wealth.[13] The analysis is applied to the theory of insurance, and Bernoulli deduces among other things the value of risk diversification.

Bernoulli's essay provided stimulus to a number of the most distinguished probabilists to discuss moral expectation and diminishing marginal utility of income (and many more to discuss the paradox). Laplace devoted a chapter (10) of his great treatise, *Théorie analytique des probabilités*, to a restatement of Bernoulli's theory. Lesser names in this literature are Fourier,[14] Quételet,[15] and Cournot,[16] and of course most writers on probability touched on the St. Petersburg parardox. In addition, writers such as Buffon, the famous naturalist, devoted considerable attention to the subject.[17]

$$\tfrac{1}{2}, \ \tfrac{1}{4}, \ \tfrac{1}{8}, \ \ldots \ \frac{1}{2^{n+1}}$$

and the expected gain for n infinite, is

$$(\tfrac{1}{2})1 + (\tfrac{1}{4})2 + (\tfrac{1}{8})4 + \ldots + \left(\frac{1}{2^{n+1}}\right)2^n + \ldots = \infty$$

12. Bernoulli, p. 25.

13. Integrating, one obtains $U = b \log (w/a)$. If the initial fortune of the player was W, his gain in utility if he wins 2^{n-1} ducats is

$$b \log \frac{W + 2^{n-1}}{a} - b \log \frac{W}{a} = b \log \frac{W + 2^{n-1}}{W}$$

and his expected gain of utility from playing the game is

$$\frac{b}{2} \ \log \ \frac{W+1}{W} \ + \ \frac{b}{4} \ \log \ \frac{W+2}{W} \ + \ldots$$

$$= b \log (W+1)^{\frac{1}{2}} (W+2)^{\frac{1}{4}} \ldots - b \log W$$

The sum D which would yield utility equal to that expected to be gained from the gamble is

$$D = (W+1)^{\frac{1}{2}} (W+2)^{\frac{1}{4}} \ldots - W$$

If $W = 10$, $D = 3$; if $W = 100$, $D = 4$; if $W = 1000$, $D = 6$.

14. See J. B. J. Fourier's remarkable essay, "Extrait d'un Mémoire sur la Théorie analytique des assurances," *Annales de Chémie et Physique*, 2d ser., 10 (1819): 177–89.

15. L. A. J. Quételet, *Letters addressed to H.R.H. The Grand Duke of Saxe Coburg and Gotha* (London, 1849), Letter VIII.

16. A. A. Cournot, *Exposition de la théorie des chances* (Paris, 1843), pp. 93, 106–9, 334.

17. G. L. Leclerc de Buffon, *Essai d'arithmétique morale*, in vol. 21 of his *Histoire*

The availability of utility theory to economists differed immensely between these two literatures. The Benthamite version was directly addressed to social life and was enunciated with the very fullest possible generality; it was known, and known well, by at least three premier economists of the age—and probably to a degree by every educated Englishman. The Bernoulli version was less available to economists, since it came in a mathematical literature in several languages and over more than a century of writing, but in certain respects these attributes increased the probability of capturing the attention and interest of some economist—after all there were plenty of mathematically literate writers on economics before 1840, including Babbage, Whewell, possibly Malthus (a ninth wrangler), Thünen, Cournot, and Canard.

There is a separate reason for believing that utility theory was fully accessible to economics: it was closely approached, occasionally formulated, and then forgotten by its author and ignored by contemporaries. We may cite Longfield,[18] Lloyd,[19] Senior,[20] and Say:[21] a list long enough and illustrious enough to make indisputably evident the accessibility of utility theory to economists, and their want of interest in it.

II. The Hypothesis

The acceptance of a theory by a science is a social act, not an individual act. The genius of Babbage could not bring a computer into being in 1830; by 1940 the introduction of the computer required no major scientific advances, and in fact could not have been much delayed by any feasible social policy.[22] Similarly, we must not explain the general reappearance and acceptance of the marginal utility theory between 1870 and 1890 as the singular achievement of a Jevons, a Menger, or a Walras—indeed their multiplicity and near-simultaneity have often and properly been used to document the importance of the scientific environment.

I propose the following explanation for the fact that the utility theory was at hand for at least three-quarters of a century before it was accepted

---

naturelle (Paris: Dufart, l'an VIII). Buffon was an independent and somewhat eccentric discoverer of moral expectation; see ibid., pp. 138–40 n.

18. M. Longfield, *Lectures on Political Economy* (1834; reprint ed., London, 1931), pp. 27–28, 45–46, 111 ff.

19. "The Notion of Value," reprinted in *Economic History, Economic Journal Supplement*, May 1927.

20. *Political Economy* (New York, 1939), pp. 11–12.

21. See the letter to Ricardo in J. B. Say, *Mélanges et correspondance* (Paris, 1833), pp. 116–17, also pp. 287–89.

22. This position is strongly argued, and in fact moderately overstated, by R. K. Merton, "Singletons and Multiples in Scientific Discovery: A Chapter in the Sociology of Science," *Transactions of the American Philosophical Society* 105, no. 5 (1961). See also my "Does Economics Have a Useful Past?" *History of Political Economy* 1 (1969): 225–27 [chap. 10, below].

76

by the science. Economics became primarily an academic discipline in the last decades of the nineteenth century. Previously it was a science conducted by non-academicians whose main interest was in the policy implications of the science; thereafter it was conducted by professors who accepted the ruling values and incentives of scholarly activity.

The academic economist shares the general tastes of academicians, and they differ in important respects from those of the journalists, politicans, bureaucrats, and men of affairs who constituted the vast majority of economists in the earlier period. In the pre-academic period, the dominant purpose was to understand and to influence public policy, and fact-gathering and theorizing were both directed to the implementation of the primary purpose. Even Ricardo's highly abstract discussion of the measure of value was important to his main dynamical proposition that economic progress would lead to a rise in rents, and to a rise in wages "which would invariably lower profits."

Few academic economists separated themselves entirely from discussions of contemporary problems, but the sovereign importance of policy questions diminished as the science became more exclusively a university profession. A dominant value of the scholarly world is a certain disengagement from the contemporary scene and a search for knowledge more fundamental and durable than that required for practical and immediate purposes. Positively viewed, the academic mind places a special premium upon *generality*. The scholar is not a handmaiden of either local commerce or this year's congress.

A lesser, related scholarly value is the emphasis upon the paraphernalia of scholarship. The form of work takes on a value independent of its content: a scholar should be literate, and his work should be pursued with non-vulgar instruments. Ancient learning is often a constituent of this paraphernalia, but so too is the command over powerful mathematical methods. Words like rigor and elegance portray this element of academic taste, whereas the world of affairs prefers words such as *effective* and *persuasive*.

These values of disengagement from the journalistic crises of the day or decade, vast generality of major results, and cultivation of scholarly techniques were reinforced by the major triumphs of the physical and biological sciences in the nineteenth century. These sciences sought and in great measure achieved deep unity of their central theoretical structures (Newtonian and Darwinian, respectively), and it became the hallmark of successful scientific work that it explained wide reaches of phenomena. Physics and astronomy already suggested that in a truly advanced science the main results lent themselves to a mathematical formalization which allowed extensive and beautiful derivations and applications.

Utility theory would have been a feeble ally to Ricardo or Mill. None of the great areas of classical economic literature would have gained much from utility theory even when it had reached the stage of development to which it was carried by Pareto and Fisher. Utility theory would have had little to say about corn laws and free trade (except that both countries gain!), about central banking and Peel's Act, about colonization and overpopulation, about Poor Laws or Factory Acts, even about Say's law or taxation. Indeed, after utility theory began to appear in the 1870's, it took no important part in any policy-oriented controversy up to World War I.

What utility theory contributed was precisely the values we attribute to the academic world and in particular to the academic sciences. The classical school had advanced one theory of value for producible goods and resorted to other theories (rent) or vague phrases ("passions of the buyer") for non-producible goods. Now the utility theory allowed a unified explanation of the value of shoes, wheat, and Shakespearean folios. The classical school had no central logic or behavior: the entrepreneur was a profit-maximizer while the consumer and laborer were opaque bundles of sociological behavior traits. Now the utility theory allowed a unified explanation of behavior: everyone was a utility-maximizer, and all economic problems became simply problems of tastes and obstacles (so, Pareto). The method of the classical school had been literary and numerical. Now the utility theory obviously permitted and even invited the use of mathematics.

There is a second stage of adoption of the utility theory: the period in which it was assimilated by the rank and file of competent economists. This period came after the theorists had developed the utility theory up to the point at which it had an operable role in substantive economic research. I also comment briefly on this process of professional adoption in the next section.

III. The Adoption of the Theory

When was the utility theory "adopted"? It is easy to give at least an approximate date for any given economist: the theory was adopted at least by 1884 by Philip Wicksteed and not later than 1892 by Irving Fisher.[23] Since we are concerned with a science, and not simply with individual scientists, however, we require a method of characterizing adoption of a theory by the science.

Let us initially state as the simple law of utility: the marginal utility of every commodity diminishes for every man, and this phenomenon underlies his demand curve for each commodity. We can now go to the literature and classify economists in each year as to whether they did or did not "know" (understand) this proposition. We can grade each econ-

23. Wicksteed, review of *Das Kapital*, reprinted in *Common Sense of Political Economy* (London, 1934), 2:705; Fisher, *Mathematical Investigations in the Theory of Value and Prices* (1892).

78

Table 1. *First Dates of Recognition of the Marginal Utility Theory by Economists*

Name	Date	Place
Jevons	1862	British Association for Advancement of Science
Menger	1871	*Grundsätze der Volkswirtschaftslehre*
Marshall	1872	Review of Jevons
Cairnes	1874	*Leading Principles*
Walras	1874	*Eléments d'économie*
J. B. Clark	1881	Article in *New Englander*
Edgeworth	1881	*Mathematical Psychics*
Sidgwick	1883	*Principles of Political Economy*
Walker	1883	*Principles*
Wicksteed	1884	Review of *Das Kapital* in *To-Day*
Wieser	1884	*Über den Ursprung des Wertes*
Böhm-Bawerk	1886	*Theorie des Güterwerts*
Cannan	1888	*Elementary Political Economy*
Auspitz and Lieben	1889	*Theorie des Preises*
Pantaleoni	1889	*Principii*
Fisher	1892	*Mathematical Investigations*
Pareto	1892	Articles in *Giornale degli Economisti*
Taussig	1893	Proceedings, A. E. A.
Wicksell	1893	*Über Wert, Kapital und Rente*
Barone	1894	Articles in *Giornale degli Economisti*
Cassel	1899	Article in *Zeitschrift für die gesamte Staatswissenschaft*

omist just as we now do in the classroom, classifying him (let us propose) under *Knows Law* and *Does Not Know Law* (and perhaps under *Knows Law* create two classes: *Accepts Law* and *Rejects Law*). Since forgetting and changing of minds are presumably uncommon, a single date will usually characterize each man: that on which he first showed knowledge of the law. We provide such a census of the leading theorists, including the main writers on utility, in the period 1860–1900 in Table 1. The dates are based upon publications; often an earlier date could be assigned for knowledge on the basis of letters, recollections, etc.

The median date of first recognition of the utility theory by the economists listed in Table 1 is 1884, but several of the men had not begun to write on economics until later.[24] Professor Richard S. Howey provides a list of numerous minor writers on utility before 1890[25] in his treatise, *The Rise of the Marginal Utility School, 1870–1889*.

24. The later beginners were Pareto, Barone, Cassel, Wicksell, Cannan, and Fisher.
25. One interesting name is G. B. Shaw, who used marginal utility theory in a review of *Das Kapital* in the *National Reformer* in 1887. His ancient foe, H. M. Hyndman, has offered an explanation of Shaw's failure to scale the heights of logical analysis: "What a pity it is that Shaw should have stunted the natural growth of his mind and rocked his intellect to fiddle-strings by his confoundedly inappropriate diet . . . Take Shaw now and feed him for a season on fine flesh foods artfully combined and carefully cooked, turn a highly skilled

Table 2. *Topics in the Marginal Utility Theory Literature*

1. The explicit relationship between utility and demand functions.
2. The implications of diminishing marginal utility for the shape of the demand curve.
3. Constancy of the marginal utility of income.
4. Definitions of complementarity in utility terms.
5. Measurability of utility with additive utility functions.
6. Measurability of utility with non-additive utility functions.
7. Indifference curve techniques.
8. The Edgeworth box.
9. Integrability problem.
10. The Slutsky equation: separation of income and substitution effects.

A later set of dates would be encountered if we raised the level of sophistication required to be classified as professional knowledge of utility theory. Some possible elements of a more complex standard of knowledge are given in Table 2. To require knowledge of even one of these elements of utility theory would remove perhaps three-quarters of the economists from Table 1, in any year. But the criterion of our simple law of utility will suffice, I belive, to support the following propositions:

1. Almost every economist who dealt seriously and professionally with utility theory in this period had an academic base. The only important exceptions are Auspitz and Lieben, and Barone, and (to a degree) Wicksteed.
2. The still substantial number of non-academic economists in this period, with the exceptions noted, ignored or rejected the theory. This list includes names such as Giffen, Bonar, Farrer, Higgs, Ackworth, the Webbs, Palgrave, Hobson, Bagehot, Macleod, and Goschen.[26] It is not coincidence that the important writers in economics outside academic posts are names which one associates primarily with "applied" and policy-oriented problems.
3. By the time the theory in even this elementary form was generally known to theorists, the science was rapidly moving toward an academic character. If we date leading English economists by their mean year of publication, we find the academic participation to be rising as shown in Table 3.[27] A not dissimilar pattern is found

French chef on to him in every department of his glorious art, prescribe for him stout, blackjack, or, better still, the highest class of Burgundy of the Romanée Conti variety, born in a good year, and Shaw would be raised forthwith to the nth power of intellectual achievement," *Further Reminiscences* (London, 1912), pp. 233–34.

26. Some violent attacks on utility theory can be found in the works of several of these men.

27. See my *Essays in the History of Economics* (Chicago, 1965), p. 38. After 1915 it is difficult to find important English economists outside academia except for Hawtrey and Stamp.

Table 3. *Number of Leading Economists and Academics*

Period	Total	Academic
1825–1850	14	0
1850–1875	10	3
1875–1900	7	2
1900–1915	8	5

in the United States, and perhaps a somewhat earlier dominance of academic economists was reached in France (see Note at the end of this article). The remarkable fact that Germany, the leading scientific nation of the world in the late Victorian period, had not a single important utility theorist (although Launhardt deserves honorable mention) is of some relevance. German economics had an established, dominant academic base before almost any other European nation—why was utility theory so neglected?

The reception of utility theory in Germany was hardly helped by Menger's intemperate attacks upon the leading German economist,[28] but personalities were at most a minor cause of German aloofness from utility theory. German economics was indeed scholarly; its emphasis upon erudition and its meticulous, highly specialized historical researches assuredly were not called for in order to use economics in the real world.

28. The attack on Schmoller in Menger's *Die Irrthümer des Historismus* (Vienna, 1884) may be quoted: "You have warned me, with friendly concern, that a dispute with Schmoller has not only a scientific side but also a very different side. There is not another scholar in Germany, or perhaps anywhere, who is so irresponsible in the choice of means when arguing with an opponent. I may be interpreted in every possible and impossible meaning of my words, and I myself have just received shocking proof that Schmoller is master equally of personality and vulgarity—incidentally, the only literary mastery which can be credited to him.

"You are right, my friend, when you look upon a scientific discussion with Schmoller as more than a scientific occasion: he is all too well known for his remarkable penchant for misinterpreting the meanings of others and equally well known as the unseemly participant in the area of scientific disputes (ibid., p. 6). . . .

"Schmoller's historical and statistical labors are in any event very shaky performances; in fact our praise of the author could be much more enthusiastic if they came from a secretary of a chamber of commerce, the editor of a trade journal, or the historical society of some provincial city of Prussia. Historical and statistical works from such sources will be used by the theorist with a measure of caution appropriate to the guarantees of their reliability and the competence of their author. It is certainly an unusual phenomenon that a professor of political economy working in fields whose technique he does not fully command nevertheless demands that work of this quality be almost the only kind of work that is done. It would border on the laughable if Schmoller held himself as a serious historian for the sake of such works.

"Truly, the example of Schmoller is not so dazzling, that any political economist should be led to abandon his own field of scientific research to become a dilettante in the area of historical scholarship" (ibid., p. 41).

German economics, however, had a profoundly antitheoretical position (which I do not attempt to explain); the disciplines of history and juris-prudence, not those of physics and biology, were the model for scientific work in the social sciences. The *Methodenstreit* was literally triggered by Schmoller's review of a book by Menger.[29] The juxtaposition of the leaders of the Austrian and the German schools was symbolic: the utility theory was the first formal, abstract, and (except in Menger's case) mathematically expressed theory of modern economics, and it empha-sized the trend toward the physical science model to a degree that the workhorse theory of the classical school had not begun to do. A German historical economist could admire Smith and Mill and vent any antifor-malism tastes upon Ricardo. With the advent of utility theory, the chal-lenge of formal theory to the historical tradition became explicit. The English historical school was equally firm in its hostility to utility theory.[30] The sharp conflict of scientific and historical methods was consistent with the acceptance by both parties of the academic values of disengagement from immediate applications, the emphasis upon scholarly techniques, the appeal of intellectual work per se. The conflict, in short, was one of the strategy of economic research.

The Use of Utility Theory in Routine Analysis

It is one thing for the theoretical innovators in a science to occupy themselves with a problem; it is quite another for the new theory to become a part of the working equipment of the competent practitioners of the science.

Utility theory was not even a fashionable topic among economic theor-ists in the first two generations after it was introduced into economics. Some measures of the attention devoted to utility theory in American economic journals are presented in Table 4. Two characteristics stand out clearly: the interest in utility did not reach a high level, and there is no apparent tendency for it to increase over the thirty years covered by the table.

A fortiori, utility was not a part of the working equipment of econo-mists during this period. An economist writing on taxes or trade or labor or the like did not introduce utility functions into his analysis and use them as a method of developing his subject. This absence of utility theory from theoretical work devoted to other subjects persisted for another two decades: not a single article in the *American Economic Review* of 1940

29. Gustav Schmoller, "Zur Methodologie der Staats- und Sozialwissenschaften," *Jahr-buch für Gesetzgebung, Verwaltung, und Volkswirtschaft* 7 (1883): 239–58.
30. J. K. Ingram believed that Jevons' researches on utility "will in fact never be anything more than academic playthings," *History of Political Economy* (New York, 1888), p. 234; see also T. E. Cliffe Leslie, "Jevons' 'Theory of Political Economy,'" in *Essays in Political Economy*, 2d ed. (London, 1888), pp. 66–72.

Table 4. *Discussions of Utility Theory in the Journal of Political Economy and the Quarterly Journal of Economics*

	1893	1903	1913	1923
1. Number of articles devoted primarily to utility	2	2	1	4
2. Fraction of all articles	2/35	2/36	1/66	4/62
3. Number of other articles with non-trivial discussion of utility	2	1	0	1
4. Articles with trivial mention of utility	2	1	0	0
5. Pages devoted to utility discussion	54	68	32	93
6. Percent of all pages	6.7%	7.1%	2.5%	6.4%

used utility theory in any fashion. It is only in the last two decades that this characteristic has emerged. A similar count of the articles in the *American Economic Review* for 1970 reveals that no fewer than fifteen of the articles introduce and utilize utility functions in the course of the analysis of other subjects. The effective acceptance of utility theory by economic theorists came almost a century after the marginal utility revolution. Science revolves slowly.

IV. Conclusion

These bits of evidence, I hope, create some support for the proposed explanation of the timing of the adoption of the marginal utility theory by the ruling theorists of economics. The explanation of the adoption in terms of the rise of new values as the discipline became increasingly academic has the additional merit that there does not appear to be any serious rival explanation.

However one views the persuasiveness of the present argument, the explanation of the adoption of theories by sciences is an important and neglected subject of scientific study. Once we accept the views that there are ruling theories in a science, and that these theories are replaced by new theories which are usually independently discovered by numerous persons, we are committed to the treatment of the change in scientific theories as a general scientific problem. We are not necessarily committed to Kuhn's particular sequence of scientific change, but we cannot any longer simply tacitly assume that genius leads its own mysterious and unpredictable life, nor that casual references to contemporary intellectual or social phenomena constitute a respectable explanation for particular changes.

The history of economics has become a nearly moribund subject in the United States, and has not failed to decline elsewhere. It is therefore a cause for rejoicing that the extraordinarily complex and subtle forces which dominate a science's evolution present a task of theoretical explanation comparable in intellectual demands to that presented by actual economic life.

Table 5. *Prominent American Economists, 1850–1915*

Mean Date of Publication	Number of Economists	
	Total	Academic
1850–1875	4	3
1875–1900	14	7
1900–1915	23	21
1915 and after	9	9

Names

Adams, C. F.	George, H.	Seager, H.
Adams, H. C.	Green, D. I.	Seligman, E. R. A.
Anderson, B. M.	Hadley, A. T.	Smith, J. A.
Atwater, L. H.	Hoxie, R. F.	Sumner, W. G.
Bellamy, E.	Johannsen, N.	Taussig, F. W.
Bowen, F.	Johnson, A. S.	Taylor, F. M.
Carey, H.	Kinley, D.	Tuttle, C. A.
Carver, T. N.	Kleene, G. A.	Veblen, T.
Clark, J. B.	Laughlin, J. L.	Walker, A.
Commons, J. R.	MacFarlane, C. W.	Walker, C. S.
Cooley, C. H.	MacVane, S. M.	Walker, F. A.
Davenport, H. J.	Mitchell, W. C.	Wells, D.
Del Mar, A.	Moore, H. L.	Will, T. E.
Dunbar, C. F.	Moulton, H. G.	Wood, S.
Ely, R.	Newcomb, S.	Wright, C. D.
Fetter, F. A.	Patten, S. N.	Young, A. A.
Fisher, I.	Perry, A. L.	

Note: The Academic Status of Economics in the United States and France

Preliminary studies have been made of the degree to which economics had become academic in the United States and France.[31]

A list of American economists was taken from Joseph Dorfman, *The Economic Mind in American Civilization*, vol. 3 (New York, 1949), and a corresponding list of French economists was taken from the well-known French textbook by C. Gide and C. Rist, *A History of Economic Doctrines* (New York, n.d.). The French list is more narrowly confined to theoretical economic literature and is therefore probably biased in the direction of overrepresentation of academic economists. In each case the mean date of publication of each economist was calculated from the usual encyclopedias, and the economists were classified as to occupancy or non-occupancy of an academic position. The results are given in Tables 5 and 6.

The American pattern is roughly similar to that of England, with academic economists becoming overwhelmingly dominant by the begin-

31. In addition to my inevitable debt to Claire Friedland, I wish to express my obligations to T. Beatzoglou and Peter Kahn.

Table 6. *Prominent French Economists, 1800–1925*

Mean Date of Publication	Number of Economists	
	Total	Academic
1800–1825	4	2
1825–1850	7	3
1850–1875	8	5
1875–1900	2	2
1900–1925	5	3

Names

Aftalion, A.	Cournot, A.	Proudhon, P. J.
Aupetit, A.	Dunoyer, C.	Rossi, P.
Bastiat, F.	Dupont-White, C.	Saint-Simon, C.-H.
Blanc, L.	Dupuit, J.	Say, J.-B.
Blanqui, J. A.	Fourier, C.	Simiand, F.
Cabet, E.	Garnier, J.	Sismondi, S. de
Chevalier, M.	Landry, A.	Walras, A.
Colson, C.-L.	Le Play, F.	Walras, L.
Courcelle-Seneuil, J.	Leroy-Beaulieu, P.	

ning of the twentieth century. Few economists were interested in utility before 1900, and indeed the prevalence of German training was such as to instill a measure of historicism and antitheory in American economics.[32] The French list seems short as well as biased: the number of prominent economists should be almost independent of the state of the science in a country! For what it is worth, the sample suggests an earlier academic base in France than in the English-speaking world.

32. J. Herbst, *The German Historical School in American Scholarship* (Ithaca, N. Y., 1965); also J. B. Parrish, "The Rise of Economics as an Academic Discipline: The Formative Years to 1900," *Southern Economic Journal*, July 1967.

8

The Scientific Uses of Scientific Biography, with Special Reference to J. S. Mill

The development of science is increasingly being viewed as a scientific problem in its own right: How do sciences evolve, and why? Do sciences admit of large and basic changes only by the revolutionary process which Thomas Kuhn has made famous? Are scientific discoveries almost always made independently by several scholars, as Robert Merton argues? Questions such as these suggest correctly that the evolution of a science is a fascinating area for study: subtle, complex, but surely obeying laws which eventually can be discovered.

One small or large problem of scientific evolution is: does the study of the lives of scientists provide useful knowledge of how sciences evolve? If we knew only that a Mr M, otherwise unidentifiable, had written a *Principles of Political Economy* in 1848 and revised it six times thereafter, would we be any less able to understand its contents and scientific role? Indeed, if we were uncertain that Mr M had survived the revolutions of 1848, so possibly the revisions had been made by a clever impostor, would we be less able to comprehend the work?

The answer to our question, one is tempted to assert, is at hand: more information is always better than less, hence biographical information must add to our understanding of science. But as Marshall said of economics, all short answers are wrong: our problem is not a trivial nonproblem. The cost of information is never zero, so less information may be better than more. More specifically, an immense number of biographies of science has been written: suppose they have yielded no understanding or even additional misunderstanding of the evolution of science? We need to examine the problem more closely.

Customary Practice

The customary use of biography in explaining scientific work is, to be quite blunt, shocking. There is no other area which is remotely scientific in its pretensions which shows half the facility and even the popularity in the use of The Hand-picked Example, The Implicit Absurdity, the Abhorrence of Evidence. These are harsh words, but I propose to document them from the actual uses made of Mill's life to explain his economic theories. This choice of illustration, I can assure you, is dictated not by some special penchant in the literature for the careless use of Mill's

Reprinted from *James and John Stuart Mill: Papers of the Centenary Conference*, edited by John M. Robson and Michael Laine (Toronto: University of Toronto Press, 1976).

biography, but simply by this felicitous occasion commemorating the resurrection of his scientific stature a century after his death.

The simplest scientific use of biography is presented in the form: to understand Mill's *Principles* "requires some familiarity with the author's *Autobiography*."[1] Unfortunately the contribution of biographical knowledge to understanding is not specified: perhaps one must know the historian's—in this case, Cossa's—life to comprehend what he meant. So much for *The Abhorrence of Evidence*.

Leslie Stephen provided an early example of the Implicit Absurdity when he wrote: "The speed with which the book [*Political Economy*] was written shows that it did not imply any revision of first principles."[2] The doctrine that the originality or heterodoxy of a volume is proportional to (or some increasing function of) the length of time the author has devoted to its *composition* (or, for that matter, its excogitation) would indeed be a wonderful hypothesis, if only it were not naked nonsense. Leslie Stephen had previously remarked that Mill's *Logic* took a substantial time to write: beginnings were made in 1830 and the book on the syllogism was written perhaps as early as 1832, but the manuscript was not completed until 1842. Does Stephen say that this work, whose writing covered more than a decade as compared to the two years for the *Political Economy*, was six times as original? Alas, no: "The coincidence with its predecessors remains far closer than the divergence. The fundamental tenets are developed rather than withdrawn."[3] Since this is what is asserted also of the *Political Economy*, Stephen should have inferred only that Mill had taken a course in speed writing sometime after 1842 and before 1847.

A less precise but no less definite association of time of preparation with results was presented by Alfred Marshall: "A critic of Mill's writings may not ignore the following facts. In the small leisure that was left to him free from official work, Mill wrote on a wide variety of questions which had already been discussed by great thinkers. On almost every one of these questions his thoughts, whatever faults they contained, were in some respect new. Therefore he had not much time for elaborating the explanations of his thoughts."[4] Putting aside the error of the assertion that Mill had small leisure, and the temptation to say that Marshall was advancing (in 1876, when the essay on Mill appeared) an apology for his own subsequent unbelievable procrastination in publishing work, one must insist that in one sense Mill had plenty of time. Between the first and last editions of the *Principles* lie twenty-three years, sufficient time to

---

1. L. Cossa, *An Introduction to the Study of Political Economy* (London 1893), 330. Other historians of thought have made the same statement, for example L. H. Haney, *History of Economic Thought* (3rd ed., New York 1936), 443.
2. *The English Utilitarians* (London 1900), III, 161.
3. Ibid., 75.
4. *Memorials of Alfred Marshall* (London 1925), 120.

correct imprecisely expressed views. Marshall was defending Mill against lesser critics, a task that must frequently be resumed, but the defence does not require the exoneration of Mill's analytical shortcomings on so implausible a ground.[5] (The number of third, fourth, and lower-class economists who complain about Mill's lack of consistency, as if they could judge it, is too extensive and painful to enumerate.)

François Trevou, a French editor of Mill's work, found Mill's view on Malthusian doctrine to be incomprehensible unless one were acquainted with his personal life. Island dwellers, said Trevou, naturally fear over-population, and Mill's father drilled the same fear into him. In addition, "the presence of 9 children in the house demonstrated to him the inconveniences rather than the pleasures of large families."[6] "Naturally he did not have children."[7]

If we can explain a view of John's by its possession by James, then we should find all doctrines of the *Elements of Political Economy* reproduced in the son's *Principles*. In fact there are important departures, which will be discussed later, so the task of determining which doctrines were inherited is unfaced. If James Mill strongly believed in the Malthusian doctrine and had nine children, why should his son's similar belief (and larger income) lead to none? (James Mill was quite familiar with the famous *Essay on Population* by 20 August 1805, the date on which, as I calculate, Stuart was conceived.)[8] Yet I must give Trevou his due: Thomas Robert Malthus had one brother and six sisters—I would conjecture that he would have produced his theory several years earlier if he had instead had six brothers and one sister.

Overton H. Taylor has found in one episode, which can be viewed as either intellectual or biographical—the two obviously overlap, as we shall argue—the explanation for an important trend in Mill's *Principles* through the various editions:

> It is of interest that in the successive editions of his *Principles* Mill lengthened and increasingly stressed the favorable parts of his comments on 'socialism.' No doubt he did so because his views were developing further in that direction, but perhaps also in part because he had disliked the misdirected praise of the first edition by a conservative reviewer. This reviewer took the work as a whole to be a sound, orthodox demonstration of the merits of the existing English economy

5. Others have given the same interpretation to the *Principles*—for example, F. W. Taussig, *Wages and Capital* (New York 1899), 217. Taussig's attribution of the wages-fund recantation in part to friendship for Thornton is too far-fetched to discuss (ibid., 248).
6. *Stuart Mill (Textes choisis et Préface)* (Paris 1953), 30.
7. Ibid., 31.
8. He had reviewed the second edition in *The Literary Journal*, Dec. 1803; see D. N. Winch, *James Mill* (Edinburgh 1966), 447.

and social order, and of *laissez faire*, and the chapters on 'socialism' to be intended simply to condemn and refute it. In an angry reply and objection to that review, in the journal which had published it, Mill avowed his opposition to the views or attitudes the reviewer had imparted to him . . .[9]

One need not dispute (1) Mill's increasingly more favourable treatment of socialism, or the interpretation of (2) the reviewer and (3) Mill's rejoinder, although in all three respects Taylor's statement is subject to severe criticism.[10] How peculiar, even with these concessions, is the proposed sequence: one review leads Mill to make several successive revisions of his treatise. Surely Mill—and Taylor—should have looked at the reactions of all reviewers and readers: if mostly they thought Mill favoured socialism more than he actually did, he should have revised the text to a more critical view of socialism.

Of course not all uses of Mill's life have been so irresponsible, and I now move on to respectable—but unsatisfactory—biographical explanations. Let us begin with Edwin Cannan, who had a sharp mind well-stocked with accurate knowledge of the classical economics: "[From 1830 to 1844] Mill's mind was extremely active, but it does not seem to have been directed towards scientific economics. When a man has been giving study and thought to a subject, he does not take rejected manuscripts which have lain fourteen years in his drawer, and print them 'with a few merely verbal alterations.'"[11] This allusion to *Unsettled Questions in Political Economy* greatly oversimplifies the problem. The five essays cover only a tiny part of economics, and give no evidence on Mill's work elsewhere. Moreover, if one has a finished manuscript, he may well publish it without reworking its exposition if its substance is still what he

---

9. *A History of Economic Thought* (New York 1960), 254–5.

10. On the latter two points, I can be brief:

(a) The "review," "Associative Progress," *The Leader*, 27 July 1850, 416, is a two-paragraph comment, signed "ion," with a passing reference to Mill's book (without mention of the author): "That recent work on Political Economy, which was first to admit the feasibility of associative views, yet foreshadowed the inanity and monotony which must supervene when the spur of animal want was conquered and withdrawn." ion had enquired concerning wealthy people driven by boredom to the "shoemaker's last," and found none.

(b) Mill's reply, "Constraints of Communism," *The Leader*, 3 Aug. 1850, 447, consisted of one long paragraph and was signed "D." It simply *corrected* the reason given for his doubts about co-operative societies: "Now, it is this bondage which I am afraid of in the coöperative communities. I fear that the yoke of conformity would be made heavier instead of lighter; that people would be compelled to live as it pleased others, not as it pleased themselves; that their lives would be placed under rules, the same for all, prescribed by the majority; and that there would be no escape, no independence of action left to any one, since all must be members of one or another community. It is this which, as is contended in the 'Political Economy,' would make life monotonous; not freedom from want, which is a good in every sense of the word . . ."

11. *Production and Distribution Theories*, 3rd ed. (London 1924), 390.

89

believes; indeed it becomes difficult to make any choice except trivial or wholesale revision.[12]

Mill's rebellion against his "dour and magerful" father has received emphasis from so learned a man as Viner.[13] In a curious essay whose ostensible occasion was the centenary of Mill's *Principles* but whose theme was a defence of Bentham, Viner explained Mill's writings on Bentham with an eye to the death of his father in 1836. The explanation may well be correct— it is one used by Mill himself[14]—but it is valueless. Unless one systematically characterizes the views of James Mill which were respected by his son—who assuredly did not share his father's view on a variety of subjects, including Harriet Taylor—one simply has not explained anything. If John's solicitude for James' feelings made random appearances, a tossed coin would be equally helpful in explaining John's tergiversations.

My final example of the misuses of biography is John Stuart Mill himself. I shall not rely upon his most famous improbability: the assessment of the influence of Harriet Taylor upon himself and his work.[15] The example I choose is the benefits of his service in the East India Company:

> I am disposed to agree with what has been surmised by others, that the opportunity which my official position gave me of learning by personal observation the necessary conditions of the practical conduct of public affairs, has been of considerable value to me as a theoretical reformer of the opinions and institutions of my time. Not, indeed, that public business transacted on paper, to take effect on the other side of the globe, was of itself calculated to give much practical knowledge of life. But the occupation accustomed me to see and hear the difficulties of every course, and the means of obviating them, stated and discussed deliberately, with a view to execution; it gave me opportunities of perceiving when public measures, and other political facts, did not produce the effects which had been expected of them, and from what causes . . . I was thus in a good position for finding out by

12. Thus, Milton Friedman began an important article: "This article was written in 1935 . . . I planned to do further work on the problem but I never did and so the paper remained buried in my files." "A method of Comparing Incomes of Families Differing in Composition," *Studies in Income and Wealth*, XV (National Bureau of Economic Research 1952). Friedman had nevertheless given some "study and thought" to economics in the intervening seventeen years.

13. "Bentham and J. S. Mill: The Utilitarian Background," *American Economic Review*, March 1949. Reprinted in *The Long View and the Short* (Glencoe 1958), 321. Others may have experienced my difficulty with "magerful": the *Oxford English Dictionary* makes "mager" a variant of "maugre," none of whose meanings (ill-will, basically) seems appropriate.

14. *Autobiography*, ed. Jack Stillinger (Boston 1969), 123.

15. Ibid., 145–60.

practice the mode of putting a thought which gives it easiest admittance into minds not prepared for it by habit; while I became practically conversant with the difficulties of moving bodies of men, the necessities of compromise, the art of sacrificing the non-essential to preserve the essential.[16]

If Mill is correct, he was an unusually successful speculative reformer because of this experience. There is no evidence, so far as I know, to justify—or contradict—the claim. If he had shown how *his* case for land nationalization, for limited liability companies, or other policies differed from the cases presented by other economists with different backgrounds, we might have some test of his view. As it stands, the claim is vacuous.

The Problem

What is biography and how may it be distinguished from scientific development? The writers of high and low science are sentient beings, and they cannot completely exclude from their scientific work their hopes and anxieties, their friendships and vendettas, their dyspepsia and their liquor—even if they tried to do so more strenuously than often they appear to do. Yet the web of mortality that ties them to their time and place is *not* science: science consists of the arguments and the evidence that lead *other* men to accept or reject scientific views. Science is a social enterprise, and those parts of a man's life which do not affect the relationships between that man and his fellow scientists are simply extra-scientific. When we are told that we must study a man's life to understand what he really meant, we are being invited to abandon science. What Mill's contemporaries did not know about his personal life—and it is well known that he was a man of few friends and few social activities—could not affect their interpretation of his words, and if we are to understand nineteenth-century economics, the details of his personal life should not affect our interpretation of his words. The recipients of a scientific message are the people who determine what the message is, and no flight of genius which does not reach the recipients will ever reach and affect the science.

Even on this view of scientific interchange, some elements of a man's milieu must be known to understand him: in particular, words undergo changes of meaning, and we should also know whether a Mr. Smith is Adam, or, say, Sydney. In short, we should seek to understand a scientist as his contemporaries understood. That understanding normally involves very little biographical information: men write for wider audiences than their neighbours and cronies, and indeed one of the lessons almost every adult learns is how remarkably few are the people who are interested in his personal affairs.

16. Ibid., 52–53.

I therefore firmly disagree with the gracious, attractive statement of the contrary position presented by one of the most distinguished of historians of economics, William Jaffé.[17] When he complains about those who "disdain the plodding labors required for understanding what Ricardo or Marx intended to say,"[18] I reply that if the labours involve biography, these scholars do right if they seek to understand the *scientific* role these men played in the evolution of economic theory: that role was played with the words they wrote, not with the ideas they intended to express.

Even if every syllable of what I have said is accepted, nothing should be inferred about the proper role of biography in the study of science. This is not a simple contradiction to the previous remarks—rather it draws a distinction between understanding a man's scientific work as it appeared to his contemporaries and understanding the evolution of science. After the sentence I have quoted, Jaffé continues: "Nor are they [who 'dabble in the history of economics'] at all interested in probing the question of how or why Ricardo or Marx came to formulate their theories. And they are still more indifferent to the question of how and why a given theory was received or rejected at the time it was first enunciated." Perhaps there are dabblers subject to these absurd beliefs, but the beliefs do not follow from the view that detailed biographical knowledge is irrelevant to the interpretation of an individual's scientific work.

The science of science (the so-called sociology of science) is concerned precisely with such questions: why some discoveries are absorbed quickly and others never; why the science of economics flourished in England and languished in France; why and when innovators need be thoroughly trained in the received tradition; and so forth without limit. There, and not in the scientific content of the work, must we look for a possible role in the study of biography.

Biography is information, but it is not the kind of information, if indeed, any information is of that kind, which speaks for itself. Enough emphasis, I hope, has already been given to the essential deception involved in handpicking congruencies between a man's life and his ideas.

The study of collections of biographies has reached that high level of achievement in which it has a special name—prosopography. Relatively few interesting applications of this technique to the history of science have come to my notice, however.[19] I made modest use of biographical

17. "Biography and Economic Analysis," *Western Economic Journal*, III, 1965.
18. Ibid., 225.
19. See Lawrence Stone, "Prosopography," *Daedalus*, winter 1971. One of the earliest applications of the method to science is R. K. Merton's *Science, Technology and Society in Seventeenth Century England, Osiris*, IV (Bruges 1938). See also J. Ben-David and R. Collins, "Social Factors in the Origins of a New Science," *American Sociological Review*, 1966, and H. Zuckerman and R. K. Merton, "Age, Ageing, and Age Structure in Science," in *Ageing and Society*, Volume 3 of *A Sociology of Age Stratification*, ed. M. W. Riley, M. Johnson, and A. Foner (New York 1972).

data to date the shift of economics to the university,[20] and no doubt other examples exist.

Certainly it is easy to propose a list of comparative biographical studies whose length and variety are limited only by one's imagination. The effects of economic incentives on the work of scholars, for example, requires a comparative biographical approach. The effects of the choice of graduate school upon one's intellectual convictions and even academic career are capable of study, and indeed I am presently in the midst of precisely this topic [see chap. 17, below].

Rather than continue with this shopping list, however, I propose to devote the remainder of this paper to the task of examining the problem of the systematic use of a single man's biography.

The Two Mills

It has been a common belief that the elder Mill indoctrinated the younger in Ricardian-Smithian economics and that his heritage was a major obstacle to the son in striking out toward a new and better economics. At a much more specific level we have already encountered the belief that after James' death in 1836 John openly abandoned some of these inherited beliefs which previously he had been unwilling to disavow publicly.

The general charge of indoctrination is an extraordinarily unperceptive one, and for two very different reasons. The first is that John was taught the best economics of his time if he was taught Ricardo and Smith. Unless one is prepared to argue that a scientist is handicapped in his future work by a thorough training in the best scientific knowiedge of his time—and despite the popularity of this view I consider it unbelievable—Mill was qualified to make contributions, not disqualified from doing so. This is not to say that all of the sound economics of 1817 could be found in Smith, Malthus, and Ricardo. In particular J. B. Say had a spacious, modern vision of the circular flow and general equilibrium that he lacked the power to push to an analytical level. But both contemporaries and modern economists must concede that John Mill was trained in *the* leading economics of his time.

The charge of indoctrination is unperceptive for a second reason. James Mill was wholly devoted to Truth and Logic, and would never teach anyone—let alone an undemonstratively beloved son—anything of which these stern masters would disapprove. Of course, the next sentence must begin, James Mill not only adhered to the truth, but believed that the devotion was reciprocated, and in this he differs from us ordinary mortals only in the intensity of this mutual esteem. Recall this passage from the *Autobiography*: "My father never permitted anything which I learnt, to degenerate into a mere exercise of memory. He strove to make

20. See my *Essays in the History of Economics* (Chicago 1965), and "The Adoption of the Marginal Utility Theory," *History of Political Economy*, IV, fall 1972 [chap. 7, above].

the understanding not only go along with every step of the teaching, but if possible, precede it. Anything which could be found out by thinking, I never was told, until I had exhausted my efforts to find it out for myself."[21] It would no doubt be bitter-sweet for James to observe his son refute a parental theory, but the sweet, I suspect, would be of the approximate intensity of the bitter.

In ascertaining the influence of James Mill on his son's economics, then, we should distinguish two levels of possible influence. There are, first, those doctrines peculiar to James Mill—extensions or departures from Ricardian economics—where the father's net influence is most easily determined. There are, second, those doctrines common to the Ricardian school, where John Stuart Mill's departures are both more fundamental scientifically and less personal.

In his *Elements of Political Economy* (3d. ed., 1826), James Mill presented a stark, pseudo-rigorous, unattractive exposition of the ruling theory, with significant differences and several improvements.[22] Although the intellectual debts to Ricardo, Malthus, and Smith were admittedly very large ("I profess to have made no discovery"), there are a number of significant departures:

1. Mill argues on essentially *a priori* grounds that capital cannot grow as rapidly as population. The argument is uninteresting: either the rich have all non-subsistence income, and *they* have no inducement to save, or many people have such a surplus, and they see the real lack of need to save (ibid., 52ff). (Mill deserves credit, at least, for facing a problem most classical economists ignored: Why should capital grow less rapidly than population?)

2. Relative values of goods are governed exclusively by relative quantities of labour used, directly or indirectly (through capital), in their production (ibid., 96ff). The profits necessary to justify the aging of wine are really measures of labour. Mill's argument is nonsense or a tautology.

3. Mill favours free competition in the issue of bank notes (ibid., 152ff). Ricardo was not hostile to the idea, but did not support it with Mill's enthusiasm.

4. Mill proposes a distinction between productive and unproductive *consumption*, which bears a closer verbal than substantive resemblance to productive and unproductive labour (ibid., 220ff). Productive consumption is that which is necessary to maintain a

21. *Autobiography*, 20.
22. Ricardo's own list of disagreements with the *Elements* was sent to Mill (*Works and Correspondence of David Ricardo*, IX, 126–33). Putting aside details and exposition, Ricardo notes my differences number 1, 2, 5, and 6. I neglect some minor innovations in Mill, such as an excellent discussion of regional price levels (*Elements*, 174–6).

man's productive capacity, unproductive consumption any surplus beyond that level.

5. Mill has two versions of Say's Law, of which he may have been an
independent discoverer.[23] In *Commerce Defended* he proposed
the proposition: total output, if properly composed of various
goods, could always be sold. If he had added "at prices equal to
costs" this would have been an equilibrium proposition. In the
Elements he presents (as Say usually did) a simple arithmetical
identity. A man's supply is defined as what he does not consume,
and supply is the "instrument" of demand, so for each man (and
hence for the nation) supply equals demand (ibid., 228ff). Mill
proceeds to reintroduce price movements to equate supply and
demand for individual commodities and effect changes in the
pattern of production (ibid., 233ff), improving upon his earlier
version—so it closely approximates Ricardo's version. Hence it is
uncertain whether Mill's view on this topic was that of Ricardo,[24]
or of Say.

6. Mill favoured the socialization, or at least the heavy taxation, of
future increments in land rents (ibid., 248ff). This was a revenue
source which on his simplistic theory of rent had no allocational
effects; the values were created independent of any efforts of the
landlord.

7. More durable income sources (eg, rent) should be taxed more
heavily than equal incomes of shorter duration (eg, salaries). The
income taxation should in effect be based upon capital values
(ibid., 270ff).

John Stuart ignored the first and rejected the second of these innovations:
neither in the *Essays on Unsettled Questions* nor in the *Principles* is the
pure labour theory of value or the ambiguous *a priori* argument on
savings adopted.[25] The free competition of banks in note issue was en-
dorsed with substantial modifications.[26] The distinction between productive and unproductive consumption was given a tolerant defence.[27] The
son was much clearer on the distinction between tautology and theorem

---

23. See my "Sraffa's Ricardo," reprinted in *Essays in the History of Economics* (Chicago
1965).

24. Some differences in detail surely existed. Thus Ricardo admitted the possibility of a
glut if everyone consumed only necessaries, whereas Mill denied a glut in this case (ibid.,
236). For Ricardo's concession, see *Principles of Political Economy*, in *Works and Correspondence of David Ricardo*, I (Cambridge 1951), ed. P. Sraffa, 292–3. On this point I side
with Mill.

25. Essay IV of *Essays on Some Unsettled Questions, Collected Works*, IV (Toronto
1967), 293ff; *Principles of Political Economy*, cw, III 477ff (III, IV).

26. *Principles*, cw, III 682ff (IV, XXIV, 5)

27. Essay III of *Essays*, cw, IV, esp. 283ff.

in dealing with Say's Law, and superior to both Ricardo and his father.[28] The rent increment socialization plan was fervently embraced in Mill's later years,[29] and the differential taxation of nondurable incomes was also accepted (and is commonly and, as we have seen, erroneously credited to the son).[30] With one exception, these were the correct positions for John Stuart to take in the light of the general level of economic theory of the time. The one unequivocal mistake was the socialization of land rent increments: both Mills believed that legitimate current investments in land should not be taxed more heavily than alternate incomes or property, and if the market in land was working efficiently (and hence predicting without bias the average future increments of rent), there would be nothing left to tax.

The treatment by John Stuart of James Mill's own innovations is difficult to interpret in any terms except of intellectual merits: there is neither systematic acceptance nor rejection, and it is easier to explain the departures of the son by a preference for superior theory than by some psychological relationship. It should be added that James Mill made revisions of his treatment of international trade and of profits in the third edition of the *Elements* in response to his son's criticisms.[31] At this stage I am prepared to argue that all one can say is that the son treated the father's views with courtesy but not with deference. It will be interesting to see if the same conclusion holds in the other main topics (psychology, government, and India) on which both wrote extensively.

The question of the existence of an uncritical devotion of John Stuart to the Smith-Ricardian economics can be disposed of summarily. In an earlier essay I claimed for Mill unusual creativity in economic theory, and listed six substantial contributions.[32] I should have added several other contributions, of which I shall name only two:

1. In a prodigious essay on "Corn Laws," written at the age of eighteen, Mill invented the compensation principle, that pillar of welfare economics.

2. In the early *Essays on Some Unsettled Questions*, he invented the theory of reciprocal demand in international trade theory, a fundamental part of that theory.[33]

28. Essay II of *Essays*, ibid., esp. 263ff.
29. See especially the essay on land tenure reform in *Essays on Economics and Society*, cw, V 689ff.
30. *Principles*, cw, III, 813ff (V, II, 4). There is an explicit disagreement with his father on one detail, ibid., 818n.
31. *Autobiography*, 108.
32. "The Nature and Role of Originality in Scientific Progress," reprinted in my *Essays in the History of Economics*.
33. Numerous lesser contributions, especially to the theory of comparative cost, are discussed by Jacob Viner, *Studies in the Theory of International Trade* (New York 1937).

There have been only a tiny handful of enormously fertile theoretical innovators in the history of economics, and Mill has full rights to membership in this regal circle along with Smith, Marshall, and Edgeworth.

Conclusion

The primary task of scientific history is to become scientific: to subject hypotheses to objective tests which the hypotheses are capable of failing. I wish I could claim that the foregoing paper constitutes much more than a sermon on methodology, because I have a singularly low estimate of the scientific value of sermons on methodology. But even if it is limited to this humble role, I hope that it will serve to remind all of us how easily illustration can be confused with evidence.

9 Merton on Multiples, Denied and Affirmed

A science is conducted by a society of scholars who jointly pursue the development of a coherent body of knowledge, including a central theoretical core. This society, using practices such as specialization and exchange which we associate with economic societies, tests received doctrines, extends their applicability, and strives to discover the explanations of phenomena presently inexplicable with received doctrines. Because the pursuit of science is a social enterprise, only knowledge shared by its members is scientific. As in other social enterprises—economic, military, political—it is superficial and misleading to view the progress of the society as the product of a few heroic figures.

No one has done more to develop the implications of this view of science and scientists than Robert K. Merton—indeed no one else has done anywhere near so much to develop the study of science as a social enterprise.[1] (Merton's contributions have been so fundamental as to constitute almost a self-refutation of his thesis of science as a social enterprise!) Among the implications which he has drawn, none is more telling than his thesis that "all scientific discoveries are in principle multiples, including those that on the surface appear to be singletons."[2] This essay examines this thesis, viewed as an explanatory principle for the scientific discoveries in economics.

The Thesis of Multiples

Rather than give a formal statement and proof of the thesis, Merton presents ten kinds of phenomena and behavior in science that are implicit or explicit suggestions that the probability is high that any important scientific discovery will be made by more than one person.[3]

These various evidences for multiples include the discoveries that proved to have one or more complete anticipations, the announcements

Reprinted from *Science and Social Structure: A Festschrift for Robert K. Merton*, Transactions of the New York Academy of Sciences, series 2, vol. 39 (New York: New York Academy of Sciences, 1980).

1. R. K. Merton, *The Sociology of Science* (University of Chicago Press, Chicago, 1973).
2. R. K. Merton, Ref. 1:356.
3. One would expect the thesis to hold even more fully for unimportant scientific discoveries. I conjecture that the lesser interest and the greater difficulty of enumerating such discoveries have kept them out of the discussion.

of duplicated researches or of nearly completed researches abandoned because of others' discoveries, the race to publish new results, and the attempts to achieve and protect priority of discovery. An inventory of multiple discoveries made in collaboration with Dr. Elinor Barber is briefly discussed.

We can produce a list of multiples in economics, the first of which was surely in Merton's list, for he quotes its mention by Macaulay:

1. ". . . the doctrine of rent, now universally received by political economists, was propounded, at almost the same moment, by two writers unconnected with each other." They were T. R. Malthus and E. West (1815).
2. The near simultaneous discovery of the marginal utility theory by Jevons (1862), Menger (1871) and Walras (1874).
3. The marginal productivity theory, discovered by Marshall (1879), Edgeworth (1881), Stuart Wood (1888), Wicksteed (1894), as well as Barone (1895), J. B. Clark (1889), and no doubt others.
4. Monopolistic and imperfect competition, discovered by Chamberlin (1934) and J. Robinson (1932).[4]
5. The modern theory of utility, including the Slutsky equation, discovered by Slutsky (1915) and Hicks and Allen (1934).
6. The theory of comparative cost, due to Ricardo (1817) and Torrens (1815).
7. Refutation of the wages-fund theory by W. Thornton (1869) and Francis Longe (1866).
8. The international factor equalization theorem, due to Lerner (1933) and Samuelson (1948).

In addition, many minor multiple discoveries are known.[5] Examples are the demonstration of the existence of a measurable utility function when the utility function is additive in its arguments (Wicksteed, 1888; Fisher, 1892), and the discovery of the kinked oligopoly demand curve by Paul Sweezy (1939) and Hall and Hitch (1939).

The Rationale of Multiples

In the basic essay on multiple discoveries, Merton does little more than hint at the reason for their existence. Of the caveats that bring this important essay to a conclusion, one states that multiple discoveries need not be chronologically simultaneous: two discoveries can be "simultaneous or nearly so in social and cultural time, depending upon the

---

4. One must apologize to Chamberlin, who spent much of his life explaining the difference between the two concepts, for combining them here.

5. Mark Blaug has called to my attention another significant (and debatable) multiple; see J. V. Pinto, "Launhardt and Location Theory: Rediscovery of a Neglected Book," *Journal of Regional Science*, 17 (1977): 17–30.

accumulated state of knowledge" in the several cultures in which they appear.[6]

In a later essay, "Multiple Discoveries as Strategic Research Site," these hints are expanded upon:

> The sheer fact that multiple discoveries are made by scientists working independently of one another testifies to the further crucial fact that, though remote in space, they are responding to much the same social and intellectual forces that impinge upon them all.[7]

In this essay a wholly different scientific function is also assigned to multiple discoveries:

> Often a new idea or a new empirical finding has been achieved or published, only to go unnoticed by others, until it is later uncovered or independently rediscovered and only then incorporated into the science. . . . Multiples—that is, redundant discoveries—have a greater chance of being heard by others in the social system and so, then and there, to affect its further development.[8]

The argument that the discoveries are called for by the preceding development of the science is surely the essential basis for expecting multiple discoveries. Previous scientific evolution has thrown up problems on methods or principles which make the succeeding discoveries necessary for continued scientific work. The rent theory of West and Malthus (and Ricardo) was appropriate to an island economy in which a rapidly growing population and rapidly expanding industrial production would put progressively stronger strains on the capacity of the domestic agricultural system. The Slutsky equation presented a fundamental relationship immanent in the theory of utility-maximizing behavior.

But if multiple discoveries are a response to generally felt scientific needs, we must *define* multiple discoveries as those which appear at a given stage in the evolution of a science. If important elements of Keynesian economics were discovered by Kalecki in Poland in the 1930s, we should hardly call this a multiple because the ruling (Marxian) economics of Poland bore little relationship to that of Great Britain.

The determination whether the state of a science in country A is the same as that in country B, either at the same or different times, is not an easy task but it is not an impossible one. If the scientists in A and B are working on the same problems, perhaps citing the same literature, they also share the implicit need for the scientific discoveries which are neces-

6. R. K. Merton, Ref. 1:369.
7. R. K. Merton, Ref. 1:375.
8. R. K. Merton, Ref. 1:380.

sary for further progress.[9] For example, was Turgot's statement of diminishing returns (1767) a multiple with that of Malthus and West in England 48 years later? I would say not, because no use was made of Turgot's theory by the Physiocrats, who were not concerned with the effect of agricultural protection on prices and incomes, as the English economists were. On the other hand, Irving Fisher and Wicksteed were concerned with the same theory of utility in their proposals to measure utility with additive functions.

There is no evidence that Merton has systematically imposed a test of similiarity of scientific environment in the determination of multiple discoveries. When we use the test, many multiple discoveries will vanish. Let us reconsider our short list from economics.

1. The theory of rent and diminishing returns *is* a true example: all three economists (for Ricardo should be included) were writing in the same scientific setting.

2. The marginal utility theory is a much more dubious example: the status and direction of economic science in France, Switzerland and Vienna were rather different than in England.

3. The marginal productivity theory becomes a much lower multiple—Wood in America and Barone in Italy, for example, are in somewhat different scientific contexts than the British economists.

4. Monopolistic and imperfect competition is a true multiple in settings, but the two theories differ in fundamental respects.

5. Slutsky writing in Russia in 1915 and Hicks and Allen in Britain in the 1930s are in quite different scientific worlds.

6. Comparative cost theory is a true multiple.

7. The refutation of the wages fund is a true multiple, but marred by the fact that the refutation was idle until a superior theory (marginal productivity) appeared somewhat later.

8. The factor equalization theorem was perhaps a multiple, although the fact that the earlier version (developed at a major center of economics) was not published raises perplexing questions.

In this very brief list, about half of the multiple discoveries appear to survive the essential requirement that they were made in similar scientific settings.

But let us now come to our main point: most of the multiple discoveries were not multiples at all, *but they nevertheless support Merton's basic thesis*. For most of the multiples were discoveries that had been made earlier but had been ignored:

1. James Anderson (1777) had the rent theory (without diminishing

---

9. This implies that two scientists in the same country at the same time would *not* make multiple discoveries if they were working in well-separated specialties.

returns in the modern sense); Turgot stated the law of diminishing returns in 1767.

2. The marginal utility theory had many early discoverers, of whom Gossen (1854) was most noteworthy.

3. The marginal productivity theory was proposed by Longfield (1832) and von Thünen (1850).

4. The theories of Chamberlin and Joan Robinson (which differ in important respects) are largely anticipated by Marshall and (later) by Sraffa.

5. Slutsky should be looked upon as an anticipator of Hicks and Allen.

6. Comparative cost theory had several incomplete anticipations (Viner, *Studies in the Theory of International Trade*, p. 440).

7. The refutation of the wages fund theory (by denying the fixity of the fund) is not credited to any earlier writers, although I am utterly confident that the main point (that the wages fund was not a fixed quantity) was common in the radical literature.

8. The factor equalization theorem lacked an earlier anticipation.

In fact, we may reasonably expect most of the multiples that survive the condition of similar scientific settings to be anticipated by earlier, less successful discoveries of the same ideas.

The unsuccessful earlier discoveries are the very evidence for the "inevitability" of scientific progress that the multiple discoveries was supposed to present. If an early, valid statement of a theory falls on deaf ears, and a later restatement is accepted by the science, this is surely proof that the science accepts ideas only when they fit into the then-current state of the science. Gossen, writing in the high tide of German Historical economics, was simply inappropriate to his scientific environment. Longfield in Ireland, and von Thünen in Germany, were presenting a marginal productivity theory for which neither German nor British economic science was ready. And similarly for Slutsky, Cournot and other unsuccessful discoverers.

On this view, Merton's secondary task for multiples of persuading a science to adopt the idea is incompatible with this basic theory. If the science is ready for an idea, it will rarely need multiple discoverers to persuade it to adopt the idea. Elaboration, repetition, and controversy will be the main vehicles of persuasion. The multiples arise because they are demanded by the evolving science.

Conclusion

On the present interpretation, multiple discoveries are indeed evidence that the advancing frontier of a science requires new analytical (or empirical) armament and the demand is being met by able scholars. But there is only one reason why full multiples—completed and tested—

should occur and that is incomplete knowledge of who is working on a problem and what his achievement will be. The better the information network of a science, the fewer will be true multiples that are separated by a significant period of time.

The unsuccessful early discoveries are equally valid evidence for the social character of science. Indeed it is probable that they are more frequent than multiples. If so, we have completed the full circle: Merton's fundamental thesis is reaffirmed, but multiple discoveries shrink to a minor support for the thesis.

Part Three   History of
Economic Thought

10

Does Economics Have a Useful Past?

The dividing line or zone between past and present economics is a matter of intention more than of time. If we go back to Marshall's discussion of demand curves, the visit is not to any important degree a response to a hope that we can learn something new about demand curves. This was not Marshall at his best, and it is highly improbable that one already reasonably well acquainted with the modern literature will profit from Marshall. But if we go back to the *Principles* and to *Industry and Trade* to learn about technological progress or economic growth, our interest need not be exclusively historical, for here Marshall may supply new ideas and suggestions even if not theories. The progress of demand theory has made Marshall's work wholly obsolete, but the progress of the theory of economic growth has been less conclusive.

I define the subject matter of the history of economics to be economics which is not read to master present-day economics (although possibly it is read to learn the path by which we have reached the present). Some historians of economics—Schumpeter is an eminent representative—believe that an understanding of the evolution of a science helps to understand its present structure.[1] This claim may be conceded and restated as the plausible hypothesis that correct knowledge never has a negative marginal product. Nevertheless, one need not read in the history of economics—that is, past economics—to master present economics.

This will not be news to the present generation of economists. The young theorist, working with an increasingly formal, abstract, and systematic corpus of knowledge, will seldom find it necessary to consult even a late-nineteenth-century economist. He will assume, just as the mathematician or chemist assumes, that all that is useful and valid in earlier work is present—in purer and more elegant form—in the modern theory. Indeed, the young economist will increasingly share the view of the more advanced formal sciences that the history of the discipline is best left to those underendowed for fully professional work at the modern level. This attitude is well described by Sir Peter Medawar in a review of James Watson's *The Double Helix*: "These matters belong to scientific history, and the history of science bores most scientists stiff. A great many highly

Reprinted from *History of Political Economy* 1 (Fall 1969). © 1969 by Duke University Press, Durham, N.C.
1. *History of Economic Analysis* (New York, 1954), pp. 4 ff.

creative scientists . . . take it for granted, though they are usually too polite or too ashamed to say so, that an interest in the history of science is a sign of failing or unawakened powers."[2] And of course these scientists are usually right in dismissing the history of science as a research weapon. The odds are 30 to 1 that Pigou will be more helpful than Senior to a modern economist interested only in increasing the power of his apparatus, and 100 to 1 that Irving Fisher will be more helpful than all the economics written before 1600. As counterevidence, after 1838 a theorist could have gained much if he had found Cournot, and after 1915 if he had found Slutsky. The economics of 1800, like the weather forecasts of 1800, is mostly out of date.

Let us return to the definition of the discipline of the history of economics as the study of earlier economics with a purpose other than the understanding of the workings of an economic system. This definition seems almost intended to deny any utilitarian purpose to the study of the history of a science, but that is not the case. The history of economics does have something valuable to teach the young economist, and this role will be described before turning to the important reason for the study of the history of science.

How to Read a Book

The definition of *literacy* is "the ability to read," and if the person is a professor who does not wish to perish, the ability also to write. Literacy is of course a matter of degree: one can "read" a newspaper in a language of which scarcely a word is known and yet learn something of the place in which it is published. Conversely, if a great book such as Smith's *Wealth of Nations* is read repeatedly, on even a fifth or tenth reading one continues to learn new things. I doubt whether anyone will ever fully apprehend all the things that Smith wished to express, and there is even more to learn from an interesting mind than its owner wished to teach us. Most professors do not know how to read a scientific work well, and this skill is developed only with purposeful practice.

To understand a man—and the nature of this understanding will be developed—one must know the subject matter of the discipline in which he is writing: it takes an economist to read an economist. Let me say at once that a large fraction of the historians of economics meet this test very imperfectly. The difficulties raised by a shaky knowledge of economic theory are illustrated by the discussion of Carl Menger by Sir Alexander Gray in his pleasant little volume, *The Development of Economic Doctrine*. The productive factors which make consumer goods are called goods of higher order by Menger and the question naturally arises, How do we divide up the value of the good of first order (say, bread) among the goods of higher order (ovens, flour, and baker's services)? Gray remarks:

2. *New York Review of Books*, March 28, 1968.

What [Menger] suggests is that the value of a higher good is represented by the difference which its presence makes, or the loss which would be sustained by its withdrawal from the group. This, however, is clearly inadmissible. It is unnecessary to go into refined arithmetical examples to realize that the withdrawal or destruction of land would have a devastating effect on agriculture, and therefore, on Menger's principles, the whole value of the product should pass to land; yet the contribution of agricultural implements and of manure cannot be denied [p. 352].

One of Menger's major claims to fame is that, unlike his codiscoverers Jevons and Walras, he applied his theory of marginal valuation directly and correctly to reach the general marginal productivity theory. Gray considers this achievement an error.[3]

The second requirement in reading an economist with comprehension is a certain measure of detachment or even sympathy. Even the best of men is a strange mixture of truth and error, of insight and partial blindness, of careful and slovenly thought and writing. One may proceed over the man's work with an analytical microscope, examining each sentence, phrase, and word with scrupulous care—and yet never understand what he is trying to say. My favorite example of this approach (among the nonliving) is Edwin Cannan, who was an acute analyst as well as an erudite student of the English classical school. For all of Cannan's intellectual power and scholarship, he simply could not understand a man like Ricardo. His five-page discussion entitled "Ricardo's Attempt to Revive the Pure Labour Theory" is a persuasive illustration of the blinding effect of hypercriticism.[4]

The opposite of hypercriticism is adulation, and it serves equally poorly as a guide in interpretation. The Marxist literature has been plagued beyond belief with this vice; I merely cite the essays on that distinguished economist theorist, Joseph Stalin, by Ronald Meek and Oskar Lange.[5] The appraisals of the economic thought of recent American presidents, I may add, have not been noticeably more attractive. The economics of kings and popes is best left to prime ministers and bishops, and funerals are not the occasion for dispassionate appraisals of great scholars.

3. Edgeworth remarks, of a similar argument by John A. Hobson: "Imagine an analogous application of the differential calculus in physics, 'put upon its broadest footing,' an objector substituting x wherever a mathematician had used dx or Δx!" *Papers Relating to Political Economy* 1:19 n.

4. *A Review of Economic Theory*, pp. 172–77; the interpretation may be compared with P. Sraffa, Introduction to volume 1 of *Works and Correspondence of David Ricardo*, or my "Ricardo and the 93% Labor Theory of Value," *Essays in the History of Economics* (Chicago, 1965), pp. 326–42.

5. Meek, "Stalin as an Economist," *Review of Economic Studies* 21 (1953–54): 232–39; Lange, "The Economic Laws of Socialist Society in the Light of Joseph Stalin's Last Work," *International Economic Papers* 4 (1954): 145–80.

The goal in the understanding of a scientific essay is the formulation of the essential structure of the author's analytical system. Our understanding is better the larger the share of the man's work we can deduce from the analytical system. Indeed, we may use prediction to test our understanding; one who understands the first five chapters of Ricardo should be able to write his chapters on taxation. Of course there will be details of inconsistent or unintegrated knowledge that we cannot reconcile with the analytical system, just as there are empirical observations which depart several standard errors from a well-established empirical relationship. The unintegrated pieces of knowledge and the errors will be fewer or more subtle the higher the scientific quality of the man's work. If a significant amount of an economist's analysis cannot be reconciled with the remainder, either that economist or his reader has failed to understand fully that portion of his work. An ad hoc "explanation" for a divergent portion of an analysis, whether venal interest or psychological illness or simple forgetfulness, is in fact no explanation at all: it is a polite way of confessing failure.

The purpose in seeking to understand the man's theoretical system is not to be generous or malicious toward him, but to maximize the probability that his work will contribute to scientific progress. Only if the analytical system is well-defined and cleansed of irrelevant digression and inessential error may we determine whether it is a worthy addition to the corpus of the science, or at least a line of investigation that ought to be explored further.

The act of reading well a piece of scientific writing will therefore be a contribution to the progress of the science: the fully professional reading has improved upon the original statement of the theory.

At no point in this discussion of how to read scientific works has the word "past" been used: the correct way to read Adam Smith is the correct way to read the forthcoming issues of a professional journal. There are good reasons, however, for believing that it is easier to learn to read if one begins with the economists of earlier times.

Perhaps the chief advantage is that it is easier to be neutral toward the work. Every major center of graduate instruction in economics has a degree of engagement in current economics. It has a faculty which is active in research and publication, and inevitably a certain amount of taking sides occurs in the graduate courses. Young Ph.D.'s come out prepared to read "good" economics uncritically and "bad" economics hypercritically. They are also aware of the fact that they will produce a major article if they find a mistake in Friedman or Samuelson. This problem is much attenuated in the history of economics: it is true that an MIT student will not have an adequate appreciation of Marshall, but his inherited attitude toward Marshall will be a much smaller block to proper

110

reading than his attitude toward Friedman. And it is harder to get a major article out of the errors of great men of the past because most of these errors have already been discovered.

A second advantage is that time identifies the economists who were worth reading properly. Most of the articles, and probably all of them, in the next issue of the professional journal are not worth a careful and costly reading.

A last advantage of earlier work is that its inherently evolutionary nature is evident and capable of study. Scientific writings are never final editions of ideas, and for that matter never first editions. This argument may be pursued along a slightly different line, to which we now turn.

Not only can the study of the history of economics teach one how to read, it can also teach us how to react to what we read. Scientific literature is to a considerable degree controversial literature. New ideas are sold very much the way new automobiles are sold: by exaggerating their superiority over the older models. There is a difference in the method of salesmanship, however: a new theory may be more important eventually than even its inventor believes and claims, but the value of the older theories is invariably greater than he acknowledges. Scientific innovation proceeds more by disparagement of rivals than by excessive self-praise, perhaps because it appears more modest.

The role of controversy is indeed to stimulate interest and animosity. Only after a theory has been subjected to hostile review do its weaknesses and limitations become identified and therefore capable of being remedied. The sterility of the early Walrasian system arose because it was ignored by most economists and adopted by a few but criticized by almost none. Milton Friedman's work is bound to be spread rapidly in the science and to achieve a wide scope and high rigor because of his wondrous gift of eliciting the probing attention of eminent contemporaries.

The young economist who reads some of the early controversies with care will surely learn one lesson, and he may learn two. The inevitable lesson is that after studying previous controversies one cannot become quite so engaged in the current controversies—one cannot become quite so convinced of either the correctness or the importance of one's new ideas. The more subtle lesson is that it does not pay to learn the first lesson: the temperate, restrained, utterly fair-minded treatment of one's own theories does a disservice to these theories as well as to one's professional status and salary. The scientist is loath to buy new models which have not been well advertised. I therefore accept the proposition of Bishop Stubbs that the study of history probably makes a man wise, and surely makes him sad.

That is all I wish to say of the utilitarian functions of the study of the history of economics. The pedagogical benefits of this study are genuine

111

and valuable, but they do not provide an agenda for the professional student of the subject. The real interest of the history of science lies elsewhere.

The Sociology of Science

The history of science provides the information to investigate the behavior of sciences. For insufficient reasons the study of the behavior of sciences is labeled the sociology of science. The behavior of sciences has been investigated by sociologists—of whom the foremost is Robert Merton—but it has also been investigated by physicists such as Thomas Kuhn, by psychologists such as Edwin Boring, and in fact by a member or two of almost every discipline. One must be a mathemetician to understand the evolution of mathematics and an economist to study the evolution of economics, and sociology puts its imperialistic title on this area of study only on the ground that sciences are practiced by human beings and therefore involve social behavior. In the same sense it would be possible and equally meritorious to describe as the economics of science the economic organization and evolution of a science.

The studies of the sociology of science may be divided into two broad categories. The first category is devoted to the development of the intellectual content of the science—its theories, its methods of measurement, its criteria of evidence, and the like. This is the more traditional kind of work in the history of science, and I shall give a few examples of it shortly. The second main branch is the relationship between the intellectual content of a science and the organization and environment of the scientists. The effects of moving the science into academic circles, the effects of foundations upon research, the relationship between the problems of the science and the problems of society are examples of this kind of research.

Let us consider first the problem studied in that fine book by Thomas S. Kuhn, *The Structure of Scientific Revolutions*, namely, How does the ruling theory of a science get displaced by a new theory? The corpus of theoretical knowledge and analytical and empirical techniques which is accepted by the dominant group of members of a science is called the paradigm of the science. This paradigm provides the consensus necessary for the existence of a community of scholars. The paradigm is open-ended and thus allows the continuing utilization of its apparatus to deal with an essentially unlimited number of unsolved problems. Kuhn's inquiry may be stated: How is one paradigm replaced by another?

With the passage of time, there appear an increasing number of what Kuhn terms anomalies or contradictions to the paradigm:

When for these reasons or others like them, an anomaly comes to seem more than just another puzzle of normal science, the transition to crisis and to extraordinary science has begun. The anomaly itself now comes to be more generally recognized as such by the profession. More and more attention is devoted to it by more and more of the field's most eminent men. If it still continues to resist, as it usually does not, many of them may come to view its resolution as *the* subject matter of their discipline. For them the field will no longer look quite the same as it had earlier. Part of its different appearance results simply from the new fixation point of scientific scrutiny. An even more important source of change is the divergent nature of the numerous partial solutions that concerted attention to the problem has made available. The early attacks upon the resistent problem will have followed the paradigm rules quite closely. But with continuing resistance, more and more of the attacks upon it will have involved some minor or not so minor articulation of the paradigm, no two of them quite alike, each partially successful, but none sufficiently so to be accepted as paradigm by the group. Through this proliferation of divergent articulations (more and more frequently they will come to be described as *ad hoc* adjustments), the rules of normal science become increasingly blurred. Though there still is a paradigm, few practitioners prove to be entirely agreed about what it is. Even formerly standard solutions of solved problems are called in question [pp. 82–83].

Eventually a new paradigm is developed which accounts for the anomalies that give rise to the crisis:

The transition from a paradigm in crisis to a new one from which a new tradition of normal science can emerge is far from a cumulative process, one achieved by an articulation or extension of the old paradigm. Rather it is a reconstruction of the field from new fundamentals, a reconstruction that changes some of the field's most elementary theoretical generalizations as well as many of its paradigm methods and applications. During the transition period there will be a large but never complete overlap between the problems that can be solved by the old and by the new paradigm. But there will also be a decisive difference in the modes of solution. When the transition is complete, the profession will have changed its view of the field, its methods, and its goals [pp. 84–85].

Kuhn's thesis is that the displacement of one paradigm by another—of neoclassical by Keynesian general theory, for example—must be abrupt and revolutionary: the previous paradigm cannot gradually and smoothly change its form and content to embrace the new paradigm:

113

When paradigms enter, as they must, into a debate about paradigm choice, their role is necessarily circular. Each group uses its own paradigm to argue in that paradigm's defense [p. 93].

That is why the change in paradigm comes by conquest rather than assimilation. The new theory explains some phenomena differently than the older theory explained them, and hence the two theories are not logically compatible. The growth of science by the unbroken cumulation of knowledge is for Kuhn fictional history.

My main quarrel with Kuhn is over his failure to specify the nature of a paradigm in sufficient detail that his central thesis can be tested empirically. If vast changes in the subject and techniques of a science can be accommodated within a paradigm, and hence do not constitute a revolution, Kuhn's assertion that a crisis is necessary to the emergence of a new paradigm is virtually a tautology.[6] If, on the contrary, large change in the science per se constitute a revolution, Kuhn asserts that there will be an abandonment of the previous paradigm which in actual fact may never have taken place. To be concrete, the marginal utility revolution of the 1870s replaced the individual economic agent as a sociological or historical datum by the utility-maximizing individual. The essential elements of the classical theory were affected in no respect. (A possible, but uncertain, aftereffect in twenty years was the development of the marginal productivity theory.) Until Kuhn gives us criteria of a revolution (or a paradigm) which have direct empirical content, it will not be possible to submit his fascinating hypotheses to test.

As a second example of studies of the nature of scientific development, let us take Robert Merton's theory of multiple discoveries of a new scientific idea.[7] He proposed the hypothesis that "all scientific discoveries are in principle multiples, including those that on the surface appear to be singletons" (p. 477). He proposes no fewer than *ten* kinds of evidence to support this view—itself a suspicious step since there are not ten good reasons for anything. I briefly quote several:

First, is the class of discoveries long regarded as singletons that turn out to be rediscoveries of previously unpublished work [p. 478].

—a class I would esteem more if it were not matched by the class of discoveries long regarded as multiples that turn out to be rediscoveries of previously unpublished or published work of *one* man.

6. The determination of whether the changes in a science are large or small is itself an extraordinarily subtle and complex task.
7. "Singletons and Multiples in Scientific Discovery: A Chapter in the Sociology of Science," *Proceedings of the American Philosophical Society* 105, No. 5 (Oct. 13, 1961). [See chapter 9, above.]

Third . . . are the cases in which the scientist, though he is forestalled, goes ahead to report his original, albeit anticipated, work . . . [p. 479].

The race to be the first in reporting a discovery testifies to the assumption that if the one scientist does not soon make the discovery, another will. This, then, provides an eighth kind of evidence bearing on our hypothesis [p. 480].

I assume that those discoverers who walk, rather than run, to the nearest journal are counterevidence, though Merton did not delay publication to discover them. And so Merton concludes that with all the facts, we might discover that all discoveries are multiples, and in fact of the 264 instances he and Dr. Elinor Barber studied, 51 were triplets, 17 quadruplets, 6 quintuplets, and 8 sextuplets. Twenty percent came within a span of one year.

The underlying rationale is of course that the discoveries are dictated by the evolving logic of the science—new ideas are not in the air, as it is often said, but near the surface of the work that has just been completed. This is a profoundly correct and illuminating view of science even if there are a substantial number of singletons.

Merton reconciles this characteristic of science with the existence of men of great genius—by two remarks. One I find unappealing for a reason soon to be given: the great man discovers ideas sooner than a lesser man. And one is surely true: a great man makes many discoveries—for example, Merton finds that Kelvin and Freud each figure in more than thirty multiples—so a great man is a large number of lesser men.

Only one aspect of Merton's central thesis seems to be questionable: he puts no time limit upon the span within which the multiples may fall. On this score he says:

The theory does not hold that to be truly independent, multiples must be chronologically simultaneous. This is only the limiting case. Even discoveries far removed from one another in calendrical time can be instructively construed as "simultaneous" or nearly so in social and cultural time, depending upon the accumulated state of knowledge in the several cultures and the structures of the several societies in which they appear [p. 486].

I find this confusing. Simultaneity is some proof of independence of discovery, but there are other and possibly better ways to prove independence. The real problem is that if two discoveries come at very different times (or at the same time in very different intellectual environments) they can no longer be said to be the ripe fruit of that season of the tree of science. The discovery of marginal productivity theory by

Longfield in Ireland in 1833 could not be a response to the same scientific environment as the discovery of the theory by Wicksteed, Clark, Barone, Wood, Marshall, Edgeworth, and others some sixty years later. The proposition that lightning strikes at least twice in every spot where it strikes once is not interesting if a test requires that we wait to the end of time.

As a third and final example of this type of study, I shall comment briefly about scientific schools. A school within a science is a collection of affiliated scientists who display a considerably higher degree of agreement upon a particular set of views than the science as a whole displays. It is essential to a school that there be many scientists outside it, or the school would have no one with whom to argue. Schools have received little study, and the following remarks are only casual impressions.

A school must have a leader, because the consensus of its members will normally be achieved and maintained by major scientific entrepreneurs. In some instances, such as the Ricardian school, the chief bond has, in fact, been admiration for the leader. I doubt whether a scientific school based upon substantive scientific views can long survive the death of its leader, except in the improbable event of the appearance of a new leader of comparable stature. New analytical and empirical challenges will continue to emerge, and only a strong leader can provide generally acceptable responses to these challenges. The Marshallian school did not survive Marshall nor did the Keynesian school survive Keynes.

If the school is united on methodology rather than substantive doctrines, its life will be longer, but also less influential. A methodology is usually not very confining with respect to substantive questions; so members of the school can more easily adjust to new problems and new challenges. Pareto could inherit the leadership of the general equilibrium school from Walras even though they agreed on almost nothing except the mistaken article of faith that general equilibrium theory was inherently better than partial equilibrium theory. The Austrian school could survive into the twentieth century only because its main bonds were opposition to historical and empirical research and loyalty to economic liberalism—the early agreement of its members on value theory did not persist, nor extend to capital theory or monetary theory.

A school may be based upon policy views rather than upon economic analysis or scientific methodology, and then its life will normally become even longer. Marxism is perhaps as much a political party as a school, but its longevity as a school is due to the fact that it is not a scientific body of knowledge (although its works have scientific content). Given its non-scientific role as an instrument of economic reform, it can ignore and has ignored almost every advance in economic theory and research which it has been unable to reconcile with its scripture. An incomparably less important but otherwise similar group is the single taxers who arose under Henry George.

The second and only loosely distinguishable category of researchers in the history of science is concerned with the effects of the organization and environment of the science upon its evolution. An example of this type of work is the thesis of Joseph Ben-David that the competitive structure of medical research in the United States was the basis of its eminence in the twentieth century.[8] I may also cite my investigations of the relationship between economic science and the social and economic developments of the society within which it is conducted,[9] and of the effect of foundations upon economic research.[10]

The role of scientific societies in the evolution of science has attracted the attention of many persons, but none more indignant than Charles Babbage. The reputation of, and knowledge about, Charles Babbage have risen greatly with the emergence of the modern computer, of which he is the unchallenged founding father. For at least three decades he was the unaging *enfant terrible* of British science, and presented his dissatisfaction with the Royal Society in two books, *Reflections on the Decline of Science in England* (1830) and *The Exposition of 1851* (1851).

Babbage believed that membership in scientific bodies should be based upon competence, and on this basis objected to the admission procedure followed by the Royal Society:

A.B. gets any three Fellows to sign a certificate stating that he (A.B.) is desirous of becoming a member, and likely to be a useful and valuable one. This is handed to the Secretary, and suspended in the meeting-room. At the end of ten weeks, if A.B. has the good fortune to be perfectly unknown by any literary or scientific achievement, however small, he is quite sure of being elected as a matter of course. If on the other hand, he has unfortunately written on any subject connected with science, or is supposed to be acquainted with any branch of it, the members begin to inquire what he has done to deserve the honor; and, unless he has powerful friends, he has a fine chance of being black-balled [*Reflections*, pp. 50–51].

8. "Scientific Productivity and Academic Organization in Nineteenth Century Medicine," *American Sociological Reivew* 25 (1960): 828–43. I find the conclusion more congenial than the evidence—the international differences in number of medical discoveries (Ben-David's key dependent variable) can perhaps be better explained by number of holders of medical and related degrees.
9. "The Influence of Events and Policies on Economic Theory," reprinted in *Essays in the History of Economics*.
10. "The Foundations and Economics," in *U. S. Philanthropic Foundations*, ed. Warren Weaver.

Babbage's law may be stated more explicitly: You'd better be good if you aren't nice.

As I understand Babbage's main (unoriginal) contribution to the subject, it is the assertion that learned bodies are each run by a self-perpetuating inner clique. I believe that this is true, and necessary to their survival. Private property not only turns sand into gold but also turns committee meetings and journal editing into careers. Babbage's violent dissatisfaction with this state of affairs is reminiscent of Ambrose Bierce's definition of the word *incumbent*: "A person of the liveliest interest to the outcumbents."[11]

Conclusion

Economics, I thus believe, has a useful past, a past that is useful in dealing with the future. Many useful commodities and services are not produced in a society because they are worth less than they cost: it remains the unfulfilled task of the historians of economics to show that their subject is worth its cost.

11. *The Devil's Dictionary* (New York: Dover, 1958), p. 65.

118

The Economist and the State

In 1776 our venerable master offered clear and emphatic advice to his countrymen on the proper way to achieve economic prosperity. This advice was of course directed also to his countrymen in the American colonies, although at that very moment we were busily establishing what would now be called a major tax loophole. The main burden of Smith's advice, as you know, was that the conduct of economic affairs is best left to private citizens—that the state will be doing remarkably well if it succeeds in its unavoidable tasks of winning wars, preserving justice, and maintaining the various highways of commerce.

That was almost two centuries ago, and few modern economists would assign anything like so austere a role to the economic responsibilities of the state. The fact that most modern economists are as confident in prescribing a large economic role to the state as Smith was in denying such a role is not necessarily surprising: professional opinions sometimes change after 188 years, and economic and political institutions are of course even less durable.

But, surprising or not, the shifts in the predominant views of a profession on public policy pose a question which I wish to discuss. That question is: on what basis have economists felt themselves equipped to give useful advice on the proper functions of the state? By what methods did Smith and his disciples show the incapacity of the state in economic affairs? By what methods did later economists who favored state control of railroads, stock exchanges, wage rates and prices, farm output, and a thousand other things, prove that these were better directed or operated by the state? How does an economist acquire as much confidence in the wisdom of a policy of free trade or fiscal stabilization as he has in the law of diminishing returns or the profit-maximizing propensities of entrepreneurs?

The thought behind these questions is simple. Economists generally share the ruling values of their societies, but their professional competence does not consist in translating popular wishes into an awe-inspiring professional language. Their competence consists in understanding how an economic system works under alternative institutional frameworks. If

Presidential address delivered at the Seventy-Seventh Annual Meeting of the American Economic Association, Chicago, December 29, 1964. Reprinted from *American Economic Review* 55 (March 1965).

they have anything of their own to contribute to the popular discussion of economic policy, it is some special understanding of the relationship between policies and results of policies.

The basic role of the scientist in public policy, therefore, is that of establishing the costs and benefits of alternative institutional arrangements. Smith had no professional right to advise England on the Navigations Acts unless he had evidence of their effects and the probable effects of their repeal. A modern economist has no professional right to advise the federal government to regulate or deregulate the railroads unless he has evidence of the effects of these policies.

This position, you must notice, is not quite the familiar one that an economist's value judgments have no scientific status—indeed I shall neither dispute nor praise value judgments. The position is rather that if a subject is capable of study, a scholar ought to study it before he advises legislators. Suppose you deplore disease or, conversely, that you greatly admire the much-persecuted germ. My assertion is that however you stand, you should not support proposals to compel or to forbid people to go to a doctor until you find out whether their attendance on a doctor will increase or decrease the incidence of disease. If this particular example strikes you as absurdly pedantic, I offer two responses. First, will your answer be the same whatever the state of medical science in a country? Second, we shall come to harder problems.

My task, then, is to ask in as hardheaded a way as possible what precisely was the evidence economists provided for their policy recommendations, evidence that successfully linked their proposals with the goals they were seeking to achieve. I begin with Adam.

I

Smith bases his proposals for economic policy upon two main positions. Neither basis is presented in a formal and systematic fashion, and there are serious problems in determining exactly why he wishes most economic life to be free of state regulation.

Smith's first basis for his economic policies was his belief in the efficiency of the system of natural liberty. There can be little doubt that this tough-minded Scotsman, this close friend of that cool and clear thinker, David Hume, had a deep attachment to the natural law of the late enlightenment. But Smith did not propose natural liberty as a lay religion of political life. Instead he argued, as a matter of demonstrable economic analysis, that the individual in seeking his own betterment will put his resources where they yield the most to him, and that as a rule the resources then yield the most to society. Where the individual does not know, or does not have the power to advance, his own interests, Smith feels remarkably free to have the state intervene.

120

Thus Smith says that to restrain people from entering voluntary transactions "is a manifest violation of that natural liberty which it is the proper business of law, not to infringe but to support"; yet he continues [11, p. 308]:

> But those exertions of the natural liberty of a few individuals, which might endanger the security of the whole society, are, and ought to be, restrained by the laws of all governments; of the most free, as well as of the most despotical. The obligation of building party walls, in order to prevent the communication of fire, is a violation of natural liberty, exactly of the same kind with the regulations of the banking trade which are here proposed.

Natural liberty seems to have been little more than a working rule, and Smith proposes numerous departures from natural liberty because the participants are incompetent or fail to consider external effects of their behavior.[1] He is quite willing to outlaw payment of wages in kind, which he believes will defraud the worker, and to put a limit on interest rates, because high interest rates encourage lenders to entrust their funds to improvident projectors, and to have a complicated tax system to change the uses of land.

The second foundation of Smith's strong preference for private economic activity was that he deeply distrusted the state. This distrust, I must emphasize, was primarily a distrust of the motives rather than of the competence of the state. Smith makes very little of inept governmental conduct—indeed he clearly believes that as far as efficiency is concerned, the joint stock companies, and even more the universities, are worse offenders than the state. His real complaint against the state is that it is the creature of organized, articulate, self-serving groups—above all, the merchants and the manufacturers. The legislature is directed less often by an extended view of the common good than by "the clamorous importunity of partial interests" [11, p. 438].

Purely as a matter of professional appraisal, I would say that Smith displayed superb craftsmanship in supporting his first argument—that free individuals would use resources efficiently—but was excessively dogmatic in asserting his second argument, which accepted the competence but rejected the disinterest of the governmental machine. He gives no persuasive evidence that the state achieves the goals of its policies, and in particular he asserts rather than proves that the mercantile system had a large effect upon the allocation of British resources. Nor does he demonstrate that the state is normally the captive of "partial interests."

1. See the essay by Viner, "Adam Smith and Laissez Faire," in *Adam Smith 1776–1926* (University of Chicago, 1928).

Smith's intellectual heirs did little to strengthen his case for *laissez faire*, except by that most irresistible of all the weapons of scholarship, infinite repetition. Yet they could have done so, and in two directions.

Where Smith finds the competitive market incapable of performing a task, they might have corrected him, for he was sometimes wrong. To a degree this was done: Smith's belief that the market set too low a value on investment in agriculture, and too high a value on foreign investment, was properly criticized by McCulloch [6, pp. 144 ff.], and the aberration on usury was of course promptly challenged by Bentham. But for each of Smith's errors that was corrected, several new ones were introduced. J. S. Mill, for example, gravely argued that the competitive market was incapable of providing a reduction in the hours of work even if all the workers wished it—a mistake I am not inclined to excuse simply because so many later economists repeated it.

What I consider to be a more important weakness in Smith's position, however—his undocumented assumption that the state was efficient in achieving mistaken ends[2]—was not only accepted, but emphatically reaffirmed by his followers. James Mill's identification of the evils of government with the undemocratic control of its instruments was an extreme example, but an instructive and influential one. The holder of the power of government would always use it to further his own ends—so argued Mill with an oppressive show of logical rigor. It followed that only a democratically controlled state would seek the good of the entire public:

> The Community cannot have an interest opposite to its interest. To affirm this would be a contradiction in terms. The Community within itself, and with respect to itself, can have no sinister interest . . . The Community may act wrong from mistake. To suppose that it could from design would be to suppose that human beings can wish their own misery.[3]

Hence a democracy, unlike a monarchy or an aristocracy, would do no unwise thing except in ignorance. And this exception for ignorance was not a serious one:

> There can be no doubt that the middle rank, which gives to science, to art, and to legislation itself, their most distinguished ornaments, and is the chief source of all that has exalted and refined human nature, is that portion of the Community of which, if the basis of Representation were ever so far extended, the opinion would ultimately decide. Of the

2. McCulloch, a somewhat underrated man, again challenged Smith here; see "Navigation Laws," *Edinburgh Review*, May 1823.

3. *The Article on Government* (reprinted from the Supplement to the *Encyclopaedia Britannica* [London]) 1829, p. 7.

people beneath them, a vast majority would be sure to be guided by their advice and example.[4]

Education of the masses, and their instinctive reverence for the wisdom of their middle class leaders, those ornaments of society, would thus insure that the democratic state would seldom stray far from the public good. The argument meant that at the time the essay was written the American government was a reliable instrument of public welfare and 50 years later England's government would become so.[5]

It would be possible to document at length this proposition that the classical economists objected chiefly to *unwise* governmental intervention in economic life, but I shall give only two instructive examples.

The first example is provided by that fine Irish economist, Mountifort Longfield. Apropos of certain dubious programs to assist the laborer he wrote, "here Political Economy is merely a defensive science, which attempts to prevent the injudicious interference of speculative legislation" [3, p. 18]. This sounds suitably conservative, but let us continue. Years later, as a witness before a Royal Commission on Railways, he complained that his timid fellow directors of the Great Southern and Western Railway underestimated the long-run elasticity of demand for rail service. To produce the necessary courage he proposed that the government appoint a director with unlimited power to vary the rates of each railroad, with the government taking half of any resulting profits and compensating all of any resulting losses.[6] Longfield wanted not *laissez faire* but half fare.

The second example is the major controversy provoked by the campaigns for the ten-hour day for women in factories, which reached success in 1847. This was one of the first of the modern English interventions in the contracts of competent adults, and it invited excommunication by the economic divines. This Factory Act was in fact opposed with vigor by two important economists, Torrens and Senior, but explicitly *not* as a violation of natural right. Torrens prefaced his criticism with a passage that reads better than it reasons:

4. Ibid., p. 32.

5. Mill's essay elicited a brilliant attack by Macaulay, who turned Mill's argument that every man seeks only his own interests against the plea for universal suffrage:

> That the property of the rich minority can be made subservient to the pleasures of the poor majority will scarcely be denied. But Mr. Mill proposes to give the poor majority power over the rich minority. Is it possible to doubt to what, on his own principles, such an arrangement must lead?

The argument is carried to an interesting prediction: "As for America, we appeal to the twentieth century," "Mill's Essay on Government," in *Critical, Historical and Miscellaneous Essays* (New York 1873), II, pp. 36–37, 40.

6. Royal Commission on Railways, *Evidence and Papers Relating to Railways in Ireland* (1866), pp. 126–30, 359–60.

The principle of non-interference can be applicable to those circumstances only, in which interference would be productive of mischief; in all those cases in which the interference of the central authority in the transactions between man and man is capable of effecting good or averting evil, *laissez faire* is a criminal abandonment of the functions for the performance of which a central authority is established and maintained.[7]

Hence Torrens, and equally Senior,[8] criticized the ten-hour bill because it would lower weekly wages, increase production costs, and reduce employment by impairing the competitive position of the British textile industry abroad.

Both Senior and Torrens died in 1864, so they had adequate time, one would think, to have tested their predictions of the effects of the ten-hour law. It is wholly characteristic of the insulation of discussions of policy from empirical evidence that no such study was undertaken by them, or by anyone else.

James Mill's oldest son, surprisingly enough, put up a stronger case against state control of economic life than his much more conservative father had. John Stuart did not follow his father in accepting the invariable wisdom of the democratic state, possibly because he was writing well after the Reform Act.[9] He rested the case much more on the defense of individual liberty, and fully three of the five reasons he gave for favoring *laissez faire* as a practical maxim were variations on the importance of the dignity, independence, self-reliance, and development of the individual [7, Bk. V, Ch. 11].

Although I reckon myself among the most fervent admirers of individualism, even for other people, I must concede that the younger Mill's position was ambiguous. He does not tell us how to determine whether a given public policy frees or inhibits individuals. Suppose I contemplate a program of public housing. If I bribe or force people into such housing, of course I have reduced their area of choice and responsibility. But I have also, I presumably hope, given a generation of children a chance to grow up in quarters that are not grossly unsanitary and inadequate for physical and moral health. Mill does not tell us whether this policy fosters or inhibits individualism—although I strongly suspect that he would have favored public housing, as he did free public education and limitation of hours of work for young people. If an economist is to be a moral philosopher, however—and I have no doubt that we would do this well

7. *A Letter to Lord Ashley* (London 1844), pp. 64–65.

8. *Letters on the Factory Act* (London 1844).

9. He did make some reference to the incompetence of state action: " . . . the great majority of things are worse done by the intervention of government, than the individuals most interested in the matter would do them, or cause them to be done, if left to themselves" [7, II, p. 511]. This argument does not play a major role in shaping his attitude, however.

too—he should develop his philosophy to a level where its implications for policy become a matter of logic rather than a vehicle for expressing personal tastes.[10]

Let us leap on to Marshall who brought up the rear of this tradition as of so many others in English economics. He conceded an expanding potential role to the state, in the control of monopoly, in the housing of the poor, and in the treatment of poverty generally. Yet he persevered in his preference for private enterprise wherever possible. The preference rested heavily on the belief that bureaucratic management would be burdensome and inefficient.[11] Marshall at this point wrote the boldest sentence of his life:

> If Governmental control had supplanted that of private enterprise a hundred years ago [1807], there is good reason to suppose that our methods of manufacture now would be about as effective as they were fifty years ago, instead of being perhaps four or even six times as efficient as they were then.[12]

Yet the "good reason" was never presented, although it was more important to demonstrate this proposition if true than to answer any other question to which Marshall devoted a chapter or a book or even his life. Marshall's other reason for his distrust of government was the fear that Parliament would become the creature of special interests, and in particular of the Trade Unions[13]—an unknowing but not unknowledgeable reversion to Adam Smith!

So much for a century of *laissez faire*. The main school of economic individualism had not produced even a respectable modicum of evidence that the state was incompetent to deal with detailed economic problems

10. Mill's famous essay, *On Liberty*, does little to reduce our uncertainty. It is here that he asserts:

> Despotism is a legitimate mode of government in dealing with barbarians, provided the end be their improvement, and the means justified by actually effecting the ends.

> The laws which, in many countries on the Continent, forbid marriage unless the parties can show that they have the means of supporting a family, do not exceed the legitimate powers of the State . . .

> As the principle of the individual liberty is not involved in the doctrine of Free Trade . . . (*The English Philosophers from Bacon to Mill* [Modern Library 1939], pp. 956, 1024, 1035).

It is not easy to avoid the conclusion that for Mill "liberty" was conveniently well correlated with the forms of behavior of which he personally approved.

11. *Memorials of Alfred Marshall* (1925), pp. 274–76, 339 ff.; *Industry and Trade* (1919), pp. 666–72.

12. *Memorials*, p. 338.

13. *Official Papers by Alfred Marshall* (1926), pp. 395–96.

of any or all sorts. There was precious little evidence, indeed, that the state was unwise in its economic activities, unless one was prepared to accept as evidence selected corollaries of a general theory. The doctrine of nonintervention was powerful only so long and so far as men wished to obey.

II

There was no day on which economists ceased to commend reductions in the government's role in economic life and began to propose its expansion. The limitation of hours of work for children was supported well before the attack on the corn laws reached its climax. The statutes liberalizing dealings in property in the 1830's followed at a distance the regulation of passenger ships to protect emigrants.

How else could it be? The distinction between ancient police functions admitted by all and new regulatory functions proposed by some was most elusive. The same economist could and did repel the state with one hand and beckon it with the other.[14]

The expansion of public control over economic life which took place in the mid-nineteenth century in England, and a trifle later in the United States, was usually of this sort: a traditional state function was expanded or a new function was adopted which had close analogies to traditional functions. Economic effects were usually incidental to protective effects: the inspection of factories and mines, the sanitation laws for cities, the embryonic educational system, and most of the controls over railroads were of this sort [9] [4].

One thing did not change at all, however, from the heyday of *laissez faire*: no economist deemed it necessary to document his belief that the state could effectively discharge the new duties he proposed to give to it. The previous assertions of governmental incompetence were met only by counter assertion; the previous hopes of wiser uses of governmental powers by a democracy were deemed too prophetic to deserve the discourtesy of historical test. I shall illustrate this persistent neglect of empirical evidence with the writings of two economists who have almost nothing in common except great ability.

The first is Jevons. Governmental operation of an industry was appropriate, Jevons believed, if four conditions were fulfilled: (1) The work must be of an invariable and routine-like nature, so as to be performed according to fixed rules. (2) It must be performed under the public eye, or for the service of individuals, who will immediately detect and expose any failure or laxity. (3) There must be very little capital

---

14. Thus McCulloch said of the post office: "It does not seem, though the contrary has been sometimes contended, that the Postoffice could be so well conducted by anyone else as by government: the latter alone can enforce perfect regularity in all its subordinate departments . . . " (*Dictionary of Commerce* [1854 ed.], article on "Postage").

126

expenditure, so that each year's revenue and expense account shall represent, with approximate accuracy, the real commercial success of the undertaking. (4) The operations must be of such a kind that their union under one all-extensive Government monopoly will lead to great advantage and economy [1, pp. 279, 338, 355]. On what is this garbled description of a municipal water system based?—mature introspection, of course.

Jevons is equally devoted to the a priori method when he discusses public regulation. The "Principles of Industrial Legislation" are illustrated first with the problem posed by a dangerous machine. Neither worker nor employer, Jevons says, generally displays due concern for the dangers that lurk in the unfenced machine.

> But there remains one other mode of solving the question which is as simple as it is effective. The law may command that dangerous machinery shall be fenced, and the executive government may appoint inspectors to go round and prosecute such owners as disobey the law [2, p.4].

Several aspects of Jevons' position are instructive. There is no showing of evidence on the failure of employers and employees to curb dangerous machinery. There is no showing of evidence that direct controls are simple and effective. Direct controls surely were not effective in factories too small to catch the inspector's eyes, and it is a completely open question whether they were effective elsewhere. And finally, Jevons does not conceive of the possible role of the price system in supplementing, if not replacing, direct inspection by a law making employers responsible for accidents.[15]

But let us recall who Jevons was; he was the economist whose supreme genius lay in his demand for empirical determination of theoretical relationships and his immense resourcefulness in making such determinations. This powerful instinct for empirical evidence spilled over into a proposal that wherever possible new policies should first be tried out at the local governmental level: "we cannot," he said, "really plan out social reforms upon theoretical grounds."[16] But, possible or not, he really so planned out his reforms.

We may learn how a theorist coped with the problem by turning to my second economist, Pigou. In *Wealth and Welfare* [8] he recited four

15. It should be a source of morbid instruction to us, that immediately after laying down this dogmatic rule on how to treat with dangerous machinery, Jevons denounces those who view the economist as a "presumptuous theorist, who is continually laying down hard-and-fast rules for the conduct of other people" [2, p. 8].

16. "Experimental Legislation and the Drink Traffic," *The Contemporary Review*, 37, 1880, 192 (reprinted in *Methods of Social Reform*, p. 275). He did not see the potentialities of empirical study in the absence of formal experiment, however, and denied the feasibility of a statistical approach ("Experimental Legislation," pp. 184–85).

reasons for distrusting the ability of legislatures to control monopolies. They were shallow reasons, but what is instructive is that all of them "can be, in great measure, obviated by the recently developed invention of 'Commissioners,' that is to say, bodies of men appointed by governmental authorities for the express purpose of industrial operation or control." Hence the government is now capable of "beneficial intervention in industries, under conditions which would not have justified such intervention in earlier times" [8, p. 250].

If time were not the most precious thing that one professor can give to another, I would follow in detail Pigou's travels from this inauspicious beginning. We would be instructed by the evidence which he found sufficient to a series of propositions on the state's competence:

> . . . laws directly aimed at "maintaining competition" are practically certain to fail of their purpose [8, p. 253].
> . . . in respect of industries, where the quality of the output is of supreme importance and would, in private hands, be in danger of neglect, public operation is desirable [8, p. 288].
> . . . the relative inefficiency of public operation, as compared with private operation, is very large in highly speculative undertakings, and dwindles to nothing in respect of those where the speculative element is practically non-existent.[17]

The evidence, you will hardly need be reminded, consisted of a few quotations from books on municipal trading.

Pigou's views of the competence of the state were, like his predecessors' views, a tolerably random selection of the immediately previous views, warmed by hope. He felt that reliance upon such loose general reflections was unavoidable. On the question of whether public or private operation of an industry would be more efficient in production, we are told "at the outset, it must be made clear that attempts to conduct such a comparison by reference to statistics are fore-doomed to failure" [8, p. 274]. How is it made clear? Very simply: by pointing out that it is unlikely that a public and a private enterprise operate under identical conditions of production. This test of the feasibility of statistical research would rule out all such research, and of course Pigou throughout his life accepted this implication.

Let me say that Pigou did not differ from his less illustrious colleagues in the superficiality of his judgments on the economic competence of the state—here he was at least as shrewd and circumspect as they. He differed only in writing more pages of economic analysis of fully professional quality than almost any other economist of the twentieth century.

---

17. The maturing fruit in a later edition; *The Economics of Welfare* (4th ed., 1932), p. 399.

Rather than sample other economists, I shall characterize more generally their role in the period of growing state control over economic life. The traditional and inevitable economic functions of the state such as taxation and the control of the monetary system are not considered in the following remarks. These functions pose no question of the desirability of state action and very different questions of the economist's role in policy. On the basis of a highly incomplete canvass of the literature, I propose three generalizations.

First, there was a large and growing range of policy issues which economists essentially ignored. If we examine the English legislation governing shop closing hours, or pure food and drug inspection, or municipal utilities, or railway and truck and ocean transportation, or the legal status of labor unions, or a host of other questions, we shall find that as a rule economists did not write on the issue, or appear before the Royal Commissions, or otherwise participate in the policy formulation. Before 1914 the detachment from contemporary policy was Olympian, thereafter it was mortal but awesome. American economists, perhaps reflecting their Germanic training, were more interested in policy, so one can cite examples like John R. Commons on regulation of public utilities and on workmen's compensation laws, J. B. Clark and a host of others on the trust problem, and so on. Even here, however, many important economic policies were (and are still) ignored, among them pure food laws, wage legislation, fair employment practices acts, the zoning of land uses, and controls over the capital markets.

Second, even when economists took an active and direct interest in a policy issue, they did not make systematic empirical studies to establish the extent and nature of a problem or the probable efficiency of alternative methods of solving the problem.

It is difficult to support allegations about the absence of a given type of scientific work; often the allegation illuminates only the reading habits of its author. I am reasonably confident, however, that the following subjects were not investigated with even modest thoroughness: (1) the effects of regulation on the level and structure of prices or rates of public utilities; (2) the extent to which safety in production processes and purity in products are achieved by a competitive market and by a regulatory body; (3) the cost to the community of preventing failures of financial institutions by the route of suppressing competition compared with the costs by the route of insurance; (4) the effects of price support systems for distressed industries upon the distribution of income, as compared with alternative policies; and (5) the effects of policies designed to preserve competition. This list is short, but I submit that the examples are important enough to give credence to my generalization on the paucity of systematic empirical work on the techniques of economic policy. From

1776 to 1964 the chief instrument of empirical demonstration on the economic competence of the state has been the telling anecdote.

Third, the economist's influence upon the formulation of economic policy has usually been small. It has been small because he lacked special professional knowledge of the comparative competence of the state and of private enterprise. The economist could and did use his economic theory, and it cannot be denied that the economist's economic theory is better than everyone else's economic theory. But for reasons to which I shall immediately turn, economic theory has not been an adequate platform. Lacking real expertise, and lacking also evangelical ardor, the economist has had little influence upon the evolution of economic policy.

III

If economists have lacked a firm empirical basis for their policy views, one might expect that guidance could be derived from their theoretical systems. In fact, to the degree that a theoretical system has been submitted to a variety of empirical tests, it is a source of more reliable knowledge than an empirical uniformity in solitary confinement. The theory allows tests of the relationship incorporated in the theory that are outside the view of the discoverer of the theory, so these tests are more challenging.

The economists' policy views have in fact been much influenced by their theories. The vast preference for free international trade is surely based in good part upon the acceptance of the classical theory of comparative costs. The general presumption against direct regulation of prices by the state is surely attributable in good part to the belief in the optimum properties of a competitive price system. The growth of support among economists for public regulation of economic activities is at least partly due to the development of the theory of disharmonies between private and social costs, and partly also to the increasingly more rigorous standards of optimum economic performance.

If it would be wrong to deny a substantial influence of economic theory on economists' policy views, it would be wronger still to suggest that the policies follow closely and unambiguously from the general theory. Our first example of free trade will suffice to illustrate the looseness of the connection. Smith supported free trade because he believed that tariffs simply diverted resources from more productive to less productive fields, and the absence of an explanation for the rates of exchange between foreign and domestic commodities did not bother him. A century later Sidgwick argued that on theoretical grounds tariffs were often beneficial to a nation, but that "from the difficulty of securing in any actual government sufficient wisdom, strength, and singleness of aim to introduce protection only so far as it is advantageous to the community" the statesman should avoid protective duties [10, pp. 485–86]. To the extent that theory was guiding Sidgwick, surely it was a theory of government rather than of economics.

There is one primary reason why the theory is not, as a rule, coercive with respect to the policies that a believer in the theory must accept: a theory can usually be made to support diverse policy positions. Theories present general relationships, and which part of a theory is decisive in a particular context is a matter of empirical evidence. Consider the wages-fund doctrine, if I may be permitted to refer to it without its almost inseparable prefix, notorious. This theory asserted that there was a relatively fixed amount to be paid in wages in the short run, and that if one group got higher wages, other groups would get lower wages or be unemployed. It followed that if a particular group of workers formed a union and managed to raise their wages, other workers would bear the burden, and numerous disciples of the wages-fund doctrine accepted this policy view.[18] But John Stuart Mill could argue, quite in the opposite direction, that since most workers would be at a subsistence level, at most the successful union would inflict only short-run harm on other workers, whereas its higher income could be permanent.[19] And obviously it is a quantitative question whether the short-run costs or the permanent benefits were larger.

What is true of the wages-fund theory is true of other theories: an empirical question always insists upon intruding between the formal doctrine and its concrete application. The truly remarkable fact is not that economists accepting the same theory sometimes differ on policy, but that they differ so seldom. The wide consensus at any time comes, I suspect, from a tacit acceptance of the same implicit empirical assumptions by most economists. All classical economists accepted as a fact the belief that wage earners would not save, although they had no evidence on the matter. All modern economists believe they will never encounter Edgeworth's taxation paradox, with no more evidence. All economists at all times accept the universality of negatively sloping demand curves, and they do so without any serious search for contrary empirical evidence.

These empirical consensuses have no doubt usually been correct—one can know a thing without a sophisticated study. Truth was born before modern statistics. Yet generations of economists also believed that over long periods diminishing returns would inevitably triumph over technological advance in agriculture, a view that agricultural history of the last 100 years has coolly ignored.

A second and lesser source of the loose connection between theory and policy has been the difficulty of translating theory into policy because of

18. For example, J. E. Cairnes, *Some Leading Principles of Political Economy* (London 1873), pp. 258–60.

19. *Principles of Political Economy*, Ashley ed. (London 1929), p. 402.

practical politics or administration. The economist refrains from drawing a policy conclusion because its implementation would pose large social or administrative costs. Mill dismissed an income tax because of the inquisitorial burdens it would put on taxpayers; one would have thought that he would remember that an earlier inquisition had been welcomed to Spain. For at least 100 years economists have recommended that a nation proceed to free trade gradually over a five-year period to ease the transition, and the period is usually lengthened if protectionism is on the ascendant. I have often wondered why we deem it necessary to tell a confirmed drunkard not to reduce his drinking too rapidly.

A third, and fortunately a moderately rare, reason for separating theory from policy is flagrant inconsistency, usually stemming from that great source of inconsistency in intelligent men, a warm heart. Marshall proved—rather unconvincingly, I must say—that the doctrine of consumer surplus instructed us to tax necessaries rather than luxuries [5, p. 467 n.]. The idea was disposed of in a footnote because it disregarded ability to pay. The economic arguments against minimum wage legislation have usually been refuted by reference to the need of poorer people for larger incomes.

The essential ambiguity of general theoretical systems with respect to public policy, however, has been the real basis of our troubles. So long as a competent economist can bend the existing theory to either side of most viable controversies without violating the rules of professional work, the voice of the economist must be a whisper in the legislative halls.

IV

The economic role of the state has managed to hold the attention of scholars for over two centuries without arousing their curiosity. This judgment that the perennial debate has refused to leave the terrain of abstract discourse is true, I believe, of the continental literature as well as the English and American literature. Economists have refused either to leave the problem alone or to work on it.

Why have not the effects of the regulatory bodies on prices and rates been ascertained, even at the cost of a 1 per cent reduction in the literature on how to value assets for rate purposes? Why have not the effects of welfare activities on the distribution of income been determined for an important range of such activities, even at the cost of a 1 per cent reduction in denunciations of the invasion of personal liberty? Why has not the degree of success of governments in bringing private and social costs together been estimated, even at the cost of a 1 per cent reduction in the literature on consumer surplus? Why have we been content to leave the problem of policy unstudied?

This variously phrased question can be considered to be a request for either a formal theory of state action or a set of empirical studies of the comparative advantages of public and private control.

Consider first the control over economic life as a formal theoretical problem. Why do we not have a theory to guide us in ascertaining the areas of comparative advantage of uncontrolled private enterprise, competitive private enterprise, public regulation, public operation, and the other forms of economic organization? This theory would predict the manner in which the state would conduct various economic activities, such as protecting consumers from monopoly or fraud, assisting distressed industries and areas, or stimulating inventions. The theory might yield rules such as that a competitive system is superior for introducing new products, or public enterprise is superior where there are many parties to a single transaction. That we have not done so is attributable, I conjecture, to two difficulties.

The first difficulty is that the issue of public control had a constantly changing focus: it was the relations of labor and employers one year, the compensation to tenants for improvements on farms and the control of railroad rates the year thereafter. At any one time few areas of economic life were seriously in dispute: most economic activites were uncontroversially private or public. That a single theory should be contrived to guide society in dealing with these various and changing problems was perhaps too great an abstraction to encourage serious efforts.

Moreover, and this is the second difficulty, the standard apparatus of the economist is not clearly appropriate. Ordinary maximizing behavior, with the ordinary rewards and obstacles of economic analysis, does not seem directly applicable to the problem. The bounds of state competence, and the areas of its superiority over variously controlled private action, are difficult to bring within a coherent theoretical system.

In short, the theory of public policy may be a difficult theory to devise, although until we have tried to devise it even this opinion is uncertain.

A usable theory of social control of economic life was not essential, however, to professional study of policy: could not the economist make empirical studies of the effects of various ways of dealing with specific problems? The state regulates machinery in factories: does this reduce accidents appreciably? The state regulated the carriage of emigrants from England and Ireland to the new world—what did the regulations achieve? A thousand prices had been regulated—were they lower or stickier than unregulated prices? The empirical answers would obviously have contributed both to public policy and to the development of a general theory of public and private economy.

Here we must pause, not without embarrassment, to notice that we could ask for empirical studies in areas traditional to economics as well as in the netherland of half economics, half political science. We need not be surprised, I suppose, that we know little of the effects of state regulation,

133

when we also know very little about how oligopolists behave. Marshall's theory that the differences between short- and long-run prices and profits are regulated by the differences between short- and long-run reactions of supply will be 75 years old next year. Despite its immense influence, this theory has yet to receive a full empirical test. If such basic components of modern economic theory have escaped tests for quantitative significance, it is hardly surprising that our antitrust laws, our motor carrier regulation, and our control of insurance company investments have also escaped such tests.

Still, there has been a difference. Empirical tests of economic theories have been made for generations, and with greater frequency and diligence than we encounter in the area of social experiments. Already in 1863 Jevons had ascertained the serious fall in the value of gold consequent upon the Californian and Australian gold discoveries—it was 26 percent over the 13-year period, 1849–62. No such diligence or ingenuity can be found in the study of state controls at that time. A half century later Henry Moore was calculating statistical demand curves; again the study of the effects of public policies was lagging.

The age of quantification is now full upon us. We are now armed with a bulging arsenal of techniques of quantitative analysis, and of a power—as compared to untrained common sense—comparable to the displacement of archers by cannon. But this is much less a cause than a consequence of a more basic development: the desire to measure economic phenomena is now in the ascendant. It is becoming the basic article of work as well as of faith of the modern economist that at a minimum one must establish orders of magnitude, and preferably one should ascertain the actual shapes of economic functions with tolerable accuracy.

The growth of empirical estimation of economic relationships, please notice, did not come as a response to the assault on formal theory by the German Historical School, nor was it a reply to the denunciations of theory by the American Institutionalists. It has been a slow development, contributed to by an earlier development in some natural sciences but mostly by the demonstrated successes of the pioneers of the quantitative method—the Jevonses, the Mitchells, the Moores, the Fishers.

It is a scientific revolution of the very first magnitude—indeed I consider the so-called theoretical revolutions of a Ricardo, a Jevons, or a Keynes to have been minor revisions compared to the vast implications of the growing insistence upon quantification. I am convinced that economics is finally at the threshold of its golden age—nay, we already have one foot through the door.

The revolution in our thinking has begun to reach public policy, and soon it will make irresistible demands upon us. It will become inconceivable that the margin requirements on securities markets will be altered once a year without knowing whether they have even a modest effect. It will become impossible for an import-quota system to evade the calculus of gains and costs. It will become an occasion for humorous nostalgia when arguments for private and public performance of a given economic activity are conducted by reference to the phrase, external economies, or by recourse to a theorem on perfect competition.

This is prophecy, not preaching. You have listened to sage advice on what to study and how to study it for well over a century. If you had heeded this advice, you would have accomplished almost nothing, but you would have worked on an immense range of subjects and with a stunning array of approaches. Fortunately you have learned that although such advice is almost inevitable on such occasions as the retirement of an officer of a professional society, it is worth heeding only when it is backed by successful examples. I have no reason to believe that you left your tough-mindedness at home tonight, and I shall respect it. I assert, not that we should make the studies I wish for, but that no one can delay their coming.

I would gloat for one final moment over the pleasant prospects of our discipline. That we are good theorists is not open to dispute: for 200 years our analytical system has been growing in precision, clarity, and generality, although not always in lucidity. The historical evidence that we are becoming good empirical workers is less extensive, but the last half century of economics certifies the immense increase in the power, the care, and the courage of our quantitative researches. Our expanding theoretical and empirical studies will inevitably and irresistibly enter into the subject of public policy, and we shall develop a body of knowledge essential to intelligent policy formulation. And then, quite frankly, I hope that we become the ornaments of democratic society whose opinions on economic policy shall prevail.

References

1. W. S. Jevons, *Methods of Social Reform*. London 1883.
2. ———, *The State in Relation to Labour*. London 1882.
3. Mountifort Longfield, *Lectures on Political Economy* (1834).
4. Oliver MacDonagh, *A Pattern of Government Growth, 1800–60*. London 1961.
5. Alfred Marshall, *Principles of Economics*, 8th ed. London 1920.
6. John Ramsay McCulloch, *Principls of Political Economy*, 1st ed. London 1825.
7. John Stuart Mill, *Principles of Political Economy*, 1st ed. London 1848.
8. A. C. Pigou, *Wealth and Welfare*. London 1912.
9. David Roberts, *Victorian Origins of the Welfare State*. New Haven 1960.
10. Henry Sidgwick, *Principles of Political Economy*. London 1883.
11. Adam Smith, *The Wealth of Nations*. Modern Library ed.

12   Smith's Travels on the Ship of State

The *Wealth of Nations* is a stupendous palace erected upon the granite of self-interest. It was not a narrow foundation: "though the principles of common prudence do not always govern the conduct of every individual, they always influence that of the majority of every class or order."[1] The immensely powerful force of self-interest guides resources to their most efficient uses, stimulates laborers to diligence and inventors to splendid new divisions of labor—in short, it orders and enriches the nation which gives it free rein. Indeed, if self-interest is given even a loose rein, it will perform prodigies:

> The natural effort of every individual to better his own condition, when suffered to exert itself with freedom and security, is so powerful a principle, that it is alone, and without any assistance, not only capable of carrying on the society to wealth and prosperity, but of surmounting a hundred impertinent obstructions with which the folly of human laws too often incumbers its operations; though the effect of these obstructions is always more or less either to encroach upon its freedom, or to diminish its security (2: 49–50 [508]).

This very quotation neatly summarizes the basic paradox which forms our subject.

The paradox is simply this. If self-interest dominates the majority of men in all commercial undertakings, why not also in all their political undertakings? Why should legislators erect "a hundred impertinent obstructions" to the economic behavior which creates the wealth of nations? Do men calculate in money with logic and purpose, but calculate in votes with confusion and romance?

To ask such a question is surely to answer it. A merchant who calculated closely the proper destination of every cargo, the proper duties of every agent, the proper bank to negotiate each loan—such a merchant would calculate also the effects of every tariff, every tax and subsidy, every statute governing the employment of labor. Indeed no clear distinc-

Reprinted from *History of Political Economy*, Fall 1971. © 1971 by Duke University Press, Durham, N.C.

1. *The Wealth of Nations*, ed. Cannan (London: Methuen, 1961), I, 313 [279]. Page references to the Modern Library edition, disfigured by a vulgar preface, are given within brackets.

tion can be drawn between commercial and political undertakings: the procuring of favorable legislation *is* a commercial undertaking.

The widely read, widely traveled, superlatively observant author of the *Wealth of Nations* need not be told so obvious a thing as that self-interest enters also political life. A list of instances in which legislation is explained by the interests of several economic groups is compiled in Table 1. The list is incomplete in two respects. Some references have no doubt been overlooked, and none is included unless Smith explicitly mentioned the interests which were served. Often Smith did not cite the economic interests which supported a law because the identity was self-evident. When the Statute of Labourers fixed wage rates in order to deal with the "insolence of servants," Smith does not even bother to mention the probable role of employers in obtaining the legislation, probably because it was self-evident.

Even an incomplete list, however, is sufficient to document the extensive role of self-interest in economic legislation. The merchants and manufacturers are singled out for the unusual combination of cupidity and competence which marks their legislative efforts. Few other economic groups are absent from the list: the great landowners jostle the parisimonious local county's magistrates and the debtors in the queue for favorable legislation, and even the sovereign is ardent in the pursuit of his private interests.

A shorter list can be compiled of policies which have been obtained by economic classes under the mistaken understanding that they are beneficial. The main examples are these:

(1) Attempts to increase the pay of curates have simply drawn more candidates into the clergy (I, 146 [130–31]).

(2) The bounty on exports of corn, first passed in 1688, has not appreciably benefited the farmers or landowners because it raises money wages (I, 219 [196–97], 418–19 [371–72]; II, 15–20 [480–84]).[2]

(3) The practice of primogeniture has lost its onetime role of achieving security of property, and injures the landowner (I, 408–9 [362–63]).

(4) The institution of slavery is uneconomic, but panders to pride (I, 411–12 [365–66]).[3]

(5) Laws against forestallers, engrossers, etc., serve only to appease popular prejudice (II, 33–41 [493–501]).

Even such mistaken uses of political power are testimony to the pursuit of self-interest in the formulation of public policy.

So far, however, we have established only two propositions in Smith's discussion of legislation:

2. There is a related argument on the taxation of necessaries (II, 402–5 [824–27]).

3. Hence the institution serves self-interest, but not production.

137

Table 1. *Economic Classes and Their Political Behavior*

Political Behavior	Beneficiary Class	Reference
1. Debasement of currency	Sovereign: to reduce debts	I, 31 [27–28], 38 [34]
2. Prohibition of combinations of workmen	Employers	I, 75–76 [66–67]
3. Usury laws	Sovereign: to reduce debt service	I, 102 [90]
4. Exclusive privileges of corporations	Members of corporations (guilds)	I, 133 ff. [119 ff.]
5. Statute of apprenticeship	Members of corporations	I, 150 [134]
6. Settlement law (poor law)	Local communities	I, 151 f. [135 f.]
7. Wage-fixing laws	Employers	I, 158 f. [141–42]
8. Opposition to turnpikes	Counties near London	I, 165 [147–48]
9. Prohibition on planting of new vineyards	Vineyard owners	I, 172–73 [154–55]
10. Restriction on planting of tobacco	Tobacco farmers	I, 176–77 [157–58]
11. Bounty on corn exports	Agricultural class	I, 219 [197]
12. Protection of woolen trade	Woolen trade	I, 256 [230–31]
13. Protection of hides	Leather trade	I, 258–59 [232–34]
14. Legal tender of paper money	Debtors	I, 347 [310–11]
15. Primogeniture	Landowners	I, 408 [361–62]
16. Varieties of tariffs	Protected industries	I, 474 [420] II, 96–97 [550–51]
17. Abolition of seignorage	Bank of England	II, 62 [519]
18. Colonial policy	Merchants	II, 87–88 [541–43] 129 [579–80]
19. Selection of "enumerated" commodities	Merchants and fishermen	II, 91–92 [546–47]
20. Free importation of raw materials	Manufacturers	II, 161 [609]
21. Grants to regulated companies	Merchants	II, 255 [691]
22. Defeat of Walpole's tax reforms	"Smuggling Merchants"	II, 412 [833]
23. Exemption of home brewing from tax	Rich consumers	II, 421–25 [840–45]
24. Use of debt to finance wars	Avoid taxpayer revolt	II, 455 [872]
25. Raising value of currency	Debtors in Rome	II, 468–69 [883–84]
26. Abolition of slavery in Pennsylvania	Quakers had few slaves	I, 412 [366]

A. Sometimes (often?) economic legislation is passed at the request of economic groups who hope to benefit by the legislation.

B. On occasion a group is mistaken in the consequences of the legislation and receives no benefit or even positive harm from its legislative program.

The first proposition is platitudinous. The second proposition is probably of wholly minor scope: some of Smith's examples are simply wrong (in particular, the corn export subsidy surely benefited landowners) and others (such as primogeniture) do not receive a convincing explanation. In any event, men make mistakes in economic life—witness the South Sea Bubble—so why not occasionally also in political life?

A much stronger proposition, one would have thought, appropriately came from the premier scholar of self-interest:

C. All legislation with important economic effects is the calculated achievement of interested economic classes.

Appropriate or not, Smith implicitly rejected the use of self-interest as a general explanation of legislation. The rejection manifested itself in various ways.

1. The most important evidence is that for most legislation no group is identified which could have fostered the law and would benefit from it. The most important area of this neglect is the discussion of taxation (II, 349–440 [779–858]). Each tax is described, its incidence explained, and its merits and demerits assessed—with hardly ever an explanation of why such a tax exists. As we shall see, this omission of consideration of the political bases of taxes had serious effects upon Smith's policy proposals.

2. Puzzles in legislation are posed where none would exist if Smith had considered systematically the role of self-interest in legislation. Consider the example of laws forbidding payment of wages in kind. Smith observes that "Whenever the legislature attempts to regulate the differences between masters and their workmen, its counsellors are always the masters. When the regulation, therefore, is in favour of the workmen, it is always just and equitable; but it is sometimes otherwise when in favour of the masters" (I, 158–59 [142]). Smith illustrates this conclusion by the just and equitable laws forbidding truck wages.

What a puzzling event! The legislature, creature of the masters, deprives the masters of the opportunity (which Smith says they sometimes exercised) to defraud their workmen with overpriced goods. Surely Smith's puzzle is connected with the fact that a legislature dominated by the agricultural class passed a law forbidding truck wages in certain nonagricultural industries (textiles, iron, apparel).[4]

---

4. We need not explore the reason truck wages were preferred in some trades; George Hilton's explanation does not appear to be completely general; "The British Truck System in the Nineteenth Century," *Journal of Political Economy*, June 1957.

Other examples are at hand. The laws forbidding the lower classes to wear fine textiles (I, 271–72 [245]) surely were not designed simply to keep them from wearing clothing that was "much more expensive"—one is entitled to suspect the support of the manufacturers of cheaper raiment. The prohibition on banks of the issue of small bank notes was more likely calculated to discourage entry into banking than to keep bank notes in knowledgeable hands (I, 343–45 [307–08]). A much more skeptical eye would have been turned to arguments such as the one that absolute governments treat slaves more kindly than republican states (II, 99–100 [553–54]).

3. Smith gave a larger role to emotion, prejudice, and ignorance in political life than he ever allowed in ordinary economic affairs. The mercantile policies directed to the improvement of the balance of trade with particular countries have their origin in "national prejudice and animosity" (I, 497 [441]). The legislation against corn traders is so perverse as to lead Smith to compare it to laws against witchcraft (II, 41 [500]); indeed, "the laws concerning corn may every where be compared to the laws concerning religion" (II, 48 [507]). In fact all unwise economic legislation from which no politically strong constituency drew benefits must be nonrational legislation.

The agricultural classes, the classes with preponderant political power in Smith's England, are singled out for their benevolence and stupidity:

> When the public deliberates concerning any regulation of commerce or police, the proprietors of land never can mislead it, with a view to promote the interest of their own particular order; at least, if they have any tolerable knowledge of that interest. They are, indeed, too often defective in this tolerable knowledge. They are the only one of the three orders whose revenue costs them neither labour nor care, but comes to them, as it were, of its own accord, and independent of any plan or project of their own. That indolence, which is the natural effect of the ease and security of their situation, renders them too often, not only ignorant, but incapable of that application of mind which is necessary in order to foresee and understand the consequences of any public regulation (I, 276–77 [249];[5] also I, 455–56 [402–3]).

Yet Smith notes often enough legislation which has been procured by the agricultural classes for their own interests (I, 416, [369], 443 [394]; II, 91, [545], 425 [844–45]).[6]

***

5. The laborers are no better: "But though the interest of the labourer is strictly connected with that of society, he is incapable either of comprehending that interest, or of understanding its connexion with his own." (I, 277 [249]).

6. In an interesting reversal of the argument, Smith argues that when tenants possess the vote, their landlords treat them better! (I, 414–15 [368]).

Little attention is paid to the political process, and that little is tantalizingly diverse. In some respects the sovereign is an incompetent manager. He cannot conduct a trading enterprise.

> Princes, however, have frequently engaged in many other
> mercantile projects, and have been willing, like private per-
> sons, to mend their fortunes by becoming adventurers in the
> common branches of trade. They have scarce ever succeeded.
> The profusion with which the affairs of princes are always
> managed, renders it almost impossible that they should. The
> agents of a prince regard the wealth of their master as inex-
> haustible; are careless at what price they buy; are careless at
> what price they sell; are careless at what expense they trans-
> port his goods from one place to another (II, 343 [771]).

Again, "the persons who have the administration of government [are] generally disposed to reward both themselves and their immediate dependents rather more than enough" (II, 395 [818]). Only the post office, Smith states in a rare moment of inverted clairvoyance, can be successfully managed by "every sort of government." In general, monarchies are conducted with "slothful and negligent profusion" and democracies with "thoughtless extravagance," but aristocracies such as Venice and Amsterdam have "orderly, vigilant and parsimonious administration" (II, 342 [770]).

Yet on other occasions Smith views political behavior in perfectly cold-blooded, rational terms. The discussion of the "recent disturbances" which constituted the American revolution provides a striking example:

> Men desire to have some share in the management of public
> affairs chiefly on account of the importance which it gives
> them. Upon the power which the greater part of the leading
> men, the natural aristocracy of every country, have of pre-
> serving or defending their respective importance, depends the
> stability and duration of every system of free government. In
> the attacks which these leading men are continually making
> upon the importance of one another, and in the defence of
> their own, consists the whole play of domestic faction and
> ambition. The leading men of America, like those of all other
> countries, desire to preserve their own importance. They feel,
> or imagine, that if their assemblies, which they are fond of
> calling parliaments, and of considering as equal in authority
> to the parliament of Great Britain, should be so far degraded
> as to become the humble ministers and executive officers of
> that parliament, the greater part of their own importance
> would be at an end. They have rejected, therefore, the pro-
> posal of being taxed by parliamentary requisition, and like

other ambitious and high-spirited men, have rather chosen to draw the sword in defence of their own importance (II, 136–37 [586]).

Smith shrewdly proposed to draw these leaders away from "peddling for the little prizes" in the "paltry raffle of colonial faction" by giving representation to the colonies in Parliament, where dazzling prizes might be won by ambitious colonists in the "great state lottery of British politics."[7]

In general, however, Smith's attitude toward political behavior was not dissimilar to that of a parent toward a child: the child was often mistaken and sometimes perverse, but normally it would improve in conduct if properly instructed.

The canons of taxation illustrate both the attitude and the fundamental weakness of Smith's position. Here are the maxims:

1. The subjects of every state ought to contribute towards the support of government, as nearly as possible, in proportion to their respective abilities; . . . .
2. The tax which each individual is bound to pay ought to be certain, and not arbitrary.
3. Every tax ought to be levied at the time, or in the manner, in which it is most likely to be convenient for the contributor to pay; . . . .
4. Every tax ought to be so contrived as both to take out and to keep out of the pockets of the people as little as possible over and above what it brings into the public treasury of the state (II, 350–51 [777–79]).

Many of the specific taxes Smith proceeds to examine fail to meet one or more of these criteria, and many reforms are accordingly proposed.

A Chancellor of the Exchequer would have found these rules most peculiar. If adopted, they would obtain for him at least the temporary admiration of the professors of moral philosophy, but this is a slender and notably fickle constituency on which to build a party. The two basic canons of taxation are surely rather different:

1. The revenue system must not imperil the political support for the regime.
2. The revenue system must yield revenue.

Smith's maxims touch on aspects of a revenue system which are relevant to its productivity and acceptability—not always in the direction he wished—but they form a wholly inadequate basis for judging individual taxes.

---

7. The retention of the unprofitable colonies by Great Britain is attributed to the interests of the administration-bureaucracy (II, 131–32 [581–82]). For a lesser example of the explanation of political behavior by interests of the sovereign, see II, 252–53 [688–89].

One may give—for generations economists have given—advice lavishly without taking account of the political forces which confine and direct policy. In the absence of knowledge of these political forces, the advice must often be bad and usually be unpersuasive. Why tell the sovereign that free trade is desirable, if one has no method of disarming the merchants and manufacturers who have obtained the protectionist measures? Why tell the French sovereign to abandon the *taille* and capitations and increase the *vingtièmes*, when only a revolution could dislodge the tax-favored classes?[8] Why believe that better turnpikes await only the appointments of a better class of commissioners (II, 248 [684–85])?

The contrast between Smith's discussions of political reform and other reforms is instructive. The dons of Oxford, he says, grossly neglect their duties of instruction. Does he preach to each don a moral reform, seeking a pledge of diligence and good sense? Smith would have considered such a remedy to be silly: the teacher is intelligently pursuing his interest, which is "to live as much at his ease as he can" because his income is independent of his efforts (II, 284 [718]). A system of remuneration based upon effort and achievement, not a weekly sermon, would bring about the changes Smith wishes.

In the political scene no corresponding search is made for the effective principles of behavior. Therefore reforms must be effected, if effected they can be, by moral suasion. At best this is an extraordinarily slow and uncertain method of changing policy; at worst it may lead to policies which endanger the society. Of course erroneous and undesirable public policies arise out of failures of comprehension as well as out of the efforts of self-serving groups, but there is little reason to accept Smith's implicit assumption that the main source of error is ignorance or "prejudice." Yet Smith's only remedy for erroneous policy is sound analysis, and that remedy is appropriate only to a minority of objectionable policies.

It may appear that Smith's failure to apply the organon of self-interest to political behavior requires no explanation. Political science had been a normative literature for 2300 years before Smith wrote and has continued to remain normative to the present day. The great Bentham, who did apply a theory of utility-maximizing behavior to political as well as other social phenomena, never stirred an inch beyond preaching, to see how well his theory actually explained legislation—and that is why his great organon remained sterile.

Yet it is uncomfortable to explain Smith's failure by the failure of everyone else, for he is a better man than everyone else. His ability to examine the most pompous and ceremonial of institutions and conduct with the jaundiced eye of a master economist—and the evident delight he

8. And Smith so recognized: II, 437 [855–56].

took in such amusement—is one of the trademarks of his authorship. The "uniform, constant, and uninterrupted effort of every man to better his condition" (I, 364 [326])—why was it interrupted when a man entered Parliament? The man whose spacious vision could see the Spanish War of 1739 as a bounty and who attributed the decline of feudalism to changes in consumption patterns—how could he have failed to see the self-interest written upon the faces of politicians and constituencies? The man who denied the state the capacity to conduct almost any business save the postal—how could he give to the sovereign the task of extirpating cowardice in the citizenry? How so, Professor Smith?

A Postscript on Failures of Self-Interest

It is in the political arena that Smith implicitly locates the most numerous and consistent failures of self-interest in guiding people's behavior, but this is not the only place where self-interest fails. Since the effective working of self-interest is so central to Smith's work, it may be useful to sketch the nature of the failures he described.

Every failure of a person to make decisions which serve his self-interest may be interpreted as an error in logic: means have been chosen which are inappropriate to the person's ends. Nevertheless it is useful to distinguish several categories of failure, all of which are found in the *Wealth of Nations*.

CLASS I: The individual knows the "facts" but fails to anticipate the consequences of his actions. The occasional behavior of the landlord is an example in Smith's book. He points out more than once that "improvements, besides, are not always made by the stock of the landlord, but sometimes by that of the tenant. When the lease comes to be renewed, however, the landlord commonly demands the same augmentation of rent, as if they had been all made by his own" (I, 162 [144–45]; also I, 414 [367–68]). The landlord is shortsighted in his greed: he removes the incentive to the tenant to make improvements which would yield more to tenant and landlord than the going rate of return. Hence there exists a system of rents which would make both tenant and landlord better off. This superior form of tenancy does not require the cooperation of any third party—only clear reasoning and a little inventiveness in writing a lease are necessary. The failure of self-interest to be served arises out of a failure to reason correctly.

The following are additional examples of the failure of individuals to reason correctly:

(1) The apprenticeship system does not give appropriate incentives to the apprentice to be diligent in his work (I, 137 [122]).
(2) Only a landlord can work no-rent land because he demands a rent from others (I, 184 [165]).
(3) The crown lands would be more valuable if they were sold off (II, 348 [775–76]).

144

One important subclass of failures due to imperfect knowledge involves the future: future gains are overestimated, or future costs underestimated. Examples are these:

(1) The possible gains are overestimated relative to the possible losses in risky ventures (I, 119 [106]; I, 124 [111]).

(2) Workers do not anticipate in seasons of plenty the higher prices of provisions in seasons of scarcity (I, 83 [74]).

(3) Workmen paid by the piece are "very apt to overwork themselves, and ruin their health and constitution in a few years" (I, 91 [81–82]).

(4) In the absence of usury laws, lenders will deal with "prodigals and projectors" (who will be unable to repay the loans?) (I, 379 [339]).

CLASS II: In an important range of situations, the employer or master is unable to control his agents so they will act in his interest. Among the examples are these:

(1) Slaves are often managed by a "negligent or careless overseer" (I, 90 [81]).

(2) Monopoly is the great enemy of good management (I, 165 [147]; II, 154 [602]).

(3) The East India Company's employees trade only in their own interest (II, 155 [603]; also II, 265 [700]).

Smith does not explain why *all* agents or employees do not display the same tendency to self-serving conduct, and it may be that this charge is made only against institutions which he objects to also on other grounds.

CLASS III: In the production of what is now called a public good, self-interest does not lead the individual to supply the correct amount of the good. Smith gives the example of the inadequate preparation by the individual citizen for war (II, 219 [658]). This is not so much a failure of self-interest as it is a failure of individual action.

The first class of (nonpolitical) failures is much the most important in the *Wealth of Nations* if importance is measured by number and variety of examples. A good number of these failures are due to incomplete factual information, and it would only be anachronistic to lament Smith's failure to discuss the problem of the optimum investment of the individual in the acquisition of knowledge. The implicit charge of inadequate analysis of known facts, it should be observed, is made against all classes: the greedy landlord, the impetuous laborer, the negligent employer, the short-sighted lender. No principle is apparent by which one can distinguish these failures from the many decisions which effectively advance these various persons' self-interests: the decisions are not especially subtle or especially demanding of information. One could make a fair case, I believe, that every alleged failure was nonexistent or of negligible magnitude. The high priest of self-interest, like all other high priests, had a strong demand for sinners.

13 The Successes and Failures of Professor Smith

The Wealth of Nations first appeared on March 9 of 1776, and perhaps sufficient time has now passed to permit a fair estimate of Professor Smith's triumphs and failures. It is a subject in which Smith himself would have displayed a vivid and natural interest. John Rae recounts his final days:

> When Smith felt his end to be approaching he evinced great anxiety to have all his papers destroyed except the few which he judged to be in a sufficiently finished state to deserve publication, and being apparently too feeble to undertake the task himself, he repeatedly begged his friends Black and Hutton to destroy them for him. . . . Black and Hutton always put off complying with Smith's entreaties in the hope of his recovering his health or perhaps changing his mind; but at length, a week before his death, he expressly sent for them, and asked them then and there to burn sixteen volumes of manuscript to which he directed them. This they did without knowing or asking what they contained. [1895, p. 434]

Only a man acutely sensitive to the opinion which posterity would hold of him would insist upon such an act. Of course Smith was wrong: there is no amount of mischief and nonsense in 16 volumes which we would not have forgiven, especially since we know he was given to neither mischief nor nonsense.

If the time is ripe, I am less certain of the qualifications of the writer. There is a game I sometimes play with children; I call it "Three Questions." If all three questions are answered correctly I promise $1 million; no doubt the Securities and Exchange Commission will eventually prohibit the game, or the Federal Reserve System will make it viable. The first two questions present no difficulty: perhaps the number of brothers and sisters the child has, and the city in which it lives. The third question is a different matter. Once I asked, "Who was Adam Smith's best friend?" The reply from this child was, "You are, Uncle George." I had someone like David Hume or James Hutton or Joseph Black in mind. Still, I have long been a good friend of Smith, though I have no right to claim priority

Reprinted from *Journal of Political Economy* 84 (1976). © 1976 by The University of Chicago.

in his circle. I do not believe that my friendship will distort the judgments I shall propose.

The task I set, in any event, is not the uninteresting one of praising or blaming Smith. The triumphs of any scholar are those of his doctrines which he persuades his contemporaries and successors to heed carefully. When Ricardo or John Stuart Mill or Torrens adopted a theory of Smith's that does not necessarily mean that they accepted it without qualifications but that their work and thoughts were directed by the formulation of Smith. Smith's failures were, correspondingly, those theories which his successors either ignored or rejected out of hand. When Smith was wrong we would naturally expect able successors to ferret out the error, but we shall also discover that some of Smith's finest theories suffered the fate of neglect. In any event, it is the judgment of the science that is decisive in judging a scholar's achievements.

There is, I hope, an intrinsic interest in Smith's triumphs and failures simply because he was as great an economist as has ever lived. There is also a broader significance to my query: can we determine the characteristics of theories that help or hurt their reception?[1]

I. The Proper Successes

A success or triumph is a proposition in economics that becomes a part of the working system (the so-called paradigm) of contemporary and subsequent economists. They accept and *use* the proposition, with heavy emphasis upon the word "use," or they reject and *dispute* the proposition, with heavy emphasis upon "dispute." In either event, their work is influenced by the successful proposition and, indeed, measures the success. So I repeat: a theoretical analysis is a success if it becomes a part of the living economics of successors, and the success is ascribable to Smith if his formulation governs the later use of the theory, whether he invented it or not. Hence I shall not attempt to determine Smith's debts to his predecessors; suffice to say they were large, but much smaller than our debts to him. One can say of Smith what Newton said of himself: "If I have seen farther, it is by standing on the shoulders of giants." That is appropriate to comparisons with predecessors but not to comparisons with contemporaries: they had the same shoulders to stand on.

Smith had one overwhelmingly important triumph: he put into the center of economics the systematic analysis of the behavior of individuals pursuing their self-interest under conditions of competition. This theory was the crown jewel of *The Wealth of Nations*, and it became, and remains to this day, the foundation of the theory of the allocation of resources. The proposition that resources seek their most profitable uses, so that in

---

1. I tried to answer this question in Stigler 1965 (pp. 66–155). The present approach is essentially independent although the answers overlap.

equilibrium the rates of return to a resource in various uses will be equal, is still the most important substantive proposition in all of economics.

I do not know whether to list as a second triumph one enormously successful application of this theory of competitive prices, namely, Smith's theory of the differentials in wage rates and profits among occupations. The famous list of cost factors which would generate apparent but not real differences in rates of wages and profits—training, hardships, unemployment, and trust—were accepted, and in fact usually quoted verbatim, by Smith's successors for a century.[2] This literature is the direct ancestor of Marshall's famous chapters on wages (1961, bk. 6, chaps. 3–5), and of the modern theory of human capital. So perhaps this special application of price theory deserves to be listed as his second success.

The third and final major success of Smith was his attack on mercantilism. I measure a success by the impact of a scholar on other scholars, not his impact upon public thinking or public policy. Smith's attack on protectionsim in all its basic forms—tariffs, subsidies, compulsory use of domestic shippers, limitations on colonial enterprise, and the like—rested squarely on his theory of competitive prices. The crucial argument for unfettered individual choice in public policy was the efficiency property of competition: the manufacturer or farmer or laborer or shipper who was seeking to maximize his own income would in the very process be putting resources where they were most productive to the nation: "Every individual is continually exerting himself to find out the most advantageous employment for whatever capital he can command. It is his own advantage, indeed, and not that of the society which he has in view. But the study of his own advantage naturally, or rather necessarily leads him to prefer that employment which is most advantageous to the society" (Smith 1976, 1:454). This application of price theory was again a corollary of the main proposition, but its development was so extensive and its success so great that it clearly deserves to be called Smith's third major triumph.

I have been most parsimonious in quoting Smith, and it is well to present a sample of the power of his argument. Here is how he describes one section of the English policy of mercantilism:

> To found a great empire for the sole purpose of raising up
> a people of customers, may at first sight appear a project fit
> only for a nation of shopkeepers. It is, however, a project
> altogether unfit for a nation of shopkeepers; but extremely fit
> for a nation whose government is influenced by shopkeepers.

---

2. The role of trust was not analysed satisfactorily by Smith and its acceptance was much less complete (for a modern interpretation of it, see Becker and Stigler [1974]). Smith's fifth source of differences, the uncertainty of success, was not a cost-based differential, and it was much disputed rather than generally accepted.

Such statesmen, and such statesmen only, are capable of fancying that they will find some advantage in employing the blood and treasure of their fellow-citizens, to found and maintain such an empire. Say to a shopkeeper, Buy me a good estate, and I shall always buy my clothes at your shop, even though I should pay somewhat dearer than what I can have them for at other shops; and you will not find him very forward to embrace your proposal. But should any other person buy you such an estate, the shopkeeper would be much obliged to your benefactor if he would enjoin you to buy all your clothes at his shop. England purchased for some of her subjects, who found themselves uneasy at home, a great estate in a distant country. The price, indeed, was very small, and instead of thirty years purchase, the ordinary price of land in the present times, it amounted to little more than the expence of the different equipments which made the first discovery, reconnoitred the coast, and took a fictitious possession of the country. The land was good and of great extent, and the cultivators having plenty of good ground to work upon, and being for some time at liberty to sell their produce where they pleased, became in the course of little more than thirty or forty years (between 1620 and 1660) so numerous and thriving a people, that the shopkeepers and other traders of England wished to secure to themselves the monopoly of their custom. Without pretending, therefore, that they had paid any part, either of the original purchase-money, or of the subsequent expence of improvement, they petitioned the parliament that the cultivators of America might for the future be confined to their shop; first, for buying all the goods which they wanted from Europe; and, secondly, for selling all such parts of their own produce as those traders might find it convenient to buy. [For they did not find it convenient to buy every part of it. Some parts of it imported into England might have interfered with some of the trades which they themselves carried on at home. Those particular parts of it, therefore, they were willing that the colonists should sell where they could; the farther off the better; and upon that account proposed that their market should be confined to the countries south of Cape Finisterre.] A clause in the famous act of navigation established this truly shopkeeper proposal into a law. [1976, 2:613–14]

From 1776 to today, the effect of this powerful attack, reinforced by the theoretical advances of Ricardo, Mill, and others, established a tradition of free international trade which even the most confirmed of economist-interventionists seldom feel equal to attacking frontally.

There is a fourth considerable success to be credited to Smith: the formulation of the wages-fund theory. This theory explained the short-run level of average wages by the ratio of funds for the payment of labor (the wages fund) to the number of laborers employed. It was saved from being a tautology by the implicit condition that over moderate periods of time the wages fund was approximately constant in size. Putting aside the question whether it was a useful theory (I have argued that it was [Stigler 1968]), there is no doubt that it dominated the next 100 years of English economics. The uncertainty is how clearly Smith formulated the theory. He definitely asserted the essence of the theory, as when he says: "The demand of those who live on wages, it is evident, cannot increase but in proportion to the increase of the funds which are destined for the payment of wages. These funds are of two kinds; first, the revenue which is over and above what is necessary for the maintenance; and, secondly, the stock which is over and above what is necessary for the employment of their masters" (1976, 1:86; also 1:110, 453). Smith's theory of wages will be shown below to rest on a wages-fund mechanism. The only real misgiving is that Smith did not explicitly define the contents of the wages fund.[3]

I am painting with a wide brush: insights and arguments of lesser scope, which would be a source of fierce pride to lesser economists, do not deserve inclusion here. The famous paradox of value concerning diamonds and water, for example, which posed in inescapable form the central problem for the marginal utility theory, would deserve attention in any lesser-man's work. But the first three of these four successes I distinguish have become a permanent part of economics.

II. The Improper Successes

An improper success is an error or an infertile and undevelopable subject or method of analysis—but one that is influential with contemporaries or successors. Most demonstrable errors, one hopes and believes, are soon ferreted out, but the analysis that somehow fails to identify and organize and exploit a useful body of knowledge can only be discovered with time.

I would propose only one significant topic in Smith's work that meets this description: his theory of productive and unproductive labor:

> There is one sort of labour which adds to the value of the subject upon which it is bestowed: There is another which has no such effect. The former, as it produces a value, may be called productive; the latter, unproductive labour. . . .
> [The] labour of the manufacturer fixes and realizes itself in some particular subject or vendible commodity, which lasts for some time at least after that labour is past. It is, as it

3. This is Taussig's main reservation in the standard history of the wages fund (1899, pp. 150–51). But the fund is not so easily defined as Smith's successors and Taussig believed—it was not simply, or all of, "the consumable goods, in dealers' hands, ready for purchase by laborers" (ibid., p. 148). The period of advance of the wages determines how "ready" the goods need be, as just one complication.

were, a certain quantity of labour stocked and stored up to be employed, if necessary, upon some other occasion. . . . The labour of the menial servant, on the contrary, does not fix or realize itself in any particular subject or vendible commodity. His services generally perish in the very instant of their performance. . . .[1976, 1:330]

The purpose of the distinction is clear: if we identify productive labor by the characteristic that its product can be accumulated, then capital formation can take place only out of the product of productive labor. The difficulties with the distinction are two. Even if Smith is correct, the extensive employment of productive labor merely *permits* the accumulation of capital, and the actual formation of new capital requires a wholly independent act of saving. Since most tangible products are not accumulated as capital but are currently consumed, there could be the loosest of connections between the share of labor that is productive and the rate of capital growth.

There is a second difficulty: there are investment acts which are not the result of productive labor. Investments in what we now call human capital do not become incorporated in a tangible, saleable commodity as commonly understood. Yet Smith agrees that one portion of the stock of a society consists of the acquired useful abilities of its inhabitants—to which he should have added the discovery of new knowledge: "The acquisition of [useful] talents, by the maintenance of the acquirer during his education, study, or apprenticeship, always costs a real expence, which is a capital fixed and realized, as it were, in his person. These talents, as they make a part of his fortune, so they do likewise of that of the society to which he belongs (1976, 1:282)." Unless we include instruction and training as productive labor—and Smith lists "men of letters of all kinds" as unproductive labor—the existence of productive labor is not even necessary to capital formation.[4]

The concept of productive labor never made a deep impression on Smith's successors. Senior and McCulloch denied the distinction and John Mill refined it almost out of existence.[5] So it was a small improper success.[6]

4. William Playfair pointed out, in his edition of the *Wealth of Nations*, that even the employment of menial servants might be a productive act: ". . . a cook, for [example] is a menial servant, but in a tavern he enriches his master just as much as any other journeyman; and on the other hand, a servant that spins or sews for the use of her master in a private family, is only acting as a menial servant; she is just supplying his wants, and contributing to his comforts in the same manner as when she lights the fire, or washes the apartments, yet she is a productive labourer by this definition" (Playfair 1805, 2:2, n.).

5. See Mill 1967, pp. 280 ff. A less influential figure, David Buchanan, was a strong supporter of the distinction (Buchanan 1817, pp. 131–36).

6. Hla Myint would wish to make the concept of productive labor, and of economic growth more generally, central to Smith's work, and a wholly proper success (1943, pp. 20–24). I would assert the contrary: that growth is not the only important path to

III. The Proper Failures

Smith's failures to persuade economists were, like his successes, of two sorts: failures that were proper, and failures that should have been successes. We consider first the proper failures. A proper failure contains an analytical error, or it presents an empirically trivial or mistaken view of the world.

The most conspicuous of Smith's proper failures was the hierarchy of employments of capital, presented in book 2, chapter 5, "Of the Different Employments of Capital": "A capital may be employed in four different ways: either, first, in procuring the rude produce annually required for the use and consumption of society; or secondly, in manufacturing and preparing that rude produce for immediate use and consumption; or, thirdly, in transporting either the rude or manufactured produce from the places where they abound to those where they are wanted; or lastly, in dividing particular portions of either into such small parcels as suit the occasional demands of those who want them" (1976, 1:361). Although all four activities are essential to one another or to "the general convenience of the society," capital is more productive—that is, sets more labor to work and augments more the annual produce of the society—if applied earlier in this sequence of operations than if applied later. The argument is simple: the capital of a retailer employs only himself and possibly a clerk—the remainder of the capital goes to purchase the goods he sells and therefore to replace the capitals of earlier stages. At the other end, "no equal capital puts into motion a greater quantity of productive labour than that of the farmer" (ibid., p. 363), for all of his capital goes to support labor, and in addition the fertility of nature is enlisted.

That Smith was in error is unequivocal. He allowed a system of financing to conceal the facts of economic life. If the consumer, instead of paying the retailer for the corn, had paid the farmer for raising it, the millwright for grinding it, the ship's captain for transporting it, and the retailer for stocking it, then everyone's capital would have gone exclusively to the direct support of production, but nothing essential would have changed.

If Smith had really incorporated this error into his theoretical system, the effects would have been disastrous. As one important example, the argument for private control over investment would have been damaged beyond repair. But it remained a local blemish (repeated however once, in Smith 1976, 2:573), duly refuted by McCulloch and ignored by Senior and J. S. Mill (McCulloch 1825, pp. 143 ff.). Only Malthus gave it warm approval (1820, pp. 30 ff.).

---

economic welfare in Smith's system, and the concept of productive labor is not important to growth. But the modesty of the success of Smith's distinction is a matter of historical record.

This error is commonly, and no doubt correctly, attributed to the influence of the Physiocrats: there is no such thing as a free trip to Paris. But this is a history of the error, not an explanation for Smith's commission of it. (Does the explanation lie in his antiluxury viewpoint?—reference will be made below to this attitude.)

A related error, and one to which Smith attached greater importance if measured by the number of times it recurs in the *Wealth of Nations*, is the assignment of a hierarchy of social usefulness to domestic trade, foreign trade, and the carrying trade for foreign nations (1976, 1:368 ff., 454, 495–96; 2:600–604, 610–11, 628–30). The internal trade, he argues, by the act of buying Scottish manufactures, carrying them to London, selling them and buying English corn to return to Edinburgh, replaces two British capitals, whereas the foreign trade replaces only one British capital and the carrying trade none. In addition, the returns of local trade are quicker than in distant trade. At this level of discourse, Smith is surely mistaken. If these various trades are yielding equal annual rates of return on capital, a shift from foreign to domestic trade would reduce aggregate national output (although the export of capital can of course affect wages). This error received no greater approval from Smith's successors (thus, Ricardo 1951, pp. 350–51).

A very different error, and possibly not an error at all, is Smith's measure of value—which came from the same source as that which may have led him to overvalue agriculture. Smith was acutely sensitive to the instability of monetary measures of value, and an appreciable fraction of the *Wealth of Nations* is devoted to the chronicle of currency debasement and inflation. He proposes as the ultimate measure of value the disutility of 1 hour of ordinary labor.

> Equal quantities of labour, at all times and places, may be said to be of equal value to the labourer. In his ordinary state of health, strength, and spirits; in the ordinary degree of his skill and dexterity, he must always lay down the same portion of his ease, his liberty, and his happiness. The price which he pays must always be the same, whatever may be the quantity of goods which he receives in return for it. . . . Labour alone, therefore, never varying in its own value, is alone the ultimate and real standard by which the value of all commodities can at all times and places be estimated and compared. [1976, 1:50–51]

Smith's error, if indeed it is an error, is to assume that the psychological cost of performing 1 hour of labor is more stable, in its significance to a person, than the psychological pleasure from the consumption of some bundle of goods. The instability of labor disutility arises from at least three circumstances: (*a*) It varies with the conditions of technology—for example, the lifting of heavy weights has been almost eliminated in a modern society. (*b*) It varies with the degree of training of the worker: the disutility of acquiring labor skills must be added to that of performing the work, and this addition was already increasing secularly with the progressive division of labor. (*c*) It varies with the hours of labor, and hence with income. The corresponding view of a bundle of consumer goods yielding constant satisfaction as the unit of value is free of the second difficulty, possibly free of the first (depending how one views new commodities), but of course not free of the third.

Smith's rejection of consumption in fixing on a measure of value is attributable to his belief that luxuries are frivolous and yield illusory pleasures that vanish in the act of realization. This view is extensively argued in his *Theory of Moral Sentiments* (1797, pt. 4, chap. 1) and receives adequate expression in the *Wealth of Nations*.[7] That Smith should attribute to almost all economic actors an illusion that greater wealth yields greater satisfactions, an illusion that is perhaps never pierced, is one of his greatest idiosyncrasies.

Smith's third error, and again perhaps we should label it a misdirection, is his monetary theory, as presented in volume 1, book 2, chapter 2, "On Money." Smith believes that there is a fixed demand for money in a society, in the special sense that only a certain quantity of money will circulate and excessive sums will be exported (if the money is gold or silver) or be presented for redemption in gold (if the money is bank notes). The theory is tenable as a first approximation if, as Smith assumes, the foreign exchanges are fixed and the paper currency is fully convertible: the theory then is implicitly a simple purchasing power parity theory.[8]

The complaint at Smith's theory is not that it is formally erroneous but that it represents a retrogression from the generality and predictive power of the monetary theory in Hume's essays.

IV. The Improper Failures

There remain the successes that Smith should have achieved, but did not. It will appear paradoxical that his immense prestige and vast powers of persuasion should have failed to obtain acceptance of ideas that were correct, profound, and fecund.

The first of these superior theories was a rejection of the subsistence theory of wages. Smith, it will be recalled, gave four explicit reasons for believing wages were not generally at a subsistence level in Great Britain:

---

7. "For a pair of diamond buckles perhaps, or for something as frivolous and useless, [the feudal lords] exchanged the maintenance, or what is the same thing, the price of the maintenance of a thousand men for a year, and with it the whole weight and authority which it could give them" (Smith 1976, 1:418–19).

8. Smith assumes the full convertibility of paper money (ibid., p. 329).

(1) Summer wages exceed winter wages, but the cost of subsistence varies inversely. (2) Subsistence varies substantially in cost from year to year, but some wages change very slowly. (3) Subsistence varies substantially from place to place, but wages vary less by place. (4) Variations over time and place in the cost of subsistence are often inverse to those of wages (1976, 1:91–93). All of these proofs, particularly the first two, suffer from a concentration on short-run correspondences of wages and the cost of subsistence, but they carry considerable weight. In addition Smith offers the powerful long-run example of the differences in real wages between England and the American colonies (ibid., pp. 87–88), an example whose persistence made it stronger with each passing year.

Smith proposed an alternative theory, and one which was surely more valid than the subsistence theory as a predictor of wage rates. He proposed that "the" wage rate of (say) unskilled labor was given by wage rate = subsistence level + $\lambda(\Delta[\text{capital}]/\Delta[\text{time}])$, $(\lambda > 0)$, that is, that population lagged changes in capital, so ". . . it is in the progressive state, while the society is advancing to the further acquisition, rather than when it has acquired its full complement of riches, that the condition of the labouring poor, of the great body of the people, seems to be the happiest and the most comfortable. It is hard in the stationary, and miserable in the declining state" (ibid., p. 99). This wage theory, despite its great plausibility, was easily vanquished for a generation by Malthus's simple theory (which set $\lambda = 0$).

A second of Smith's theories took slightly more than a century to achieve currency—it was his theory of rent. He consistently treated the rent of land as it should be treated: any one use of land had to pay a rent, which was a cost of production, to draw the land away from other uses; whereas for all uses combined, rent was a residual. This theory is present in volume 1, book 1, chapter 11, "The Rent of Land," with hardly any ambiguity but with hardly any explicitness. Indeed, I used to suspect my own reading of it until I discovered an early and wholly concordant treatment by D. H. Buchanan (1929). It is difficult in retrospect to see how the many recognitions of the alternative cost theory received so little attention, as when Smith says, "As an acre of land, therefore, will produce a much smaller quantity of the one species of food [meat] than of the other [corn], the inferiority of the quantity must be compensated by the superiority of the price. If it is more than compensated, more corn land would be turned into pasture; and if it was not compensated, part of what was in pasture would be brought back into corn" (1976, 1:165, 168, 175, etc.). John Stuart Mill gave this theory timid recognition, and Marshall refused to give it full credit. But unlike the other theories of Smith under discussion, the correct theory here is only partly explicit and was fragmented in presentation, so he rather than his successors deserve the larger blame for its neglect.

The last of Smith's regrettable failures is one for which he is overwhelmingly famous—the division of labor. How can it be that the famous opening chapters of his book, and the pin factory he gave immortality, can be considered a failure? Are they not cited as often as any passages in all economics? Indeed, over the generations they are.[9]

The failure is different: almost no one used or now uses the theory of division of labor, for the excellent reason that there is scarcely such a theory. The description of division of labor was much enlarged in Babbage's account of manufactures, and the phenomenon lies at the base of that part of Marshall's theory of external economies which attends to localization of industry. There are more praises and even mild use of Smith's theorem that the division of labor is limited by the extent of the market in essays by Allyn Young and myself, and Ronald Coase's work on the firm is clearly in the line of descent (Young 1928; Coase 1937; Stigler 1951). But there is no standard, operable theory to describe what Smith argued to be the mainspring of economic progress.

Smith gave the division of labor an immensely convincing presentation—it seems to me as persuasive a case for the power of specialization today as it appeared to Smith. Yet there is no evidence, so far as I know, of any serious advance in the theory of the subject since his time, and specialization is not an integral part of the modern theory of production, which may well be an explanation for the fact that the modern theory of economies of scale is little more than a set of alternative possibilities.

V. The Recognition of Success and Failure

It is a general rule of scientific work that a scholar's successes and failures are judged by his contemporaries, and their judgment is accepted by later scholars. Allowing for the fact that Smith wrote when there were few even part-time economists, so we may perhaps treat the early nineteenth century as near contemporary, his experience confirms this rule. Certainly all of Smith's successes, proper and improper, were achieved within 50 years of their initial publication. All of his failures, proper and improper, were similarly achieved in this period. It is almost (but not quite) tautological that proper successes and proper failures be promptly recognized at such, but it is not inevitable that an improper success (recall that Smith's on productive and unproductive labor was a modest success) will soon be dispatched.

As for improper failures, the interesting point is that they do not influence the later adoption of the neglected contribution. When the theory of rent was finally set straight—a development which took place primarily in the period from 1890 to 1910—the correct formulation owed

9. Babbage reports the dramatic story of how M. Prony was enabled, by reading Smith on this subject, to plan the great mathematical tables of the French revolutionary government (1842, pp. 191–95).

nothing to Smith's profound but inarticulate insight. When the Malthusian wage theory was abandoned, as it was on an ever-widening scale from 1825 on, it was not Smith's highly plausible theory of population lags that was adopted. In fact, for a long time no alternative theory was adopted, and population receded from economic attention. It is perhaps rash to complete the trilogy, for these are three scientific tragedies, by asserting that when a theory of specialization comes it will owe little to Smith; but on historical grounds it is even rasher to assert the converse.

There are, of course, exceptions to the rule that much later scientific descendants accept the judgment of a man's contemporaries: perhaps Cantillon, von Thünen, Cournot, and Gossen are the leading exceptions in the history of economics. These exceptions were for Schumpeter the source of considerable lament at the closed minds and narrow visions of contemporaries (Schumpeter 1954, pp. 463 ff., and elsewhere), but it seems unfruitful to expect of a science that it immediately value all scientific work at its ultimate worth, never erring in deficit or in excess.

The rule of the dominance of contemporary judgments, however, rests upon another basis: science is a *social* pursuit of knowledge, not a census of independent individuals. A scholar who does not influence his contemporaries—who does not persuade them to work differently—is not an effective member of that science. Occasionally he may indeed have been too farsighted—inventing disk brakes before the internal combustion machine was known—but this is so rare a cause of failure that there cannot be many less efficient ways to discover good unexploited ideas than by reading earlier literature. The overwhelming cause of failure of scholars is that their ideas were erroneous or infertile or their development too primitive to provide useful guidance to their contemporaries. That is the proper reason for a judgment of failure in a social enterprise, and later scholars are quite sensible in accepting the verdict in perpetuity.

VI. The Sources of Success and Failure

In the long run nothing is more essential to a theory than that it be right, but we cannot even pause for a new sentence before remarking that rightness means limited wrongness. The theory must help in explaining to the world that economics is attempting to understand, and a partial explanation is better than none.

Logical error is sometimes enough to disqualify a theory—that is why Smith's four-layered hierarchy of employments of capital never had a prospect of scientific prosperity. Usually, however, it is possible to retain the substance of a theory in a logical reformulation. Perhaps that is the reason that logical criticisms of Smith's hierarchical theory were not common—economists like Ricardo simply ignored this theory, and it is difficult to doubt that their aversion was at least partly due to a belief that the whole approach was infertile and contrived.

Blemishes, however, will exist in every theory: the logic may be reasonably rigorous—although standards of rigor are not unchanging—but the very formulation of a problem will, in time, prove to be obtuse.

The acceptability of Smith's theories, logic aside, was very little influenced by the strength of the *specific* evidence he gave in their support. His strong empirical arguments against a subsistence theory of wages were ignored, whereas his support for the theorem on equalization of rates of return under competition was only casual and anecdotal. To say that a proof is nonspecific and nonquantitative is not to say that it is unweighty: if the theorem was congruent with widely observed phenomena—the growing number of members of prosperous trades, the fall of prices of new goods over time—then one was prepared to follow the theorem into unobserved places. A century later, however, when Cliffe-Leslie denied the tendency of rates of return to approach equality, there was precious little documented evidence to refute him.

But the proof of the ubiquity of the division of labor certainly also met this test of congruence with common observation: in fact, irresistibly so. Ask a modern economist to name an instance of *non*specialization of labor and he will be lucky to remember Robinson Crusoe. Yet, as we saw, there has been scarcely any systematic or regular use of this concept in economic analysis.

We have already hinted at the difference between the fates of the theorems on division of labor and on rates of return. The latter was a generalization of enormous power and could be used immediately on the most obtrusive and important questions: why some occupations earned more than others; why mercantilism and similar state interventions, as well as private monopoly, led to misallocations of resources; and who would bear various taxes. The theory of division of labor is not devoid of consequences—that it is limited by the extent of the market makes it relevant to protectionism, for example—but the uses were few and far between.

So Smith was successful where he deserved to be successful—above all in providing a theorem of almost unlimited power on the behavior of man. His construct of the self-interest-seeking individual in a competitive environment is Newtonian in its universality. That we are today busily extending this construct into areas of economic and social behavior to which Smith himself gave only unsystematic study is tribute to both the grandeur and the durability of his achievement.

References

Babbage, C. *On the Economy of Machinery and Manufactures*. London: Knight, 1842.

Becker, G. S., and Stigler, G. J. "Law Enforcement, Malfeasance, and Compensation of Enforcers." *J. Legal Studies* 3 (January 1974): 1–19.

Buchanan, D. *Observations on the Subjects Treated of in Dr. Smith's Inquiry into the Nature and the Cause of the Wealth of Nations.* London: Ogles, Duncan & Cochran, 1817.

Buchanan, D. H. "The Historical Approach to Rent and Price Theory," *Economica* 9 (June 1929): 123–55. Reprinted in *Readings in the Theory of Income Distribution.* Philadelphia: Blakiston, 1946.

Coase, R. "The Nature of the Firm." *Economica,* n.s. 4 (November 1937): 386–405.

McCulloch, J. R. *The Principles of Political Economy.* Edinburgh: Tait, 1825.

Malthus, T. R. *Principles of Political Economy.* London: Murray, 1820.

Marshall, A. *Principles of Economics.* London: Macmillan, 1961.

Mill, J. S. *The Collected Works of John Stuart Mill.* Vol. 4, *Essays on Economics and Society.* Toronto: Univ. Toronto Press, 1967.

Myint, Hla. "The Welfare Significance of Productive Labour." *Rev. Econ. Studies* 9 (Winter 1943): 20–31.

Playfair, W., ed. *The Wealth of Nations by Adam Smith.* London: Cadell & Davies, 1805.

Rae, John, *Life of Adam Smith.* London: Macmillan, 1895.

Ricardo, D. *Works and Correspondence.* Vol. 1, *Principles of Political Economy,* Cambridge: Cambridge Univ. Press, 1951.

Schumpeter, J. A. *History of Economic Analysis.* New York: Oxford Univ. Press, 1954.

Smith, A. *The Theory of Moral Sentiments.* Dublin: Beatty & Jackson, 1797.

——. *The Wealth of Nations.* Oxford: Clarendon, 1976.

Stigler, G. J. "The Division of Labor Is Limited by the Extent of the Market." *J.P.E.* 59, no.3 (June 1951): 185–94.

——. *Essays in the History of Economics.* Chicago: Univ. Chicago Press, 1965.

——. "Mill on Economics and Society." *Univ. Toronto Q.* 28 (October 1968): 96–102.

Taussig, F. W. *Wages and Capital.* New York: Appleton, 1899.

Young, A. A. "Increasing Returns and Economic Progress," *Econ. J.* 38 (December 1928): 527–42.

14 Mill on Economics and Society

Lord Robbins, in an introductory essay which is as fair as the mature Mill, justly complains of the arrogance and dogmatism of the most youthful work of John Stuart. I shall lament later a basic deficiency in Mill's latter-day major essays on labour and economic reform. But Lord Robbins' complaints leave plaintless a large number of splendid essays, which fill most of these two volumes and spill over into forthcoming volumes on related subjects. There can be little doubt that Mill's reputation as an economist, which reached a nadir in the generation between the world wars, is on the ascendant and will be given a thrust upward by this splendidly presented collection of his economic essays.

Mill's reputation as an economist inevitably declined after his death. His reputation suffered also as economics became more formal in both its abstract and its empirical work and thus moved away from his style and shared less his interest in the relationship between political and economic institutions. And it suffered because this modest man did not shout his analytical achievements.

Increasingly Mill became known as a faithful, enormously talented defender of the Ricardian economics to which he attached (but could not really join) a broad and compassionate social philosophy. Sir Erich Roll will serve as an example of a patronizing critic:

> In short, his economic theory lacks the logical rigor and his social philosophy, the unflinching consistency which are nowadays more frequently demanded.
>
> But although he was not original as an economist, and although he did not leave behind one of the great systems of political philosophy, Mill is not to be dismissed as unimportant. His significance lies precisely in the fact that he was able to make eclecticism in theory and compromise in politics into something like a generally accepted system. (*A History of Economic Thought,* New York 1942, 388.)

The picture of a mind without razor edges was drawn in writings vastly more authoritative than the textbooks: one may cite Schumpeter (*History of Economic Analysis*, New York 1954; especially Part III, Chaps. 5 and 6); who nevertheless was on the whole an admirer of Mill; Blaug (*Ricar-*

Review of *Collected Works of John Stuart Mill*, vols. IV, V: *Essays on Economics and Society*, edited by J. M. Robson (Toronto: University of Toronto Press, 1967). Reprinted from *University of Toronto Quarterly*, October 1968.

dian Economics, Chap. 9, New Haven 1958); and the very dean of historians of economics, Viner ("Bentham and Mill," *American Economic Review*, March 1949).

I have argued elsewhere that Mill was an extraordinarily creative theoretician ("The Nature and Role of Originality in Scientific Progress," *Economica*, 1955; reprinted in *Essays in the History of Economics*, Chicago 1965). The volumes under review reinforce the case. Indeed the case could be rested upon an essay (new to me) on "Corn Laws" published in Mill's eighteenth year (1825)! First hear Mill on the objection to a tariff:

> Having proved the Corn Laws to be injurious to all the rest of the community, and beneficial to the landlord alone, we might here close our remarks. . . .
>
> . . . if whatever is lost by the consumer and by the capitalist were gained by the landlord; there might be robbery, but there would not be waste . . . The evil of the Corn Laws admits not even of this alleviation: they occasion in all cases an absolute loss, greatly exceeding the gain which can be derived from them by the receivers of rent . . .
>
> The consumer is taxed, not only to give a higher rent to the landlord, but to indemnify the farmer for producing, at a great expense, that corn which might be obtained from abroad at a comparatively small one.
>
> We seriously propose, therefore, as a great improvement on the present system, that this indirect tax should be commuted for a direct one; which, if it still gave an undue advantage to the landlords, would, at least, give them this advantage at a smaller cost to the public: or that the landlords should make an estimate of their probable losses from the repeal of the Corn Laws, and found upon it a claim to compensation. (IV 50, 51, 52)

That this is superb analysis is perhaps sufficiently documented by the fact that the identical argument including the reintroduction of the compensation principle was independently published in 1939 by Nicholas Kaldor, stirring up an immense controversy in welfare economics. ("Welfare Propositions of Economics and Interpersonal Comparisons of Utility," *Economic Journal*, September 1939.) This single analysis of Mill's would entitle him to fame as a theorist. Some of his best work, including the *Essays on Some Unsettled Questions of Political Economy*, is reprinted in these volumes.

One may and should carry the argument to the other camp: Mill's wisdom and tolerance were logical rather than intuitive. An instinctively wise man (such as de Tocqueville) is one whose subtle, inarticulate, mental assessments of scattered fragments of evidence and logic yield a profound understanding of an event too complex to be analyzed in

161

systematic, explicit terms. Wisdom such as Mill's was wholly different: he sought to reach most probable positions on complex questions by conscious and explicit rational processes. Disciplined wisdom is admirable, but unfortunately it is severely limited in useful scope and beyond that scope becomes superficial and unstable. It is in fact not wisdom but analytical power. And Mill's judgments were often superficial and unstable.

Consider his proudest achievement in the *Principles*: the distinction between the immutable laws of production and the politically and socially malleable laws of distribution. That some relationships in economic life are beyond parliamentary reach, and that others are easily tortured on a legislative rack, is certainly true. But these types of relationships do not correspond at all closely with, respectively, production and distribution. (We have not yet discovered which economic relationships are malleable.) Consider again his advocacy of socialization of future increments of land rent (V, 671–95), an attempt to combine an uncongenial mixture of Ricardian rent theory (and mistaken, at that, because the future increments were already in the present price of land), respect for previous commitments, and egalitarian ethics. A man of wisdom would have made some estimate of the costs and returns of the scheme—and dropped it cold. In fairness to the fairest of economists it must be added that even less wisdom was shown by the parliaments of 1931 and 1947 which incorporated variants of this quixotic scheme into laws. This same lack of a profound wisdom is apparent in Mill's vacillating treatment of the comparative claims of private property and socialism, important parts of which appear in these volumes.

Mill's recantation of the wages-fund theory, however, is the example I would like to explore. The wages-fund doctrine presented a short run theory of wages, which can be stated as follows:

(1) The fund for the employment of labour—the wages-fund—is approximately constant in the short run.

(2) The average wage rate will be given by the simple formula,

$$\text{Average Wage Rate} = \frac{\text{Wages-Fund}}{\text{Number of Workers Employed}}$$

(3) The wage rate in any occupation will differ from the average by an amount which was not discussed, but could be analysed with Mill's theory of reciprocal demand in international trade. (There was a well-developed theory of long-run wage rate differences, to which Mill's theory of non-competing groups was a major contribution).

Perhaps the most important, and beyond any doubt the most heretical, remark to be made about this theory was that it was correct.

The theory was correct: it yielded correct predictions of the effects of changes in wage rates, capital, and population. It predicted:

(1) A rise in unemployment, if an effective minimum wage were set by law.

(2) The main short-run burden of a rise in wage rates by one group would usually be a fall in wage rates elsewhere.

(3) A rise in wage rates, if a portion of the labor force were removed by pestilence (the Black Death).

The theory could not cope with many questions—such as the structure of wage-rates—and deserved to be supplanted by the marginal productivity theory, as it was in the 1890s—but it was much better than no theory at all.

In 1869 Mill's long-time friend in the East India Company, William T. Thornton, published *On Labour*, in which the wages-fund doctrine was subjected to discursive attack. The vehicle of Thornton's criticism was an assemblage of peculiar instances of supply and demand (involving discontinuities or multiple equilibrium) which yielded indeterminate prices. The market for labour was presented as the premier case of highly inelastic demand and supply, and a substantial scope was allowed to arbitrary power in the setting of wages. Thornton's work was not of good analytical quality, and its historical role as a trigger aside, it would long since have fallen into oblivion.

Mill correctly analyzed the peculiarities of Thornton's cases, in his reply, but then went on to accept the view that a combination of short-run supply and demand curves each with zero elasticity *was* appropriate to the labour markets:

> Does the employer require more labour, or do fresh employers of labor make their appearance, merely because it can be bought cheaper? Assuredly, no. Consumers desire more of an article, or fresh consumers are called forth, when the price has fallen: but the employer does not buy labour for the pleasure of consuming it; he buys it that he may profit by its productive powers, and he buys as much labour and no more as suffices to produce the quantity of his goods which he thinks he can sell to advantage. A fall of wages does not necessarily make him expect a larger sale for his commodity, nor, therefore, does it necessarily increase his demand for labour. (V, 644)

Mill earned an hour in purgatory with this passage, because lower wages make for lower costs and larger sales of the product, and hence for more employment—this is a conclusion which is essentially exceptionless.

Mill generalizes the argument: he denies that there is a "fixed amount which, and neither more nor less than which, is destined to be paid in wages" (V, 644). He now acknowledges that the labourer competes with the capitalist's expenditures or savings, so the maximum amount that labour could wring from an employer is "not only [his] capital but the whole of what can be retrenched from his personal expenditure" (V, 645). And so, within a few lines, we reach the conclusion that the doctrine that "trade combination can raise wages" must be shifted from the list of errors to that of truths of political economy (V, 646). The powerful union could advance the full length of the employer's wife's pearls.

The recantation did not convince Cairnes, and it does not convince us. One may raise a formal objection that unless the union had a ubiquitous jurisdiction, the capital could move outside its reach, and then consumers, not capitalists, would pay the higher wages, a point which Mill himself later elaborates (V, 658, 661–2). The basic complaint which Mill invites, however, is that his recantation did not face the significant version of the theory which asserted only the approximate constancy of the wages-fund. Nor did Mill provide a substitute theory. The recantation must be attributed to non-analytical considerations, perhaps an attempt to construct a defense of labour unions or a wish to enlarge the role of the state in assisting the labourer.

There was a fundamental scientific irresponsibility in Mill's behaviour towards the wages-fund doctrine. He capitulated to a debating point without having explored its consequences for the general theory, and without providing any coherent theory to replace the abandoned portion. It is no doubt admirably honest to acknowledge error openly and quickly, but error is as elusive as truth—in fact, error implies the existence of truth—and Mill did his science no service by his acceptance of Thornton's "truth," which now serves as a compendium of analytical fallacies. Mill was a great man and a superb theoretician, but he was not a wise man.

A final word on the nature of the editions which are here presented. The scrupulous critical editions of these essays serve two very different purposes: to make accurate and meticulously complete texts available for research now and forever; and to make the works of a great man easily accessible to a circle of non-hair-splitting readers. The two purposes conflict when the man wrote many trifles, or when he made many trifling changes in his works over time, for then to serve the research scholar is to disserve the general scholar. (It is as if sentences alternate in English and German, to help Bavarian readers.) Scholarship vacillates between these audiences: in the nineteenth century even tolerable carefulness was sure to be labelled "heavy Germanic," and today the literary scraps of every second-rate American president must be immortalized. (In fact, the present edition, by abandoning the original pagination, has already compromised the research function.) I hope that technology will soon come to our rescue and preserve every misprint in some efficient way for the specialist, and permit tasteful, intelligently edited editions of great works on spacious pages for the more general reader.

These animadversions, even if acceptable, bear more lightly on the present volumes than on the *Principles*. If they are not acceptable—and the present canons of scholarships emphatically reject them—there is nothing but praise due to Professor Robson and his colleagues in this noble venture.

15 Henry Calvert Simons

Henry Calvert Simons was the Crown Prince of that hypothetical kingdom, the Chicago school of economics, and even at this late date it is desirable to present the main facts about the man and his career.

Simons was born into an upper middle class family in Virden, Illinois, on October 9, 1899. His father was an attorney, his grandfather an English immigrant who had become a church organist and then a successful grain merchant; his mother was a southern belle whose imperious ambitions caused Simons to escape from home as soon as he completed high school in 1916.

The first stop was the University of Michigan, where he specialized in economics and received the AB in 1920. The brilliance and capacity for boredom that marked his entire life were already present: he was an excellent student (9 A's, 5 B's, in economics) and a poor accountant (1 A, 1 B, 2 C's, 1 D).

He moved on to the University of Iowa in January of 1921, beginning as an assistant in principles and railroads ($700 per year), rising to assistant professor with a salary of $2750 in 1926–27. At Iowa he met and eventually became the premier student of Frank Knight. He began the pursuit of a Ph.D., first sampling Columbia in the summer of 1922 and then shifting to Chicago (summers, 1923, 1924, and the academic year, 1925–26). A thesis on personal income taxation was launched, and when he followed Knight to Chicago in 1927 as a lecturer, he was given a leave to learn German in the first half of 1928. He spent the time in Germany, partly at the University of Berlin, and readers of his *Personal Income Taxation* (1938) will remember his perverse pleasure in quoting the German literature only in the original.

He returned to Chicago in 1928 as an assistant professor and Chicago was his home for the remainder of his life. By external signs he was a desultory, aimless student (that is, well ahead of his time!). No prelims were taken, and up to 1932 he had published only three book reviews. Paul Douglas led a strong opposition to the renewal of his appointment, beginning in 1932. Simons' main and perhaps only defender, unreason-

This essay is a by-product of the preparation of a much briefer sketch on Simons for the *Dictionary of American Biography*. Further genealogical details will be available there. Reprinted from *Journal of Law and Economics* 17 (April 1974). © 1974 by The University of Chicago.

able and intransigent and successful, was Frank Knight. But it was all Knight could do to preserve Simons' position, and it was 1942 before he was promoted to associate professor—and then only with the backing of the Law School, where Simons had begun teaching economic theory in 1939. The further delay in reaching his professorship (1945) was due to the opposition of a dean who was incensed by Simons' attack on labor unions in his famous essay, "Some Reflections on Syndicalism."

The actual facts concerning his industry were different: by 1933 Simons had worked out the main elements of his position in virtually every respect. A famous unpublished memorandum, "Banking and Currency Reform" (of which he was the main author) has the fundamental elements of his monetary theory and hints of much of the remainder, and in the *Positive Program for Laissez-Faire* (1934) all the elements are present. The success of this pamphlet presumably insured his continuance at Chicago, although Douglas' last effort to terminate the appointment came in 1935. There is no evidence that he ever received an offer from another university.

Simons seemed to everyone a confirmed bachelor, but sanity triumphed and he married Marjorie Powell (to whom I had introduced him) in 1941. For years his recordings—he was a classicist also in musical taste—accompanied by rye old-fashioneds had been a fixture of the Quadrangle Club. He was also excellent at billiards, formidable at bridge, and a lackadaisical tennis player. In my time as a student, Simons was too sophisticated and subtle to be a widely popular teacher: he could not bring himself to emphasize the important if it were moderately obvious; this changed later, as we shall see. He was primarily an introspective philosopher of economics: he was uninterested in empirical economics (a trait shared with Knight), and found it more congenial to study economic life by reflection than by wide reading (the antithesis of Knight). There was, indeed, a basic conflict between his philosophy and that of his teacher: Simons was a strong believer in the possibility of purposive, disinterested reform, with the intellectual playing a great role in such reform,[1] whereas Knight believed that social life was basically non-rational and hence not improvable (and hence ideal!).

Simons was a soundly trained theorist, and his *Materials for Economics 201* was a remarkably thorough training in the most important elements of price theory. In this material, which was never formally published, he developed also a lucid analysis of cartels, which was elaborated and

---

1. A strong example: "If we (responsible economists) could achieve agreement among ourselves—excluding those who would use all proximate means, fiscal and other, to prevent survival of this kind of a system—we might easily exercise decisive influence and rapidly induce a popular, political consensus." Henry C. Simons, *Economic Policy for a Free Society* 207 (1948).

published (with due acknowledgement) by Patinkin.[2] He did not teach the graduate theory courses, however—always introductory courses (including that in the law school) and public finance.

His participation in the Law School deserves a remark. It began in 1939, and continued until his death, and it is the Law School which instituted the memorial lectures which have been given, chronologically, by me, Viner, Carter (of the Canadian Tax Commission), Friedman, Tobin, and H. G. Johnson (all appearing in the *Journal of Law and Economics*). Although Simons initiated the practice of having an economist in the law school at Chicago, the relationship was somewhat didactic in his time: there was no visible impact of his law school associations upon his own work, although he became an extremely popular teacher and had a substantial influence upon several of the law faculty. Simons' primary interest was in macroeconomic policy, not allocative price theory, and the reciprocal relevances of monetary policy to the law and of the law to monetary policy are severely limited. Only when Simon's friend, Aaron Director, succeeded him did the effect of the collaboration reach fruition. Director entered into the instruction of law (especially in the famous course on antitrust law, with Edward Levi) and in the process solved important problems in industrial organization such as the economics of tie-in sales, predatory competition, and patent licensing restrictions. The inauguration of the remarkable collaboration between law and economics which persists to this day at Chicago is one of Simons' major contributions.

The *Positive Program for Laissez-Faire* was Simons' *Manifesto*, and it contained all of the major ideas which he was to elaborate in the next decade. Completed in the trough of the deepest depression of modern times, it had an urgency which never left his work: Western society was near the point of no return.

The central philosophy of the *Positive Program* was highly individual. Simons believed that it was essential to the preservation of personal freedom that a large sector of economic life be organized privately and competitively—this was a fundamental element of the liberal position that many, perhaps even an increasing share of us, still believe. With it, however, he joined an extensive and intricate set of tasks for the state:

1. The positive pursuit of competition by limitist laws as well as by antitrust policy.
2. Public ownership and operation of "natural" monopolies (preferably by local governments where possible).
3. Severe restriction of advertising and merchandising.
4. Elimination of tariff barriers.

---

2. As part of Don Patinkin, "Multiple-plant Firms, Cartels, and Imperfect Competition," 61 *Q.J.Econ.* 173 (1974).

5. The elimination of all forms of public debt except long-term bonds and of almost all forms of private debt except short-term credit, to strengthen the weapons of monetary policy and eliminate the forced liquidations consequent upon business downturns. (The 100 per cent reserve plan was already fully developed in the 1933 memorandum.)

6. A monetary authority committed to maintain stability in the quantity or value of money.

All these policies, with the possible exception of the limitation of advertising, could be argued to be necessary to the preservation of a large and efficient private enterprise sector. To this theme, Simons adds a second major one which is surely independent: that there should be a large movement toward income equality, achieved primarily by reliance upon a personal income tax of elegant analytical simplicity. Income should include capital gains, inheritances, gifts—everything that increased a person's relative command over resources. This strong egalitarian element separated Simons from most conservatives, and indeed one could make a strong case that Simons was a modern liberal who understood price theory. Certainly no other economist accepted so fully Mill's proposition that the distribution of income was a matter of free social choice.[3]

Simons hardly ever departed from normative economics, and yet he had a vague and contradictory picture of the state as an instrument of economic policy. This state, which historically had been complaisant to strong minorities in granting tariffs and stupid in its grants of corporate license, was assigned arduous tasks such as the operation of railroads and insurance companies and the administration of a tax system of unprecedented intellectual elegance and fiscal severity. Simons had a theory of the demand for governmental services, but none of its capacity to perform these services. Only the former student of Leo Sharfman could have written of the Interstate Commerce Commission as "an unusually competent and scrupulous public body" and only a nonstudent could have had Simons' 1934 faith in the Federal Trade Commission, which "must become perhaps the most powerful of our governmental agencies."

The little volume on *Personal Income Taxation* (1938) was an elegant (his favorite word) and ingenious monograph. It contains, in addition to a consistent application of a comprehensive income measure, an early and influential case for income averaging. He once said that the Hicks, Hicks, and Rostas' book, *Taxation of War Wealth*, belonged in the 5-inch shelf of

---

3. "Moreover, the control of the distribution of income through taxation represents a form of control which democratic governments can be expected to exercise somewhat correctly, i.e., without undermining the foundations of their own existence. No fundamental disturbance of the whole system is involved." Henry C. Simons, *Personal Income Taxation* 29 (1938).

good books in public finance; surely his own also belonged in this tight space.

The famous essay, "Rules versus Authorities in Monetary Policy" (1936), which Simons once said was the best piece of writing he had produced, is the fullest exposition of his monetary and cyclical views. Here I am content to refer to Milton Friedman's perceptive study of Simons' monetary theory, which gives the monetary theory high marks but criticizes the policy proposals, for whose faults Friedman assigns a large role to Simons' (mis)understanding of the causes of the 1933 monetary collapse.[4]

Henry Simons was closely tuned to the time and place in which he lived: America in the Great Depression. It was a time for great fears and bold reforms—indeed bold reforms require great crises, and Simons frequently invoked imminent and utter catastrophe as the justification for his proposals. Could it be that his tragic death in 1946 was an inevitable final bond with the disappearing era to which he had devoted his mind and heart?

The "Chicago School" has always been a phrase whose accuracy varied inversely to its content. The leading figures of the School in the 1930's were highly diverse: Knight was the great philosopher and theoretician, almost in a Marxian sense; Viner was studiously non-dogmatic on policy views; Mints was a close historical student of money, and restricted himself to that field; Simons was the utopian. None of the school had any interest in quantitative work, and indeed—like the rest of the economics profession—none (except Viner) had serious reservation that his understanding of economic life was incomplete or mistaken. At a doctrinal level, the one specific idea that carries over to the present day in Friedman's writings is Simons' demand for a fixed rule for the conduct of monetary policy. In forming most present day policy views of Chicago economists, Director and Friedman have been the main intellectual forces.

The evolution of institutions and theories has moved them beyond Simons' positions—and beyond those of contemporaries such as Keynes, Hansen, and Tawney. Yet Simons' central goal is as vital and as irresistible today as it was forty years ago: to devise a decentralized, unpoliticized world in which personal freedom and economic efficiency find wide scope and strong defense.

4. Milton Friedman, "The Monetary Theory and Policy of Henry Simons," 10 *J. Law & Econ.* 1 (1968).

Part Four   Quantitative Studies

16

The Pattern of Citation Practices in Economics

with Claire Friedland

1. Introduction

Citations are an external, objectively (more or less!) measurable characteristic of the writings of scholars, and that alone is enough in this quantitative age to incite their study. These citations could be ceremonial and stereotyped, so that they displayed the acknowledgments that good manners decreed. In fact our manners are not that uniform, and citation analyses have shown that citations are measures of intellectual influence and of the development of subjects.

The quality of a scholar's work is properly related to frequency of its citation by his colleagues. Thus, the Coles found that in 1961 the average physicist was cited 5.5 times, those who received the Nobel prize between 1956 and 1960, 42 times, and those who would shortly be receiving the prize between 1961 and 1965, 62 times.[1] Price theory is scientifically more mature than monetary and fiscal theory; this is confirmed by the greater commonality of the citations by doctorates of different universities in the former field than in the latter.[2]

We shall study a variety of characteristics of the citation practices of economists since 1885. We shall compare the citation practices of prominent economists (measured by professional office) and the less prominent. We shall explore the little-studied characteristics of citations to books versus those to articles. The inevitable list of most cited economists will be presented, and we shall examine the influence of volume of publications on the frequency with which an economist is cited. Finally, we shall look at self-citation and the changing role of foreign languages in economic citations.

Reprinted from *History of Political Economy* 11 (1979). © 1979 by Duke University Press, Durham, N.C.

We are indebted to David F. Mitch and Stephen R. Weisbrod for invaluable assistance in collecting the citation data.

1. Jonathan R. and Stephen Cole, *Social Stratification in Science* (Chicago, 1973), p. 22.
2. G. Stigler and Claire Friedland, "The Citation Practices of Doctorates in Economics," *Journal of Political Economy*, June 1975 [chap. 17, below].

The sample of articles, taken from the AEA *Index of Economic Journals*, whose citation practices we describe, is summarized in Table 1.1.

Table 1.1. *Numbers of Economists, Articles, and Citations Included in the Study*

	Period I:[a] 1886–1925	Period II:[a] 1925–1969
A. Presidents (Presidents of AEA and Clark Medallists)		
Number of authors	42	44
Articles sampled	76	97
Works cited:		
Articles	148	458
Other	390	683
Total	538	1141
B. Other economists (random sample excluding A)		
Number of authors	47	47
Articles sampled	76	97
Works cited:		
Articles	137	275
Other	351	408
Total	448	683
C. Average citations per source-article		
Presidents	7.08	11.76
Other	6.42	7.04
D. Percent journal citations to total citations		
Presidents	27.5	40.1
Other	28.1	40.3

[a]Throughout the article we write time and other class intervals, such as 1886–1925, to mean from (including) 1886 to, but not including, 1925.

The sample incorporates several basic decisions:
1. Because each citing article must be analyzed with respect to its citations, limitations of resources dictated samples which did not permit classification by shorter time periods or more than two levels of professional prominence of the authors of the citing articles.
2. The unit of citation was the author-work: all references in an article to Smith's *Wealth of Nations* would be counted as *one* citation, and a reference to his *Moral Sentiments* would be counted as a second citation. Only references appearing in footnotes and bibliographies, but not in sources of statistical tables, are treated as citations. For an analysis of the reason for prefer-

ring "at least one" citation to counts of citations, see our previous article (note 2 above).

3. Two groups were sampled: Presidents (and Clark Medallists) of the American Economic Association, who will be referred to simply as Presidents) and other economists. A limit of 9 articles (randomly chosen) by any one author was allowed in the sample, stratified by age-period for the "Presidents' group and, for the "other" group of economists (for whom biographical information is often unavailable), stratified by publication period.[3]

2. Articles and Books

The historian of economics encounters relatively few famous articles, in contrast to books, in the period up to, say, 1870: none by Smith or Ricardo or Cournot, few by Malthus and Senior (although some by Mill and McCulloch). Partly this was a difference of detail, for the pamphlets of the time were often written and published with a speed that arouses the envy of present-day authors. Not much of the economics of the period would be lost if all articles published before 1850 were destroyed, but one suspects that a great deal would be lost if the articles since 1930 were destroyed.

The convenience of analyzing articles, and the inconvenience of analyzing books, reinforce and no doubt greatly exaggerate this impression. The articles since 1886 are presented and classified in the *Index of Economic Journals*, and *current* analyses of citations in articles are rendered easy by *Social Science Citations*, which since 1973 has recorded all citations in all articles appearing in some 100 economic journals.

Books have declined relative to journal articles as the form of initial publication of economic work since, one would estimate, roughly 1885. Since that time there has been a continuous increase in the number of journals devoted to professional (academic) economics. The date of

---

3. For the "Presidents" group, no more than three articles were drawn from each of the individual's age periods: under 40, 40–60, 60 and over. With these restrictions our sample is 76 articles in 1886–1925 and 97 in 1925–69. For the "other" group, authors were chosen at random from the *I.E.J.* author sections within the before and after 1925 classes (Periods I and II, respectively). The year 1925 was chosen as the start of Period II for convenience in using the *I.E.J.* volumes. The sample size precluded the use of finer time divisions in most of our analyses. In Period II, for approximately half of the authors chosen our selection rule was mistakenly applied to the author of a randomly chosen article, rather than to a randomly chosen author, and hence more prolific economists were somewhat oversampled in this period: this bias is quantitatively unimportant in most uses we make of the data. A maximum of 3 articles per "other" author was included for Period I and a maximum of 9 for Period II, with a limit of not more than 3 articles from each of the sub-periods, 1925–40, 1940–55, and 1955–69; the total numbers of articles chosen in Periods I and II for this group are the same as for the Presidents. For both groups, we excluded obituaries, review articles, rejoinders, and survey articles.

initial publication of the journals indexed by the *Index of Economic Journals* (*I.E.J.*) is compiled in Table 2.1. If foreign-language journals were included we would be able to increase the relative numbers in early years, but the pattern of growth would not be much affected. We do not have a corresponding count of publication of books on economics, but their relative decline is suggested by some sample tabulations given later (Tables 2.4 and 2.5), and also by the time classification in Table 1.1: the percentage of citations to journals increased by a half between the two periods. An appreciable share of contemporary books are collections of previously published articles.

Table 2.1. *Number of English-language Economic Journals Indexed in the I.E.J. by Year of Initial Publication*

Year of Initial Publication	Number of Journals
Before 1890	3
1890–1900	2
1900–1910	0
1910–1920	4
1920–1930	11
1930–1940	11
1940–1950	15
1950–1960	22
1960–1968	31
	99

Whether the citation patterns we shall discuss would be affected by the inclusion of a proper sample of books is something only further research can determine. (The citation practices in famous books in economics would be a suitable and interesting way of beginning the study of citations in books.)

The converse problem is the comparative citation *to* books and articles by the journal articles comprised in our sample. We see at least one good reason for distinguishing between the two types of citations. The journal article is generally more specialized than a book, and the period between writing and publication is on average possibly one-half to one-fifth as long as the corresponding period of gestation for a book, putting aside G. D. H. Cole and Seymour Harris. Hence the journal article represents a different style of research both in scope and pace, one in which currency, competition, and controversy are more prominent. Indeed, with the Xerox circuit of papers in the major universities, even journal publication is becoming a sort of public certification of a paper's existence.

These differences between books and articles in their currency may be correct, but the differences apparently do not lead to large differences in the ages of cited articles and books at the time of citation. For three

Table 2.2. *Age of Citations*

	AER Dec. 1975	JPE Dec. 1975	QJE Nov. 1975
Number of citations to			
Books	83	50	27
Articles	226	124	89
Age of citations (years), Average			
Books	12.4	13.2	12.5
Articles	8.7	9.0	11.5
Standard deviation			
Books	12.9	10.9	10.9
Articles	9.2	9.7	13.0

recent journal issues we have compiled the average age of the citations to works written after 1899 (Table 2.2).

We have examined the relative frequency of citations to journal vs. non-journal sources in the articles constituting our basic sample (see Table 2.3). Citations to non-journal sources include much more than books, of course: pamphlets, government publications with authors, etc.[4] Except in the most contemporary (fashionable?) of fields such as economic theory, non-journal sources are still the dominant type of citations.[5] It has become customary to treat journal publication as representative of all publication,[6] and Table 2.3 suggests that this is not a plausible assumption. We can give one emphatic indication of how loose the relationship is between journal and total citations when we determine the most frequently cited economists on the two bases—which will be examined at length in Section 4. For the period 1886–1925, the rank correlation between the frequency of citations to the 21 leading authorities' publications in non-journal sources and publications in journal articles was .06; for the period 1925–1969 the rank correlation was − .05 for the leading 41 authorities.[7] We may conclude that the two types of citations are poorly related among the leading authorities—a result easier

4. The present tabulations treat all citations to non-journal articles as other, or loosely, "books," but the tabulations of book publications in Tables 2.4 and 2.5 and the counts of book publications in the regressions in Section 4 are restricted to books.

5. A similar pattern of relative citation in journal articles held before 1925, so the characteristics of the subject areas that favor or disfavor journal publication seem fundamental. The sample sizes are small, especially for numbers of articles, but the stability of the general pattern (rank correlation of .83 for fraction of journal article citations in the two periods) is reassuring.

6. For example, M. C. Lovell, "The Production of Economic Literature," *Journal of Economic Literature* 11 (1973): 31.

7. In this second period, the correlation would have been somewhat better (but not large) if it had not been for the numerous citations primarily to books for Keynes, Fisher, and Marshall, and primarily to articles for Douglas, Leontief, and Samuelson.

Table 2.3. *Citations to Journal and Non-journal Sources by Selected Subject Classification of Citing Article, 1925–69*

AEA field classification	Number of Citing Articles	Total Citations	Citations to Journal Articles as Percent of Total Citations
Economic theory	59	648	50.9%
Mathematical, statistical and other tools of analysis	10	119	42.9
International economics	9	79	41.8
Agriculture	16	73	41.0
Scope and method	7	101	32.7
Industrial organization	23	134	30.6
Money, credit, and banking, exc. theory	14	109	29.4
History of economic thought	4	94	26.6
All fields	194	1824	40.2

to report than to understand. Until citations to and in books are fully explored, the existing citations studies must be considered to possess large and unknown biases.

The Output of Articles and Books

A list of "authorities"—economists selected on the basis of frequency of citation in our previous citation study plus a sample drawn for this purpose (see note 11 below)—was compiled, and the citations to these individuals are analyzed in Section 4 below. For this group we compiled complete records of economic articles published from 1886 through 1968, and nearly complete records of books published through 1968.[8] Because the book publications of economists have been relatively unstudied, the results of these inventories will be presented briefly.

The first general finding is that the number of books has been falling steadily relative to the number of articles, from 1 to 3 in the early period to 1 to 5 or more at the end. The rates of publication per publishing economist per 5-year period are reported in Table 2.4 in order to adjust for variations in both numbers of authorities and years covered. When the authorities are classified by their year of birth, the movement away from book publication is even more marked (Table 2.5). If we compare the outputs of books and of articles of individual authorities in successive periods, there is a small but persistent decline in the correlation of the two types of output.

8. The book source was Regenstein Library at the University of Chicago. Tests of Library of Congress catalogues indicate that our count is fairly complete. Only the first edition of a book is included. For some authors, Library of Congress was used to supplement Regenstein listings.

Table 2.4. *Output of Articles and Books in Economics by the "Authorities" by Period*

Period	Number of "authorities" publishing in period	Output per person publishing, adjusted to 5-yr. average rate in periods 1, 2, and 10		Ratio:
		Articles	Books	Articles/Books
1. 1886–1905	28	2.2	0.68	3.2
2. 1905–1925	46	2.8	0.72	3.9
3. 1925–1930	47	3.8	0.85	4.5
4. 1930–1935	59	4.5	0.95	4.7
5. 1935–1940	72	5.3	0.71	7.5
6. 1940–1945	66	5.9	0.83	7.1
7. 1945–1950	74	5.4	0.77	7.0
8. 1950–1955	80	5.6	0.83	6.8
9. 1955–1960	76	5.8	0.88	6.6
10. 1960–1964	80	6.1	0.75	8.2
11. 1964–1969	72	5.2	0.94	5.5

Table 2.5. *Lifetime Output of Books and Articles, through 1968, by "Authorities" Classified by Period of Birth*

Period of Birth	Number	Mean Year of Birth	Average output per person through 1968		Ratio:
			Articles	Books	Articles/Books
1815–65	22	1850	20.5	8.2	2.5
1865–90	21	1878	46.3	9.1	5.1
1890–1915	49	1904	36.5	6.0	6.1
1915–36	28	1922	29.1	3.1	9.4

Our second finding is that even though we have restricted the selection of writers to "authorities" of probable influence, the variation in output of individual scholars is large (see Table 2.6). The average number of books published was 6.0, the standard deviation 4.7; the average number of articles published was 33.8, the standard deviation 26.0 The numbers are not very different if we restrict the measures to those who had reached age 70 by 1968—a group for whom one hopes for their sake and ours that their main contributions have been made.

3. The Leaders and the Non-followers

Our prominent economists consist of a sample of the Presidents of the American Economic Association and its Clark Medallists (we note that 5 of the 13 Medallists became Presidents by 1968); our "other" category consists of a random sample of other writers except the "authorities."[9]

9. In retrospect, our sample of Presidents might have been improved by inclusion of the kingmen of the Royal Economic Society.

Table 2.6. *Distribution of Publications of Authorities, 1886–1968 Inclusive*[a]

	Books		Articles	
Number of		Excl. Those under		Excl. Those under
Items	All	Age 70 in 1968	All	Age 70 in 1968
0–3	26	9	3	3
3–6	40	20	6	5
6–9	26	10	8	4
9–12	15	6	8	6
12–15	5	5	8	2
15–20	5	4	11	3
20–30	2	2	20	4
30–40			15	8
40–50			10	5
50–75			18	8
75–100			9	7
100 and over			3	1
Total authors	119	56	119	56

[a]Excluding economists born before 1825.

Table 3.1. *Total Articles Published in Indicated Period by Economists Sampled in Our Study*[a]

	1886–1925		1925–1969	
Number of articles	Presidents	Others	Presidents	Others
1–6	12	36	2	21
6–11	9	7	0	12
11–16	9	3	7	2
16–21	3	1	2	2
21–26	4	0	3	5
26–51	4	0	21	5
51–76	1[b]	0	7	0
76–101	0	0	0	0
Over 100	0	0	2[c]	0
Total	42	47	44	47
Mean	14.0	5.1	36.7	9.8
σ	13.7[d]	3.1[d]	23.2[d]	9.9[d]

[a]Only those economists sampled, and hence writing, in a period are included in that period's tabulation. [b]F. W. Taussig. [c]J. D. Black and P. Samuelson. [d]Calculated from ungrouped data.

The first and most obvious difference between the two groups is the number of articles they published. It is a tolerable hypothesis that fame and energy are, not cousins, but twins. Not identical twins. In any event, the articles written by Presidents are four times as numerous as those of the "randomly" chosen authors (see Table 3.1).[10]

10. Who, it will be recalled, are a moderately upward-biased selection in output relative to all non-Presidential writers (Section 1, note 3).

The subject matter fields of the articles (Table 3.2) display two well-known facts about economic writing. The first is that the Presidents write extensively in economic theory—especially in the second period, when almost half their articles are in economic theory. A related difference holds even more strongly for methodology, although here the causation may well be reversed: only Presidents can get their writings on methodology published! The corresponding emphasis of the other writers is on industrial organization, agriculture, labor economics.

Table 3.2. *Subject Fields in Which the Sampled Articles Are Written*

AEA Classification		Number of Articles				
		1886–1925		1925–1969		Grand
Code	Field	Presidents	Other	Presidents	Other	Total
1.	Scope and method	5	0	6	1	12
2.	Economic theory	17	5	47	13	92
7.	Mathematical and statistical tools	1	1	4	6	12
8.	Social accounting	0	1	2	8	11
9.	Money, credit, banking	10	7	2	8	27
10.	Public finance	7	13	2	4	26
11.	International economics	2	3	4	8	17
15.	Industrial organization	8	17	5	17	47
18.	Agriculture	2	4	5	11	22
19.	Labor economics	8	13	2	4	27
	Other	16	12	18	17	63
	Total	76	76	97	97	346

4. Who is Cited?

A master list of cited economists was prepared in the course of the study, and the frequency of citations to names on this list was compiled. This list contained 85 leading "authorities" of our earlier citation study augmented with 65 names, particularly for the earlier period, provided by a sample of articles drawn for this purpose.[11]

The mortality of fame is emphasized by the list of authorities for the two periods, given in Tables 4.1 and 4.2. Of the 1824 citations in 194 articles published between 1925 and 1968, Malthus and Petty are cited once, Walras and Ricardo twice, Adam Smith 4 times, and Cournot not at all. Of the 20 leading authorities in the pre-1925 period, only 3 (Fisher, Marshall, and Pigou) appear among the 20 leaders of the second period, and 2 (Fisher and Pigou) lived on for several decades into the later

11. A sample of 100 articles (50 by Presidents and 50 by our other authors) was drawn at random and 65 authorities were added to the master list comprising those names cited by two or more authors in this sample.

Table 4.1. *Most Frequently Cited Economists, 1886–1925*

| | Number of Citations | | |
| | | Cited by | |
Name	Total	Presidents	Other
I. Fisher	32	20	12
J. B. Clark	17	13	4
E. Böhm-Bawerk	16	11	5
F. W. Taussig	13	6	7
F. A. Fetter	12	9	3
A. Marshall	12	9	3
D. Ricardo	11	10	1
E. R. A. Seligman	11	7	4
T. N. Carver	10	5	5
F. Y. Edgeworth	9	0	9
J. S. Mill	9	7	2
A. C. Pigou	8	6	2
A. Smith	7	5	2
F. A. Walker	7	5	2
S. N. Patten	6	5	1
S. Webb	6	1	5
E. Cannan	5	1	4
H. J. Davenport	5	2	3
H. R. Seager	5	4	1
D. Friday	4	2	2
J. A. Schumpeter	4	2	2

period. Indeed not a single economist whose main work was done before 1900 except Marshall is among the top 41 for the 1925–69 period: the historic figures of economics would appear not to be personal participants in contemporary research.

There is a substantial illusion in this disappearance of famous ancestors that needs to be emphasized. A thoroughly successful contribution may become so widespread that its authorship is at first taken for granted and then forgotten. Such Marshallian concepts as "the" short run, elasticity of demand, quasi-rents, and external and internal economies have gone through these stages. Friedman's concepts of permanent and transitory incomes, and Muth's rational expectations, are more recent examples.

There would perhaps be an endless sequence of citations if they carried the history of the literature that had influenced a person. A famous article by John Clapham begins as follows:

> Picture an economist, well-educated in the dominant British school, going over a hat-factory. On the shelves of the store, the first room he enters, are boxes containing hats. On the shelves of his mind are also boxes. There is a row labelled Diminishing Return Industries, Constant Return Industries, Increasing Return Industries [1]. Above that a dustier row

Table 4.2. *Most Frequently Cited Economists, 1925–1969*

Name	Total	Presidents	Other
		Number of Citations	
		Cited by	
J. M. Keynes	32	23	9
Irving Fisher	21	21	0
P. H. Douglas	20	20	0
J. R. Hicks	20	10	10
D. H. Robertson	19	16	3
P. Samuelson	18	17	1
W. Leontief	16	9	7
G. Haberler	15	14	1
A. Marshall	15	12	3
R. M. Solow	15	12	3
A. C. Pigou	14	13	1
R. F. Harrod	13	11	2
S. Kuznets	13	9	4
J. M. Clark	12	10	2
M. Friedman	12	9	3
F. A. Hayek	12	6	6
W. A. Lewis	12	7	5
J. K. Galbraith	11	9	2
H. G. Johnson	11	8	3
A. H. Hansen	10	8	2
W. C. Mitchell	9	8	1
J. Robinson	9	9	0
R. Hawtrey	8	5	3
A. P. Lerner	8	8	0
J. A. Schumpeter	8	7	1
G. J. Stigler	8	6	2
J. D. Black	7	5	2
E. Cannan	7	3	4
E. H. Chamberlin	7	5	2
F. H. Knight	7	7	0
F. Machlup	7	6	1
N. Kaldor	7	5	2
R. Nurkse	7	3	4
T. B. Veblen	7	7	0
J. W. Angell	6	5	1
F. A. Fetter	6	5	1
W. I. King	6	5	1
H. Leibenstein	6	4	2
S. H. Slichter	6	5	1
J. Viner	6	4	2
J. H. Williams	6	5	1

The many with 5 citations are R. G. D. Allen, K. J. Arrow, S. Fabricant, W. J. Fellner, Z. Griliches, J. S. Mill, C. Snyder, F. W. Taussig, J. Tobin. Among those with 4 are J. B. Clark, A. Smith.

labelled Monopolies (with discrimination of all three degrees) in Diminishing Return Industries, Constant Return Industries, Increasing Return Industries [2].[12]

The sentence we have numbered [1] is a pious reference to Marshall—but he is not cited. The sentence we have numbered [2] is as clear a reference to Pigou—but he is not cited. Any article in modern economics which cited its direct sources would perhaps name modern articles and books, but they would soon be traced back to Marshall, and then to earlier writers. Perhaps no proposition is invoked more often in economics than that resources are allocated so that they receive equal rates of return in different uses, but never with a reference to the economist who put this proposition in the center of economics.[13]

We should notice also that the frequency of citation changes over time. In the articles sampled in this study, the percentage of articles without any citations was as high as 30 in 1886–1925, and again in 1935–45, but has since fallen to 10.3 percent in 1964–69. Correspondingly, the average number of citations in an article (including those with no citations) has risen from about 5 in the 1886–1925 period to 10.8 in 1964–69. The rise in citations marks the transition toward more formal standards of scholarship in recent times than in the nineteenth century. Economic literature is becoming more professional and more interdependent (more specialized).

Our lists of citations display a difference between American and English authorities: the Americans are usually the authors of textbooks. In the earlier period every leading name except Clark falls in the textbook class, although the fame of (say) Fisher does not rest on this basis. Even in the later period the international difference is marked. The explanation surely turns on the size of the markets for textbooks in the two countries, and the apparent need for translation between American and English.

The early list adds to our confidence in the relevance of citations to influence and quality of work. Fisher was the best economic theorist in the United States in this period (and quite possibly in our history to date) and he dominates the list. But the other two premier theorists of that period were surely Marshall and Edgeworth, and it is a measure of the numerical dominance of recent literature by American economists, we believe, that they are not ranked higher.[14] And of course our lists reflect much more than prowess in theoretical analysis, because all branches of the literature are included.

12. "Of Empty Economic Boxes," *Economic Journal* 32 (1922): 305, reprinted in *Readings in Price Theory*, ed. Stigler and Boulding (Homewood, Ill., 1952), p. 119.

13. *We* shall cite him: A. Smith, *The Wealth of Nations*, Book I, chs. 7–10.

14. The "other" economists are not biased against English or other non-American economists (if English-speaking or frequently translated), and Edgeworth is second to Fisher here.

Even with the sampling of the full list of subjects the lists are dominated by the general theorists. Only two major empirical workers, Douglas and Kuznets,[15] are among the 20 leaders in the later period—although Mitchell is the next name in the list. It is noteworthy also that not a single economic historian has made the list: they have become a separate craft.

We are naturally curious to determine why some economists are cited so much more than others. Are the citations due to the volume of writings of an authority? We seek to answer this question by examining how closely the number of citations is related to the number of books and articles that an authority has published. Thus for the 1886–1925 period we calculate the regression

$$C' = a_1 + b_2 \text{ books before 1905} + b_3 \text{ books, 1905–25}$$
$$+ \ b_4 \text{ articles, 1886–1905} + b_5 \text{ articles, 1905–25}$$

where C' is a transformation of the number of citations, namely $C' = \sqrt{C} + \sqrt{C+1}$, a transformation suited to binomial and Poisson distributions, which the distribution of number of citations approaches.[16] The results, with t-values given in parentheses, are

$$C' = 2.29 + .200 B_{\text{to }05} + .070 B_{5,25}$$
$$(1.68) \qquad (.60)$$
$$+ .064 A_{\text{to }05} - .0047 A_{5,25}.$$
$$(1.05) \qquad (.05)$$
$$R^2 = .237 \qquad n = 53$$

The coefficients have relatively large standard errors, but they form an interesting pattern. Older books are more effective in eliciting citations than recent books, and similarly with articles; presumably this result is partially a by-product of the fact that early books and articles could be cited throughout the period, whereas later items could be cited only in later articles. Judged by the earlier period, a book is three times as important as an article in eliciting citation. The low R^2 suggests that quality of publications plays a much larger role than quantity.[17]

For the later period we divide publications into three periods, to 1925, 1925–50, and 1950–69. The regression equation is

$$C' = 3.00 - .066 B_{\text{to }25} + .162 B_{25,50} - .0081 B_{50,69}$$
$$(1.28) \qquad (2.09) \qquad (.10)$$

15. Perhaps Leontief should be added, since the ratio of quantitative work to analytical work possibly exceeds unity in input-output analysis.

16. The distribution of residuals approaches normality for our longest period regressions, with this transformation. See F. Mosteller and C. Youtz, "Tables of the Freeman-Tukey Transformation for the Binomial and Poisson Distributions," *Biometrika* 4 (1961): 433, and references there cited.

17. The large positive residuals were Fisher, Böhm-Bawerk, J. B. Clark, and Ricardo, in that order.

$$+ .028 A_{\text{to}\,25} + .046 A_{25,50} - .263 A_{50,69}$$
$$(1.89) \qquad (3.73) \qquad (2.67)$$
$$R^2 = .398 \qquad n = 126$$

The curious time pattern of influence of the earlier period partly persists here also: recent books had a negligible influence on total citations, but citations of articles show regular increase of influence with recency. Except in the recent period, books have coefficients 2 to 3 times those of articles. The articles written between 1925 and 1950 are about one-sixth $(.046/.263 = .175)$ as influential as those between 1950 and 1969, which would suggest a depreciation rate of about 7.7 percent a year.[18] The residual pattern suggests that the following (in order) were most cited in excess of the regression prediction: Marshall, Keynes, Solow, and Robertson; and the following (in order) least cited relative to prediction: T. N. Carver, Black, Kalecki. The R^2 is substantially higher than in the earlier period, but still makes factors other than volume of publication more important in determining number of citations.

In order to explore the ambiguity involved in analyzing citations to people of widely different ages, a final regression was run for cumulative citations to 1969, of all authorities between the ages (in 1968) of 50 and 70, in our sample. The regression equation for this more homogeneous group is

$$C' = 2.343 + .0363 A_{\text{to}\,69} + .178 B_{\text{to}\,69}$$
$$(3.69) \qquad (2.83)$$
$$R^2 = .378 \qquad n = 48$$

and thus yields a relative weight of books to articles of 5 to 1. This equation does not differ greatly from that for all authorities.[19]

5. By Himself

Self-citation is an interesting aspect of citation practices. It would be highly unusual if a person did not cite his previous work; he is well informed of its existence and this work is often on the same subject as his present work. A sequence of articles may be the form in which a monograph on a subject is published, and then self-citation is inevitable. Moreover the self-confidence necessary to do scientific work—which is risky in proportion to its interest and potential importance—insures that the scholar does not easily disavow his previous efforts. One must of

18. $(.1749)^{1/22} = .923$, for the 22-year average difference in appearance of articles in the two periods.

19. The corresponding equation for all authorities is

$$C' = 3.237 + .0296 A_{\text{to}\,69} + .137 B_{\text{to}\,69}$$
$$(t = 4.15) \qquad (t = 3.41)$$
$$R^2 = .268 \qquad n = 126$$

course recognize that these explanations are reinforced by a desire to advertise the earlier works, which—almost every author will admit after modest persuasion—are not fully appreciated by his contemporaries.

Whatever the motives, self-citation is much practiced: one-tenth of the citations by Presidents are self-citations and among other writers the fraction is rather less (see Table 5.1). Those Presidents who cite themselves most frequently are reported by name in Table 5.2. This group does not coincide with our "authorities" (although 38 Presidents and Clark Medallists are in that group), but they surely are or were cited by other economists. Nevertheless the fraction of all citations to an author that are self-citations sometimes reaches such levels as to commend the practice of eliminating self-citations.

Table 5.1. *Self-Citation in Articles*

	Before 1925	1925–68 (incl.)
Presidents		
Total citations	538	1141
Self-citations	56	112
Percent	10.4	9.8
Others		
Total citations	488	683
Self-citations	38	53
Percent	7.8	7.8

Do more productive scholars cite themselves relatively often? We seek an answer to this question by regressing the percentage of self-citations to all citations on the total volume of publications. Since we have a count of books as well as articles, we sum the two, but experiment with various relative weights (number of equivalent articles) of books. The effect of additional book weights is negligible after a relative weight of 6 is reached:

$$\text{Percent of self-citations}$$
$$= 6.67 + .050 \ (\text{articles} + 6 \ \text{books})$$
$$(t = 2.22)$$
$$R^2 = .065; \ n = 73$$

where only those Presidents with 10 or more citations are included.[20] It is apparent that there is only a weak relationship between a scholar's output and the extent to which he cites himself. The quality of his work, the breadth of his researches, his vanity, and other factors must explain most self-citation.

20. This regression employs 446 sampled articles by Presidents (chosen as indicated in Section 1, note 3) for which self-citation practices were tabulated, including the 173 articles on which Sections 2 to 4 are based.

187

Table 5.2. *Relative Frequency of Self-Citation by Presidents,*
for 25 Most Frequent Self-Citers

Name	Birth Year	Total Citations in Sampled Articles	Percent of Citations to Self
David Kinley	1861	12	33.3%
Thomas S. Adams	1873	16	31.2
Irving Fisher	1867	94	30.9
J. W. Jenks	1856	7	28.6[a]
W. Z. Ripley	1867	18	27.8
I. L. Sharfman	1886	4	25.0[a]
John H. Williams	1887	83	22.9
Simon Kuznets	1901	73	21.9
Fritz Machlup	1902	95	21.1
T. W. Schultz	1902	96	20.8
Franklin Fisher	1934	20	20.0
P. A. Samuelson	1915	60	20.0
S. H. Slichter	1892	21	19.0
E. W. Kemmerer	1875	37	18.9
Carl C. Plehn	1870	11	18.2
Henry R. Seager	1867	11	18.2
Paul H. Douglas	1892	94	18.1
M. A. Copeland	1895	67	17.9
E. R. A. Seligman	1861	39	17.9
Frank A. Fetter	1863	86	17.4
K. E. Boulding	1910	12	16.7
Frank W. Taussig	1859	30	16.7
W. Leontief	1906	19	15.8
F. C. Mills	1892	13	15.3
J. R. Commons	1862	22	13.6

Number with 10–13.5% self-citations: 7; Number with 5–10% self-citations: 19; Number with under 5% self-citations: 32.

[a]Base < 10.

6. Which Language?

Until the 1950's the conventional requirements for the Ph.D. included a modest, not to say self-effacing, knowledge of French and German, which have since been replaced by mathematics. This change reflected more than it influenced the change in the practice of economic writing. Before 1925 one-fifth of the citations were to foreign-language sources, chiefly German and French, and in the more recent period the share has fallen more than in half (see Table 6.1).

Even these modest levels of foreign-literature citation are probably overestimates of the frequency with which English and American economists cited foreign languages. Some of the articles in our sample were written by foreigners; thus Heinrich Dietzel wrote two articles (sampled in the randomly selected group) in the earlier period, and they contained one-third of the German citations in the earlier period.

Table 6.1. *The Language of Citation*

	English	German	French	Italian	Other	Total
Presidents:						
Before 1925	435	51	32	8	11	537
percent	81.0	9.5	6.0	1.5	2.0	100.0
After 1924	1,035	51	44	7	5	1,142
percent	90.6	4.5	3.9	0.6	0.4	100.0
Others:						
Before 1925	374	52	44	1	17	488
percent	76.6	10.7	9.0	0.2	3.5	100.0
After 1924	642	19	12	8	2	683
percent	94.0	2.8	1.7	1.1	0.3	100.0
Total of Presidents and others:						
Before 1925	809	103	76	9	28	1,025
percent	78.9	10.0	7.4	0.9	2.7	99.9
After 1924	1,677	70	56	15	7	1,825
percent	91.9	3.8	3.1	0.8	0.4	100.0

Indeed we can turn the argument around: given the linguistic knowledge of the earlier economists, it is remarkable how little they cited foreign literature. In our sample there were 16 Presidents of the earlier period who had studied and often taken degrees abroad, usually in Germany: Jenks, Patten, James, Fetter, Gray, Gay, Plehn, Bogart (all the preceding, German Ph.D.'s), Seligman, Fisher, Seager, Mitchell, Dunbar, Taussig, and Farnum. They cited foreign literature only once in every 4 citations.

The decline of foreign languages in the citations in English-language articles is not mere chauvinism, for economics is now pre-eminently an English-language science. To demonstrate and to measure this trend, the language of sources cited in selected foreign-language journals has been analyzed for the three years, 1900, 1935, and 1970 (see Table 6.2). Not only has the share of English citations risen substantially over the seventy years in each journal, but also (i) English is more often cited than the native language (the German journal being the sole exception); (ii) the citations to all non-native languages except English have declined sharply and/or are near zero, though French citations appear to be holding their own at a low level in *Schmoller's Jahrbuch*. If one takes account of both citation practices and the number of journals published in each language, it is probable that over 90 percent of the cited work in economics is now English.

7. Conclusion

Two important characteristics of citation practices are established in the foregoing pages.

Table 6.2. *Percentage Distribution of Citations by Language of Source in Selected Foreign Economic Journals, 1900, 1935, and 1970*

Journal and Language	1900	1935	1970
Revue d'Economie Politique			
English	16.9%	20.8%	58.8%
French	67.5	55.0	34.9
German	15.0	13.9	1.7
Italian	.6	7.6	.3
Scandinavian	.0	.3	.0
Other	.0	2.4	4.3
(Total citations)	(360)	(331)	(347)
Schmoller's Jahrbuch			
English	5.0	31.6	30.1
French	6.9	10.0	9.0
German	82.8	57.2	59.2
Italian	.7	.0	.6
Scandinavian	1.0	.7	1.0
Other	3.6	.5	.1
(Total citations)	(419)	(402)	(691)
Giornale degli Economisti			
English	13.1	20.8	52.3
French	13.1	13.9	4.7
German	13.1	8.3	1.8
Italian	60.2	56.6	41.1
Scandinavian	.6	.4	.0
Other	.0	.0	.0
(Total citations)	(176)	(505)	(384)
Ekonomisk Tidskrift[a]			
English	15.9	30.1	79.0
French	4.3	4.1	1.3
German	40.6	12.3	.0
Italian	.0	.0	.0
Scandinavian	39.1	53.4	19.6
Other	.0	.0	.0
(Total citations)	(69)	(73)	(153)

[a]Published in English in 1970.

The first is the transitory nature of practice of citing a work. Successful scholarly work becomes a part of the corpus of the science, and its paternity is soon ignored. A few concepts are labeled with men's names, for example Edgeworth's box (but not his indifference curves), Pareto optimality, Knightian risk vs. uncertainty, and Keynesian theory. Yet even or especially when these labels become universal, they are seldom documented by specific reference to the originals (and hence seldom included in our citation counts). Almost always they eventually become distant in scope or meaning from the original usage.

The second finding is that volume of work published is a minor determinant of how often a man is cited. Perhaps if we measured article length the association would improve, because a book is definitely more influential on citations than an article. We suspect that *quality* is a larger source of the discordance between citations and quantity of publication, and our analysis of residuals from the regression equations relating the two is favorable to this interpretation. There is also an implicit hierarchy of fields of specialization in economics—witness the relative distribution of fields in the writings of the Presidents, with its heavy concentration in economic theory, and of the other economists in our sample.

17

The Citation Practices of Doctorates in Economics

with Claire Friedland

Schools of thought have been a popular concept—or perhaps one should say, label—in economic discussion. The Physiocrats, the Ricardians, the Austrians, the Marshallians, and the Keynesians are famous examples, but we are almost as willing to speak of smaller groups such as the schools of workable competition, public choice, and Chicago.

Yet the degree of harmony in the views of a group of men necessary for them to qualify as a school is not easily specified. As a field develops, a large area of agreement—made famous by Kuhn as the paradigm—comes to be shared by all qualified practitioners, whatever their "school."

Conversely, a school of scientific thought cannot be expected to display the specificity of belief and the intolerance of dissent that a religious body or a policy-oriented group will insist upon. After all, a science pays homage to originality and to independent verification, and these are engines of change. Still, in closely knit schools it is possible to make excellent predictions of a person's views on certain controversial issues simply by knowing that he is a member.

This paper began with the question: Are the major centers of graduate instruction in the United States "schools" in the sense of leaving distinctive imprints upon their doctorates? More precisely, does the graduate of Chicago differ in significant scientific respects from the graduate of Harvard? Even when we answer this second question, the source of any observed differences—whether instilled by graduate schools or due to basic attitudes which influenced their choice of graduate schools—will be largely outside our purview.

The basic approach was as follows. Lists of articles in two main areas of economic theory—value theory (as we shall term the theory of prices and resource allocation) and monetary and fiscal economics (often abbreviated by us as monetary theory)—written by doctorates from each of six major schools were compiled for the period, 1950–68[1] (table 1). Even the fifth largest school we included in each area has so few doctorates writing in these two fields that we are forced to skate on statistically thin ice.

Reprinted from the *Journal of Political Economy* 83 (1975). © 1975 by The University of Chicago.

1. One Chicago influence is already evident. Many economists would refer to these as micro- and macroeconomic theory, respectively.

Table 1. *Institutions, Doctorates (1950–55), and Articles (1950–68) Comprising the Universe for This Study*

Institution	Total Doctorates	Doctorates Publishing Articles in		Articles Published in	
		Value Theory	Monetary Theory	Value Theory	Monetary Theory
Berkeley	80	16	14	32	23
Chicago	106	26	27	82	73
Columbia	116	19	15	61	35
Harvard	225	38	32	127	77
M.I.T.	30	8	*	17	*
Wisconsin	143	*	8	*	19

*Too few for analysis.

In the course of our study other aspects of the citation practices of economists naturally arose, and even though our sample was not designed to deal with them, some preliminary inquiries were made. The most important of these additional topics is the citation practices of leading economists.

We begin with a survey of the academic backgrounds of these doctorates and their subsequent professional careers. After an examination of some problems in the use of citations, we shall then turn to our central question: the influence of choice of school on the doctorates. Thereafter we examine the relationships among the cited leading economists revealed by *their* citations.

I. The Doctorates

Our necessarily brief survey of the characteristics of the doctorates included in our study will often consider all 1950–55 doctorates from the chosen schools, not only those writing in the two subject areas included in the citation study.[2]

Who Are the Doctorates?

We begin with the baccalaureate origins of the doctorates. In general the graduate public institutions recruit primarily from public institutions and the graduate private institutions primarily from private institutions (see table 2). The segregation goes farther. In every case except M.I.T. the leading source of a graduate school is its own undergraduate college (see table 3). Perhaps the most striking characteristic of the recruitment

---

2. The biographical record on the doctorates—where they came from and where they are now—is seriously incomplete. In particular, the doctorates who never publish (a third of the total, as we shall see) and those who are not members of the American Economic Association (AEA) are poorly reported.

Table 2. *Types of Undergraduate Schools Attended by the Doctorates*
(Percentage Distribution)

Type of Undergraduate Institution	Berkeley	Chicago	Columbia	Harvard	M.I.T.	Wisconsin	Total
United States:							
Private	21.7	53.8	44.2	55.1	43.3	19.6	41.6
Public	68.1	30.2	40.7	30.9	26.7	63.8	43.0
Total U.S.	89.8	84.0	84.9	86.0	70.0	83.4	84.6
Canada	5.8	7.5	2.7	6.3	13.3	3.6	5.6
Other foreign:							
Europe	4.3	3.8	7.1	1.0	6.7	1.4	3.2
Asia...........	0.0	2.8	2.6	3.4	6.7	5.8	3.5
Total foreign ..	4.3	8.5	12.4	7.7	16.7	13.0	9.8
Total known	100.0	100.0	100.1	100.0	100.0	99.9	100.0
Unknown*	13.8	0.0	2.6	8.0	0.0	3.5	5.3

*Percent of all doctorates.

Table 3. *Leading Individual Undergraduate Schools Attended by Doctorates*

Undergraduate School	Berkeley	Chicago	Columbia	Harvard	M.I.T.	Wisconsin	Total
Harvard	1	5	3	39*	1	0	49*
Wisconsin.........	2	2	2	5	0	29	40
Chicago	1	25	2	2	0	0	30
Berkeley..........	15	2	1	2	1	0	21
CCNY...........	0	1	17	2	0	1	21
Columbia	1	1	17	1	0	0	20
Univ. of Washington	3	2	2	4	0	2	13
Univ. of Illinois ...	0	0	3	3	0	3	9
Iowa State	2	0	1	2	1	3	9
Univ. of Minnesota	2	2	4	0	0	1	9
Univ. of Texas	0	0	5	3	0	1	9
Oberlin...........	1	1	1	5	0	0	8
NYU.............	0	1	3	2	0	1	7
Northwestern......	0	4	1	1	1	0	7
Princeton	0	3	1	2	1	0	7
Brooklyn	0	1	3	1	0	1	6
Ohio State	1	3	0	1	1	0	6
Cornell	0	2	1	2	1	0	6
Swarthmore	1	0	0	4	1	0	6
Univ. of Arkansas..	0	0	0	2	0	3	5
Kansas State	0	1	0	2	0	2	5
Queens College....	0	1	3	1	0	0	5
Amherst	0	1	1	3	0	0	5
Rochester.........	1	0	0	2	1	1	5
Pomona	2	0	1	1	1	0	5

*Includes five Radcliffe B.A.'s.

Table 4. *Doctorates by Primary Field (Percentage of School Totals)*

School	Primary Field	
	Value Theory	Monetary and Fiscal Theory
Berkeley	23.4	3.1
Chicago	20.2	19.1
Columbia	20.0	14.4
Harvard......	18.9	11.1
M.I.T.	21.7	0.0
Wisconsin	11.9	23.9
Total	19.1	13.3

Table 5. *Type of Employers of Doctorates in 1969 (Percentage Distribution)*

Type of Employer	Berkeley	Chicago	Columbia	Harvard	M.I.T.	Wisconsin	Total
Academic	86.4	74.2	68.8	59.1	58.6	63.9	66.8
Business	6.8	7.2	10.7	13.4	24.1	7.3	11.0
Government.....	3.4	11.3	5.4	18.8	10.3	12.1	12.3
Nonprofit	1.7	3.1	6.4	3.4	3.4	3.6	3.7
All other........	1.7	4.1	8.6	5.2	3.4	13.2	6.3
Total known...	100.0	99.9	99.9	99.9	99.8	100.1	100.1
Unknown*	27.5	8.5	19.8	7.6	3.3	42.0	18.7

*Percent of all doctorates.

patterns is that geographical proximity could explain a large fraction of the pairings of undergraduate and graduate schools.

The graduate schools differ substantially in the distribution of students among major fields, so the restriction of our study to articles in value theory and monetary and fiscal theory has a large influence upon the share of doctorates of each school represented in the citation study. The distribution of doctorates by the primary fields in which they work is shown in table 4.[3]

In 1969 the differences among schools in the type of employment of doctorates was surprisingly large (table 5). Only one Berkeley doctorate in 30 entered government service, but almost one in five from Harvard did so. A fourth of M.I.T.'s small number of doctorates entered business, against only one-fourteenth for Berkeley, Chicago, and Wisconsin.

The differences among schools would have been modified if our information had been more complete. Our chief source has been the

3. The classification is based upon self-description in the 1969 *Handbook* of the AEA, supplemented by assignments on the basis of publications and 1964 *Handbook* self-descriptions. The categories of "Value Theory" and "Monetary and Fiscal Theory" are described in the *Handbook*. Figures are percentages of all doctorates with information available.

Table 6. *Leading Academic Affiliations of Doctorates in 1969 by Individual School*

1969 Affiliation	Berkeley	Chicago	Columbia	Harvard	M.I.T.	Wisconsin	Total
Berkeley	3	1	2	2	1	...	9
Chicago	...	6	...	...	...	...	6
Columbia	...	2	6	2	1	...	11
Harvard.........	1	...	1	7	...	...	9
M.I.T.	...	1	2	2	2	...	7
Wisconsin	4	1	2	2	1	4	14
CCNY	1	1	6	1	...	...	9
Univ. of Illinois ..	1	2	1	2	...	2	8
Univ. of Michigan.	2	...	3	2	1	...	8
Northwestern	1	3	...	1	1	1	7
NYU	...	...	3	3	...	1	7
Univ. of Washington....	3	2	...	...	...	1	6
Yale............	...	...	...	5	1	...	6
Miami Univ......	...	1	...	1	...	3	5
Univ. of Missouri	1	...	...	1	...	3	5
Rutgers	...	...	4	1	...	...	5
Pittsburgh	...	1	1	1	1	...	4
Princeton........	...	1	...	3	...	...	4
Stanford	...	1	...	3	...	...	4
UCLA	1	1	...	2	...	...	4
Wayne	...	2	...	1	...	1	4

Handbook of the American Economic Association (AEA), but this has been supplemented by alumni records of several universities. This latter source suggests that those not belonging to the AEA are much more likely to be in business, government, and other professions or deceased or retired, and less likely to be in academic work.[4] The information on doctorates was especially incomplete for Wisconsin and Berkeley, and appreciably so for Columbia. For Columbia, we can employ the occupational distribution from alumni records to distribute the unknown group; this procedure yields a slightly lower academic percentage, about 65. Alumni information is not available for Berkeley or Wisconsin but we infer that with fuller information these schools would have relatively fewer academicians, so Berkeley would approach the other schools and

4. The differences are illustrated by the percentage distribution by occupation from the two sources:

	AEA *Handbook*	Alumni Records
Academic	74.8	44.0
Business	10.2	16.0
Government	10.5	23.0
Nonprofit bodies	3.8	4.0
Other professions	0.0	5.0
Retired or deceased	0.7	8.0

Wisconsin fall below them in this area. Similarly, the share of doctorates of each school in business and government would probably have become less unequal.

The two-thirds of the doctorates who enter academic life are more widely dispersed among schools than they were in their undergraduate days. Nevertheless there is a marked penchant of the schools to hire their own doctorates. In our sample there is only one exception to the rule that the graduate school attended is the largest single employer of its doctorates (see table 6). The explanation for this home recruitment is probably that the information possessed about one's doctorates is much more intensive and reliable than that provided by other schools. This argument applies primarily to young doctorates, but it is also true that an assistant professor at any school has 10 or 20 times as large a probability of promotion at that school as a comparable scholar elsewhere.

The detailed analysis of geographical location of doctorates confirms the belief that there is a certain regionalism in the academic market: 52 percent of the Harvard doctorates were (in 1969) teaching in schools in the northeast; 46 percent of the Berkeley doctorates were in the west; 55 percent of Wisconsin doctorates were in the north central area; etc. A strikingly similar geographical segmentation held for the baccalaureate origins of the doctorates, so one may assert that there is a surviving element of the doctrine of noncompeting groups.[5]

Publication by the Doctorates

The total number of doctorates conferred by the schools during 1950–55 is reported, together with their aggregate journal publications during 1950–68, in table 7. The enumeration of publications is a trifle chauvinistic because we are limited to English-language journals, but apparently correction for this distortion would be minor.[6]

5. The full tabulation is

Ph.D. Institution	Region	Percentage of Doctorates Who Were Located in Region as	
		Undergraduates	College Teachers
Berkeley	West	53.2	46.0
Chicago	North central	56.1	41.5
Columbia	North east	61.5	62.7
Harvard	North east	49.4	52.4
M.I.T.	North east	42.9	46.2
Wisconsin	North central	61.7	55.1

6. Columbia gave 13 doctorates to students with foreign-language degrees, but eight of the 13 remained permanently in the United States. The fraction of foreign-language degree holders was similar in M.I.T. and Wisconsin (12%–14%) and somewhat smaller in Berkeley, Chicago, and Harvard (4%–8%).

Table 7. *Journal Publications of All Doctorates from Selected Schools, 1950–68*

	Berkeley	Chicago	Columbia	Harvard	M.I.T.	Wisconsin
Doctorates, 1950–55..	80	106	116	225	30	143
No. publishing at least one article........	58	79	82	153	18	68
% publishing at least one article........	72.5	74.5	70.7	68.0	60.0	47.6
Total articles per doctorate:						
All doctorates	4.65	5.56	3.66	4.94	4.17	2.06
Doctorates with publications	6.41	7.46	5.18	7.26	6.94	4.32
No. of articles published........	372	589	425	1,111	125	294
% of articles in value and monetary theory	14.8	26.3	22.6	18.4	N.A.	N.A.

The fraction of doctorates who publish is large in the major schools: about two-thirds publish at least one article. The articles per doctorate are highest for Chciago graduates, nearly equal for Berkeley, M.I.T., and Harvard graduates, and at a much lower level for Wisconsin doctorates— only the last difference is statistically significant.

The inequality among doctorates is immense (tables 8, 9). In the fields of value and monetary theory, half of those who published published only one article; the corresponding figure for articles on all subjects is 21 percent. The most prolific two doctorates wrote 13.8 percent of the

Table 8. *Doctorates by Total Articles Published on All Economic Subjects, 1950–68*

	Doctorates						
Articles	Berkeley	Chicago	Columbia	Harvard	M.I.T.	Wisconsin	Total
0	22	27	34	72	12	75	242
1	10	14	24	26	1	23	98
2	5	4	10	20	5	10	54
3	2	14	12	15	0	9	52
4	9	6	5	15	0	5	40
5	7	6	4	11	0	4	32
6–10	16	17	15	28	8	10	94
11–15	4	9	10	22	3	5	53
16–20	3	3	0	8	1	1	16
21 and over*	2	6	2	8	0	1	19
Total..........	80	106	116	225	30	143	700

*Doctorates with maximum number of articles published are as follows: Berkeley, K. Fox, 22; Chicago, E. Mishan, 41; Columbia, K. Arrow, 36; Harvard, R. Solow, 44; M.I.T., G. Strauss, 18; Wisconsin, R. Lampman, 26.

Table 9. *Doctorates by Articles Published in Value and Monetary Theory, 1950–68*

Articles	Berkeley	Chicago	Columbia	Harvard	M.I.T.	Wisconsin	Total
Value theory:							
1	8	13	8	16	4	...	49
2	5	3	5	6	3	...	22
3	...	3	3	3	...	...	9
4	1	2	1	4	...	...	8
5	2	1	...	1	...	...	4
6–10	...	3	1	6	1	...	11
11–15	...	...	...	2	...	...	2
16–20............	...	1*	...	...	...	...	1
21 and over	...	...	1†	...	...	...	1
Total...........	16	26	19	38	8		107
Monetary and fiscal theory:							
1	9	10	8	20	...	7	54
2	3	6	4	2	...	...	15
3	1	4	1	4	...	...	10
4	...	3	1	...	...	...	4
5	1	1	...	2	...	...	4
6–10	...	3	...	4	...	...	7
11–15	...	...	1	...	...	1	2
Total...........	14	27	15	32		8	96

*Mishan, 20 articles.
†Arrow, 24 articles.

articles in value theory, and the top 15 (of a total of 107) wrote 45.8 percent of the articles; the corresponding percentages in monetary and fiscal theory were 10.6 and 46.3 (and a total of 96 doctorates). If egalitarianism ever reaches the domain of scholarly research, the journals will fall into evil days.

Our study covers approximately a half-life of the doctorates—an average of 16 years of publication. Writing and not writing are both strongly habit forming, so the skewness of the profile of publication will increase with time.

The skewness of the distribution of articles of the doctorates raises a troublesome question in measuring attributes of the citations of the doctorates. Should we reckon Mishan the equal of 17 less prolific Chicago doctorates, or Arrow the equal of 15 less prolific Columbia graduates? We shall generally employ a method of counting citations (described below) which does not allow multiple citations from one article but allows each article an equal voice. Some comparisons with the one-man one-vote methods of measurement will also be made.

II. The Citation Approach

The citation practices by and toward a scholar are becoming a popular source of information on his intellectual debtors and creditors. Citations are of course a fallible index for any one person: styles of citation vary enormously. The erudite scholar (rightly or wrongly associated with an older Germanic tradition) who displays his learning in his footnotes is hardly recording the strong intellectual influences which have acted upon him. The ostensibly casual scholar (surely trained at Oxbridge) considers citation beyond a name, preferably misspelled, to be a pedantical display. The scholars of all schools are united in their penchant for citing themselves. Some men are careful not to cite their greatest debts. All such differences, one is entitled to believe, are much reduced in magnitude when we combine the citation practice of a substantial number of scholars, as we shall do.

To say that individual idiosyncrasies are submerged in a statistical aggregate is not to say that the aggregate is a correct measure. The nature of intellectual influence is most varied. The direction and, perhaps, the extent of influence are reasonably clear when we follow Friedman and employ permanent and transitory income concepts in a study, or invoke Samuelson on revealed preference. An innovator's work is accepted and used by others. The influence may be most powerful when we simply do not cite at all, and Marshall's theory of long- and short-run equilibrium prices is a fine example. Economists constantly use this distinction, often unaware not only that Marshall introduced it into economics but also that its empirical significance has not been established by Marshall or anyone else. Citation analysis probably works best for fairly recent work which has not had time to be fully absorbed within the literature.

We do not wish to exaggerate the possible weaknesses of citations as a measure of influence. Controversy attracts attention and hence citations, and attention influences scholars. Citations are an easy way to transfer the exposition of a theory or problem from your paper to someone's else, so in the larger view citations reveal a form of intellectual collaboration. To some degree citations *are* influence, for they influence the reading by readers of the citing paper.

The Domain of Citations

Two large areas of economic literature were chosen for the citation analysis: "value" theory (as we term it) and monetary and fiscal theory. In terms of the categories of the *Index of Economic Articles*, the areas covered are:

I. Value Theory
    2.1   Value, Price and Allocation Theory
    22.2   Factors of Production and Distributive Shares
    15.23 Monopoly. Concentration. Competition

II. Monetary and Fiscal Theory
  2.3 Aggregative and Monetary Theory
      (Specifically 2.30–2.33)
  9.6 Prices. Inflation. Deflation
  9.9 Monetary Policy
      (Specifically, 9.90–9.93)
 10.2 Fiscal Policy for Economic Stabilization and Growth
 10.5 Public Debt and Debt Policy
 13.3 War Finance and Stabilization Policies
      (Specifically, 13.32–13.33)

For each article (in the indexed journals) written between 1950 and 1968 by those receiving doctorates between 1950 and 1955, the number of times each economist is cited and the type of citation (favorable, unfavorable; or neutral) has been compiled. The publication period has been divided into three periods (1950–57, 1958–62, and 1963–68) in order to study the changes in citation practices—usually without significant result, perhaps because of small sample sizes. It is on this body of evidence on influence and attitude that our main study rests.

How Should Citations Be Counted?

The literal number of times a man is mentioned is one possible measure, in a given article, of the extent of his influence. It is a lax measure, since a man's name may be cited a dozen times in one paragraph on one point and then dropped. In our count of total citations we have counted all citations subject to the limitation of one citation of any authority per paragraph.

    The total number of citations, however, is not necessarily the proper measure of a person's influence. The leading doctoral citers have strong enthusiasms, so they heap large hills of citations upon favored (or disfavored!) fellow economists. That compulsive citer, E. J. Mishan, cites Hicks 66 times, Little 55 times, and Kaldor 43 times; Myron Gordon thinks often of Modigliani (55 citations); and similar things can be said of Robert Dorfman (Leontief, 41 times), Robert Strotz on Von Neumann and Morgenstern (each 31 times), etc. Some indication of this concentration of attention is given by the tabulation of leading doctorate citers in value theory in reference table 1.[7]

7. A set of the following reference tables may be obtained by writing to the authors: (1) Most Frequent Doctorate-Citers, Economic Theory, 1950–68; (2) Number of Citations in Articles on Value Theory to the Most Frequently Cited Authorities, 1950–68; (3) Number of Citations in Articles on Monetary and Fiscal Theory to the Most Frequently Cited Authorities, 1950–68; (4) Number of Articles in Price Theory Published by the Leading Authorities; (5) Number of Articles in Monetary and Fiscal Theory Published by the Leading Authorities; (6) Citations of Authorities in Price Theory of Doctorates and Authorities: Number of Articles in Which Cited (at Least Once); (7) Citations of Author-

Table 10. *Citations in Value theory*

Name	Total Citations	Citations from Three Most Frequent Citers of Each (%)
Hicks	268	50.4
Samuelson	209	39.7
Walras	160	80.0
Little	151	73.5
Marshall	107	44.9
Kaldor	83	79.5
Von Neumann	68	83.8
Stigler	67	31.1
Lange	63	79.4
Knight	49	38.8

These bursts of enthusiasm are perhaps a source only of mild surprise, but they raise a question: What kind of influence do we wish our citations to measure? We shall find that Walras is the third most frequently cited name in value theory with 160 citations, of which 93 came from Kuenne (and only 10 other of the 30 most prolific doctorate citers even mention Walras). That seems a much narrower impact than that of Alfred Marshall, who was cited only 107 times but who received only 18 citations from the most frequent citers (Mishan and H. Levin) and was cited by 17 of the 30 leading doctorate citers. There are numerous other examples of narrow and of wide circles of citation. Consider the sample from citations in value theory shown in table 10.

There are various ways in which we can choose our citation count in order to measure better the breadth of influence of the authorities. The count of number of doctorates ever citing an authority, already employed previously, seems too severe. On the other hand, if Kenneth Arrow repeatedly cites Samuelson (40 times) in various articles, that ought to count for more than his single citations of Bain and Marschak. A fully rational weighting of citations would be based upon an acceptable measure of intellectual influence, which we utterly lack.

As a compromise among the available measures, we shall use as our fundamental measure of citations the number of articles in which an authority is cited at least once. For the purpose of our primary interest, the measurement of the impact of institutional choice upon doctorates, it is desirable to have a measure of impact which does not allow a few heavy citers to overwhelm the results. The use of "at least one" citations compromises by eliminating multiple references to an authority within one article and yet allows the more prolific doctorates a louder voice,

ities in Monetary and Fiscal Theory by Doctorates and Authorities: Number of Articles in Which Cited (at Least Once).

which we believe they should have, in revealing intellectual influence.[8] When we say (table 11) that Samuelson was cited 72 times, we mean that there were 72 articles written by the doctorates in which he was cited at least once.

Favorable and Unfavorable Citations

The two graduate students who performed the citation analysis were requested to classify the citations as "favorable," "unfavorable," and "neutral"—using the last category if there was serious doubt whether a citation was favorable or unfavorable. Of the 5,581 citations they classified, some 648 were favorable and 566 unfavorable—mild contradiction of Hugh Dalton's famous remark that economists take in each other's dirty laundry to wash.

Usually a citation is easy to classify. For example, Eckstein (with Wilson) is surely being favorable toward H. M. Levinson when he states: "We are considerably indebted to the pioneer work of Levinson, who emphasized the importance of wage rounds and key bargains in his qualitative account. Levinson discovered the central significance of profits from his analysis of annual data for two-digit manufacturing industries. He also made the important negative discoveries that productivity and output changes were not significant variables in the explanation of wages" (Eckstein and Wilson 1962, p. 402).[9] Often, however, the classification taxes one's casuistical skill. Consider Hicks's review article on Patinkin, which begins by stating: "The main things I have learned from [the book] are not what the author meant to teach me" (1957, p. 278). It is not complimentary to be told that one did not understand his own message; it is complimentary for an economist to be able to teach Sir John anything—so the passage is classified as neutral. Although there is no unambiguously correct classification, we believe the classification has been fairly consistent.[10]

---

8. The count of names cited at least once is much more accurate than that of total citations. In experimental replications we found that an eligible authority was seldom omitted, but the count of citations was systematically too low by roughly 4%–5%. The top 30 names cited at least once in value theory and the top 30 names in total citations in value theory, a combined total of 35 names, has a rank correlation of .76.

9. An unequivocally unfavorable citation may be illustrated by S. C. Tsiang (1956, p. 540) on Lerner: "Abba Lerner's proof of the equivalence of the liquidity preference and loanable funds theories was achieved only at the expense of total distortion of the latter. For to establish the identity of the two theories, he interpreted the two main components of the demand and supply of loanable funds, viz., savings and investment, in the *ex post* sense in which they are always identical. This made nonsense of the loanable funds theory. . . ."

10. In a small replication of the classification of citations, the differences, which ran around 7 percent, were systematic. We consistently classified more citations as neutral and fewer as favorable than did Glen Gilchrist and Richard Ippolito, to whom we are indebted for the analyses of the citations.

Who Is Cited?

It would be possible to tabulate, in our universe of articles written by the doctorates in economics between 1950 and 1968, the frequency with which every economist (or other person) is cited. For the purpose of determining academic loyalties and intellectual affiliations, this list of potential authorities was curtailed in the interest of economy in tabulating the basic data. Accordingly, we tabulate only citations to publications of (1) members of the 1950–55 faculties of the schools under study and (2) leading figures in the literature.[11]

The selection of authorities was narrower than, in retrospect, we wish it had been. The nonfaculty authorities were compiled from fairly brief surveys of the appropriate literature. Thus Don Patinkin, one of the most cited monetary economists, was not in the list of eligible price theorists by our criterion, so citations to him were not tabulated in articles on price theory. It follows that we have excluded many citations, and in particular those to many of the faculty at schools whose doctorates are not included in our study. The omitted names, to be sure, would have appeared chiefly in the bottom halves of the distributions.

The citations by doctorates are of course not typical of the journal literature. A given age-cohort will be more homogeneous in its interests, reading, and writing than the profession at large, and this homogeneity is strengthened by the restriction to a few major schools. However, these schools produce a large share of the leading economists, and it could be argued that the citation practices of doctorates of these schools during their prime years of scientific work provide better measures of influence than a broader group would.

The citation counts are also much influenced by the immense concentration of writings and of citations in a few unusually prolific doctorates. In this respect the doctorates are not very different from the profession at large: most economists write little, a few write much; and of the writers, some cite parsimoniously and others as if every name will yield a job offer.

The frequencies of citation we shall report in the next section will inevitably invite interpretation as measures of the importance or influence of the cited authorities. This is in good part an inescapable inference. In monetary and fiscal economic theory we report as the leaders Keynes, 61 citations; Friedman, 45; Hicks, 34; Patinkin, 31; and Pigou, 31. No one can dispute that the first four of these were among the most influential intellectual leaders in this subject area in the postwar decades. (Pigou probably owed his popularity to discussions of the Pigou effect.) Yet our measures may be quite inaccurate when we drop farther down the lists. An economist, you must be reminded, was not counted among the citees, no matter how often he was cited, unless he was

11. The leading figures were identified by the frequency of citation in Ellis (1948), Haley (1952), and *Surveys of Economic Theory* (1965 and 1966).

mentioned several times in the survey articles or was on the faculty of one of the schools included in our study (five schools in each area, with four appearing in both lists).[12]

III. The Influence of Schools on Doctorates

We come at last to the citations. Let us present at once the two samples of articles which we have analyzed: those dealing with value theory and with monetary and fiscal economics. These lists of leading "authorities" (this good Victorian word must not lead us to forget that some were, to those citing them, adversaries or dunces) are presented in tables 11 and 12 on the basis of "at least one" citation per article, and the corresponding total citation lists are presented in reference tables 2 and 3. More economists are cited in articles on value theory than in those on monetary theory, so we carry the listing of names farther in the former field.

We emphasize for the last time that many distinguished names are omitted from the lists because of the nature of the criteria for inclusion. Even with this large proviso, it is safe to call the following the leaders of general economic theory so far as the doctorates are concerned:[13] Hicks, 105 citations in the two tables; Keynes, 91; Samuelson, 90; Friedman, 78; Pigou, 56. (The first four names would be the same if we used total citations; the fifth would be Patinkin.) If we had broadened our canvass to the other fields of economics, many names would have risen in relative frequency: Gardiner Means probably would have dominated industrial organization; Johnson, Metzler, Meade, Nurkse, and Viner, international trade; Slichter and Douglas, labor economics; and so on. If we had broadened the canvass to other schools, the effects are more problematical, but probably the ranking of names near the tops of the lists would be little changed.

There is enough resemblance between the lists of authorities of the various schools to suggest that there is needed only one theory of value and one theory of monetary and fiscal economics. Thus the doctorates of each of the three large schools (Chicago, Columbia, and Harvard) cited each of the 26 leading authorities on value theory and each of the 18 leading monetary and fiscal theorists. As a more summary measure of the concordance among the schools, we tabulate the correlation coefficients (calculated from $\log [C + 1]$ where C is the citation count) in table 13.[14]

---

12. The following are illustrative names omitted from our master lists in both value theory and monetary economics: Böhm-Bawerk, Eisner, Hawtrey, Houthakker, Jorgenson, Lipsey, Tinbergen, and Wicksell. In addition, Otto Eckstein and Edwin Kuh were inadvertently omitted from the monetary theory list.

13. For evidence that citations measure the *quality* of scientific output, see Cole and Cole (1973, chap. 2). The evidence seems much weaker to us than to the Coles.

14. The log transformation reduces the correlations but yields much more plausible scatter diagrams. With actual citations the regression line goes through the origin and has a slope determined by citations to a few leading authorities.

Table 11. *Articles on Value Theory in Which Authorities Were Cited at Least Once, 1950–68*

Authority	Ph.D.'s from					Five-School Total
	Berkeley	Chicago	Columbia	Harvard	M.I.T.	
P. A. Samuelson	6	15	17	27	7	72
J. R. Hicks	9	18	13	25	6	71
A. Marshall	4	16	10	14	2	46
G. J. Stigler	1	15	14	9	1	40
K. J. Arrow	0	11	5	15	2	33
M. Friedman	1	9	12	11	0	33
W. J. Baumol	4	5	6	16	1	32
J. M. Keynes	3	7	4	13	3	30
L. Walras	6	5	7	9	1	28
T. Scitovsky	3	10	5	7	2	27
F. H. Knight	5	9	7	5	0	26
F. Modigliani	0	6	3	16	1	26
V. Pareto	1	7	10	7	1	26
A. C. Pigou	2	10	5	6	2	25
W. Leontief	4	4	1	13	1	23
J. von Neumann	1	5	9	8	0	23
O. Morgenstern	0	5	9	8	0	22
R. M. Solow	3	5	4	8	1	21
N. Kaldor	2	8	2	8	0	20
O. Lange	0	3	8	7	2	20
K. E. Boulding	2	7	3	7	0	19
I. M. D. Little	0	10	5	3	1	19
H. Hotelling	0	5	5	7	0	17
H. A. Simon	0	3	6	8	0	17
A. P. Lerner	1	5	4	6	0	16
J. Robinson	5	2	1	7	1	16
J. S. Bain	0	0	8	6	1	15
T. Koopmans	2	4	5	3	1	15
J. Marschak	3	2	2	8	0	15
J. A. Schumpeter	2	1	3	8	1	15
A. Bergson	0	2	7	5	0	14
E. H. Chamberlin	2	2	2	8	0	14
J. Duesenberry	3	2	3	5	1	14
M. W. Reder	0	3	4	7	0	14
R. G. D. Allen	1	4	2	4	1	12
A. Cournot	1	1	5	4	1	12
R. Dorfman	1	1	0	9	0	11
R. F. Harrod	0	2	2	6	1	11
L. R. Klein	2	0	1	8	0	11
E. Kuh	0	1	1	9	0	11
J. Tobin	0	2	2	7	0	11
G. S. Becker	0	1	2	5	2	10
J. M. Clark	1	1	4	4	0	10
P. H. Douglas	2	2	0	6	0	10
J. T. Dunlop	0	1	1	8	0	10
O. Eckstein	0	2	1	7	0	10

206

Table 11 (*cont.*)

Authority	Ph.D.'s from Berkeley	Chicago	Columbia	Harvard	M.I.T.	Five-School Total
W. J. Fellner	1	0	0	8	1	10
L. A. Metzler	0	2	5	3	0	10
D. H. Robertson	3	4	0	3	0	10
Other persons cited: 5 or more times (39 persons)	22	52	57	115	9	255
1–4 times (75 persons)	18	28	32	70	4	152
Total (163 persons)	127	325	324	595	59	1,430

In value theory the various correlation coefficients (for the 49 leading authorities) generally fall within the range of .3 and .4, with three conspicuous exceptions: Berkeley and Columbia are uncorrelated, and Chicago and Columbia are closely correlated. In monetary and fiscal economics the correlations are lower—the first of the evidences we shall find of a lesser agreement on authorities in this branch of economics.[15]

Aside from the penchant of doctorates in citing their own faculty, to which we shall shortly turn, it is difficult to find systematic differences among the schools in citation practices. In value theory, it is possible to distinguish a set of economists who make relatively large use of mathematics: the doctorates of all schools cited them with about equal relative frequency. Again, it is possible to distinguish a set of economists who are relatively active in welfare economics: here the differences were larger, but only the doctorates from M.I.T. showed a morbid interest in the subject. Finally, if one distinguishes economists who have done extensive empirical work, they are about equally frequently cited by doctorates of each school—possibly somewhat less by those from Berkeley and M.I.T. In general this finding is in keeping with the impression held by many economists (including ourselves) that value theory is a reasonably well-defined body of knowledge which most competent economists accept.

In the monetary and fical area the differences among schools are larger. If we loosely classify a group as Keynesians,[16] there is no important difference among the doctorates of the various schools—about one-fifth of each school's citations are to this group (indeed Chicago is highest with

15. In interpreting these correlation coefficients it is desirable to note a fairly high measure of instability in the rankings. When we correlated citations of one half of the doctorates against the other half (the division being random), the correlation coefficients for 49 authorities in value theory were Berkeley .56, Chicago .28, Columbia .27, and Harvard .07!

16. Keynes, Hansen, Tobin, Lerner, Samuelson, Goodwin, Klein.

Table 12. *Articles on Monetary and Fiscal Theory in Which Authorities Were Cited at Least Once, 1950–68*

Authority	Berkeley	Chicago	Columbia	Harvard	Wisconsin	Five-School Total
J. M. Keynes	6	26	11	17	1	61
M. Friedman	1	21	14	9	0	45
J. R. Hicks............	4	13	5	11	1	34
D. Patinkin............	3	18	5	5	0	31
A. C. Pigou	1	18	6	6	0	31
A. H. Hansen	3	7	5	8	2	25
J. Tobin..............	1	8	4	8	3	24
A. P. Lerner	4	7	6	3	1	21
G. Haberler	3	1	5	11	0	20
A. Marshall	3	7	3	5	0	18
P. A. Samuelson	3	5	2	5	3	18
E. S. Shaw	3	2	5	7	1	18
J. Duesenberry	1	4	3	8	1	17
R. M. Goodwin........	2	2	1	12	0	17
J. Gurley..............	2	2	2	9	2	17
W. L. Smith...........	0	4	5	7	1	17
L. A. Metzler..........	2	8	1	5	0	16
L. R. Klein............	3	7	2	2	0	14
D. H. Robertson.......	3	5	0	5	0	13
R. M. Solow...........	1	4	3	5	0	13
W. J. Baumol..........	1	0	2	8	1	12
M. Bronfenbrenner.....	2	0	4	4	2	12
J. M. Clark............	3	3	0	6	0	12
A. Smithies............	0	3	2	6	1	12
A. F. Burns	3	1	1	4	1	10
E. D. Domar	2	3	0	5	0	10
I. Fisher	0	7	1	2	0	10
A. G. Hart............	0	2	4	3	1	10
S. C. Tsiang	2	1	1	6	0	10
R. F. Harrod	2	1	1	5	0	9
H. G. Johnson.........	1	3	1	4	0	9
J. A. Schumpeter	2	1	1	4	1	9
K. Brunner............	0	4	3	1	0	8
S. Kuznets	0	3	0	5	0	8
O. Lange..............	0	3	1	3	1	8
R. T. Selden...........	2	1	5	0	0	8
D. G. Johnson.........	3	3	1	0	0	7
F. H. Knight	1	4	0	2	0	7
T. Koopmans..........	0	3	0	4	0	7
E. R. Rolph...........	1	2	2	2	0	7
S. H. Slichter	0	2	1	4	0	7
W. J. Fellner	4	0	1	1	0	6
W. Leontief	1	2	1	2	0	6
A. W. Marget	1	2	2	1	0	6
A. E. Rees............	0	2	0	4	0	6
R. Turvey.............	0	1	1	4	0	6

Table 12 (*cont.*)

Authority	Ph.D.'s from					Five-School Total
	Berkeley	Chicago	Columbia	Harvard	Wisconsin	
J. W. Angell..........	1	1	2	1	0	5
O. Brownlee..........	0	4	1	0	0	5
J. T. Dunlop	2	1	0	2	0	5
J. K. Galbraith	1	0	1	3	0	5
E. J. Hamilton........	1	4	0	0	0	5
F. Machlup...........	0	0	0	5	0	5
L. W. Mints	0	3	1	1	0	5
A. W. Phillips	0	1	0	4	0	5
Other persons cited 1–4 times (56 persons)....	16	36	19	40	3	114
Total (110 persons)...	101	276	148	294	27	846

Table 13. *Correlation Between Schools in Citation of Authorities: Articles in Which Cited (at Least Once)*

	Chicago	Columbia	Harvard	M.I.T.	Wisconsin
Value theory, leading 49 authorities:					
Berkeley..........	.36	.07	.33	.39	...
Chicago	...	.60	.39	.42	...
Columbia	...	...	.27	.39	...
Harvard	...	...	...	.47	...
Monetary and fiscal theory, leading 54 authorities:					
Berkeley..........	.19	.31	.23	...	.21
Chicago	...	.46	.25	...	.09
Columbia	...	...	.31	...	.42
Harvard	...	...	...	...	.40

NOTE.—Correlations between $\log (C_i + 1)$ and $\log (C_j + 1)$, *where C_i is the number of* citations of doctorates from school *i*.

22.5 percent). But a similar grouping of monetarists[17] reveals large differences: one-tenth of Harvard and Berkeley doctorates cite the monetarists against one-sixth for Columbia and one-fifth for Chicago.

Parochial Loyalty

The doctorates of a school naturally cite relatively frequently the publications of the faculty of that school. Familiarity alone would lead to this result and it is reinforced by friendships and possibly by indoctrination.

17. Friedman, Patinkin, Robertson, Tsiang, Brunner, Marget, Hamilton, Mints.

Table 14. *"At Least One" Citations in Value Theory (Percentage Distribution)*

Doctorates	Authority on Own Faculty	Authority on Faculty of Other Four Schools	Authority Elsewhere
Berkeley	7.1	41.7	51.2
Chicago	13.2	26.8	60.0
Columbia	9.6	32.1	58.3
Harvard.........	13.7	31.1	55.2
M.I.T.	15.3	27.1	57.6

The same factor of familiarity—greater knowledge—leads to a preference of English economists for citing Englishmen, and similarly for Americans, as we shall see later. Knowledge probably also leads to the relatively heavy concentrations of the citations of the doctorates on the faculties of the other leading schools. To give one sample from value theory, the distribution of "at least one" citations is shown in table 14. Of course our universe of authorities excludes many economists, all outside these schools, but nevertheless the concentration of citations on the faculties of the largest producers of doctorates is substantial.

We present the cross-tabulation of doctorates by faculties in tables 15 and 16. An index of "parochialism" has been calculated as follows: (*a*) Calculate the percentage distribution of school *i*'s citations in the publications of the three other large schools, excluding citation by the doctorates of their own faculty.[18] (*b*) Average these unweighted ("expected") distributions of citations for the four large schools, and adjust to 100 percent. These are the "expected" relative frequencies of citations of the faculties of the five schools.[19] (*c*) Divide this expected percentage of citations into the actual percentage for that school's doctorates. This procedure yields an index of parochialism. For example, in value theory, Berkeley doctorates cited ("at least once") their own faculty 14.52 percent of the total citations to the five faculties. The average Berkeley faculty share in the citations of the doctorates from the other large schools was 19.20 percent, so the index (14.52/19.20 = 0.76) shows *negative* parochialism in this category. The indexes of parochialism are a trifle parochial because they rely on the doctorates' citations of faculty of other schools, but it would require a complex study of citations (perhaps by leading scholars) to improve upon them.[20] The "at least one" indexes of parochialism, together with the patterns of citations, are also given in tables 15 and 16.

18. The school with the smallest number of articles is omitted.
19. The larger schools are unweighted to reduce the influence of the largest schools.
20. See the discussion of citations by authorities, below.

Table 15. *"At Least One" Citations among Faculties of Five Schools:*
Value Theory (Percentage Distribution)

School of Doctorates	Faculty Cited					
	Berkeley	Chicago	Columbia	Harvard	M.I.T.	Total
Berkeley	14.5	32.3	8.1	27.4	17.7	100.0
Chicago	13.8	33.1	13.8	20.8	18.5	100.0
Columbia	17.0	29.6	23.0	12.6	17.8	100.0
Harvard.........	20.4	19.6	10.7	30.4	18.9	100.0
M.I.T.	12.0	16.0	8.0	28.0	36.0	100.0
Indexes of parochialism ...	.76	1.19	1.89**	1.44**	1.83*	

*Significantly different from unity at 10% level.
**Significantly different from unity at 5% level.

Table 16. *"At Least One" Citations among Faculties of Five Schools:*
Monetary and Fiscal Theory (Percentage Distribution)

School of Doctorates	Faculty Cited					
	Berkeley	Chicago	Columbia	Harvard	M.I.T.	Total
Berkeley	23.1	25.0	17.3	28.8	5.8	100.0
Chicago	3.6	61.8	10.0	23.6	0.9	100.0
Columbia	16.2	29.4	17.6	30.9	5.9	100.0
Harvard.........	9.4	24.5	10.8	51.8	3.6	100.0
Wisconsin	7.7	15.4	15.4	38.5	23.1	100.0
Index of parochialism ...	1.87*	2.05**	0.98	1.49**	4.95**	

*Significantly different from unity at 10% level.
**Significantly different from unity at 5% level.

All of the statistically reliable indexes of parochialism are above unity.[21] Harvard is consistently parochial, and Chicago (money) and Columbia (value) also strongly so. The indexes are generally high in the schools with few articles by doctorates (M.I.T. and Wisconsin). If one analyzes total citations—the tables are based upon "at least one" citations—the evidence of parochialism is usually even stronger.

When the period is divided into three subperiods, the parochial indexes become less stable but show no clear tendency to decline with the passage of time.

Parochial indexes were also calculated for doctorates publishing (1) three or less articles and (2) four or more articles. It is a plausible

21. The tests of differences of proportions from unity are not exact because it is not possible to specify the precise number of degrees of freedom: the ratios of the other three schools (whose unweighted average we use) are based upon differing numbers of citations.

Table 17. *Classification of Citations (Percentage Distribution)*

	Five Faculties	Other Authorities	Total
Value theory:			
Favorable.............	9.4	4.8	6.7
Neutral...............	84.6	86.6	85.8
Unfavorable..........	6.0	8.6	7.6
Monetary and fiscal theory:			
Favorable.............	24.1	18.2	20.6
Neutral...............	60.3	67.5	64.5
Unfavorable..........	15.6	14.3	14.8

conjecture that the more productive scholars will be less parochial because they are more extensively engaged in research—and less dependent upon their doctorate institution for academic support. No such difference was found.

The classification of citations as favorable or unfavorable (or neutral) yields further information on the intellectual associations among schools.[22] In value theory, the favorable to unfavorable citations run three to two for faculties of the five schools, about even for all authorities, and most references are neutral; opinions are much stronger in monetary and fiscal economics (see table 17). The much higher fraction of nonneutral citations is additional evidence of the controversial nature of that literature. The detailed tabulations are given in table 18.

If we accept the observed ratio of roughly three favorable to two unfavorable references as the standard, there are few important differences among the schools in value theory. Chicago doctorates are unfavorable in their references to Harvard (an attitude which Chamberlin frequently credited to Knight's influence),[23] and similarly M.I.T. doctorates are unfavorable to Chicago, but the general pattern is one of random fluctuation. In monetary and fiscal theory, as usual, the story changes. There is evident parochialism (Harvard doctorates are favorable to their faculty in 44 percent of the citations, unfavorable in 6 percent; and Berkeley is as extreme). Ideological battles are also hinted at by cross-citations: on average, Berkeley and Columbia doctorates' citations of Chicago faculty are unfavorable one-fifth to one-third of the time.

IV. The Authorities and the Doctorates

The leading authorities cited in our studies were themselves examined in some detail. A preliminary question which almost asks itself is: Does one

22. When analyzing attitude in citations, we necessarily use total citations, not the at-least-one citation base used elsewhere.

23. As an early skeptic of monopolistic competition, George Stigler can testify that Knight devoted even less time than compliments to Chamberlin so students had to read the book on their own.

Table 18. *Favorable and Unfavorable References in Citations by Doctorates* (Percentage Distribution)*

	Faculty Cited									
	Berkeley		Chicago		Columbia		Harvard		M.I.T.	
	Favorable	Unfavorable	Favorable	Unfavorable	Favorable	Unfavorable	Favorable	Unfavorable	Favorable	Unfavorable
Value theory:										
Berkeley.........	20.0	5.0	7.5	9.4	14.3	0.0	10.4	0.0	4.0	4.0
Chicago	7.1	7.1	10.9	7.3	5.6	11.1	2.0	18.0	10.6	2.1
Columbia	3.3	11.5	4.3	8.7	7.8	4.7	2.9	0.0	9.8	0.0
Harvard	16.4	7.8	8.0	6.8	8.5	2.1	10.6	4.0	15.2	2.2
M.I.T............	10.0	0.0	10.0	35.0	0.0	0.0	0.0	0.0	3.0	6.1
Monetary and fiscal theory:										
Berkeley.........	31.6	0.0	12.7	34.5	12.5	6.2	22.7	0.0	...	...
Chicago	20.0	0.0	22.6	14.5	14.3	14.3	15.6	23.4	...	...
Columbia	23.1	0.0	13.8	22.5	6.2	0.0	24.0	4.0	...	...
Harvard	38.7	32.2	27.0	23.0	13.2	21.0	44.2	6.5	...	...

*Wisconsin excluded because of sample size.

213

become an authority by writing a good deal, or is citation largely independent of writing? The omission of books from our analysis means that our answer must be somewhat partial and biased, but even a partial answer is not without interest. The numbers of articles in value and monetary theory written from 1886 to 1968 are given for each authority in reference tables 4 and 5.[24]

We expect, and observe, some correspondence between publications and citations even though the restriction of our list to leading authorities obscures the influence of publication on citations. Robert Merton has discussed the "Matthew Effect" ("For unto every one that hath shall be given . . .") in science and given it the interpretation that larger increments of recognition are given a piece of work, the more famous the author already is (Merton 1973, pp. 439–59). As he points out, the fame of the author is a valuable guide to a prospective reader in choosing from the flood of literature that which he will study. It is *not* evident that the acceptance, in contrast to the knowledge, of a piece of work is influenced by its authorship. In any event, the most cited authorities are prolific authorities: the number of articles on price theory published by the five leading authorities was 112, and in monetary economics the corresponding number was 73.

When we regress the number of "at least one" citations in price theory on price theory articles before and after 1950, we find

$$\text{citations} = \quad 11.8 \quad + \quad 0.93 \text{ articles}_{1886-1949}$$
$$(t = 2.55) \quad (2.40)$$
$$+ \quad 0.95 \text{ articles}_{1950-68} \ (R^2 = .327).$$
$$(2.78)$$

The comparable equation for citations in monetary and fiscal economics is

$$\text{citations} = \quad 8.09 \quad + \quad 1.10 \text{ articles}_{1886-1949}$$
$$(t = 2.31) \quad (3.19)$$
$$+ \quad 0.58 \text{ articles}_{1950-68} \ (R^2 = .254).$$
$$(1.69)$$

Thus the price theory citations give equal attention to publications before and after 1950 and the monetary citations place a higher weight on earlier publications, which is contrary to one's belief that articles should and do depreciate with time. Presumably, the inclusion only of authorities who are cited frequently after 1950 overcomes the depreciation of articles. The linearity of the relationship between citation and publications has also been examined, and there is a trace of increasing returns to articles.

24. We omit a few names (Walras, Marshall, Pareto, von Neumann) where for reasons of language or period or discipline, the count would be meaningless. Schumpeter might have been added to this list.

The elasticity of citations with respect to articles exceeds unity after the number of articles reaches 19 in price theory and 11 in monetary theory.[25]

The individual schools do not differ much in the citations of their doctorates with respect to articles published by authorities. In price theory the correlation coefficients for individual schools range from .431 (Columbia) to .601 (Berkeley); in monetary economics the level is lower and the variation wider (from .189 [Berkeley] to .432 [Chicago]). The lower influence of publications upon citations in monetary and fiscal economics than in price theory is in keeping with our consistent finding of greater variability of relationships in the former field.[26]

Relationships among Authorities

The citations of active authorities (those writing after 1950) on each other were studied with a view to discovering what might be called allies and antagonists in scientific work. The hypothesis we propose is that numerous citations, unless they are heavily unfavorable, reveal allies, especially if they are reciprocated. The relationships between authorities have usually been easy to classify even on this simple hypothesis.

First let us begin with the simple relationships. We deem the following to be clear cases of allies (all in price theory):

1. Samuelson (1)-Solow (2). Let $_1C_2$ be citations of (2) by (1). Let F be percent favorable, U percent unfavorable. Then

$$_1C_2 = 20\,(F = 10; \quad U = 0),$$
$$_2C_1 = 19\ (F = 15.8; U = 0).$$

2. Arrow (1)-Solow (2):

$$_1C_2 = 6\,(F = 0; \quad U = 0),$$
$$_2C_1 = 9\,(F = 22.2; U = 0).$$

3. Arrow (1)-Samuelson (2):

$$_1C_2 = 40\,(F = 10.0; U = 0),$$
$$_2C_1 = 20\,(F = 15; \quad U = 5).$$

---

25. For the entire period, 1886–1968, the equation in price theory is:

$$\text{citations} = 26.7 - 1.54 \text{ articles} + 0.073 \text{ (articles)}^2 \ (R^2 = .531),$$
$$\quad\quad (4.50)\ (1.96) \quad\quad\quad (3.30)$$

In monetary economics, there is no relationship for the entire period, but a strong one on publications before 1950, which follows:

$$\text{citations} = 17.0 - 1.24 \text{ articles} + 0.13 \text{ (articles)}^2\ (R^2 = .354),$$
$$\quad\quad (5.94)\ (1.51) \quad\quad\quad (2.87)$$

where the articles are those published 1886–1949.

26. In both areas the correlations are consistently higher for "at least one" citations than for total citations, which reinforces our arguments for the former measure.

Probably one should add two pairs:

4. Hicks (1)-Samuelson (2):

$$_1C_2 = 8\,(F = 12.5; U = 12.5),$$
$$_2C_1 = 56\,(F = 12.5; U = 16.1).$$

5. Bergson (1)-Little (2):

$$_1C_2 = 9\,(F = 33.3; U = 11.1),$$
$$_2C_1 = 6\,(F = 0; U = 0).$$

The clear instances of antagonistic relationships are more numerous if the following qualify:

1. Samuelson (1)-Lerner (2):

$$_1C_2 = 16\,(F = 0; U = 12.5),$$
$$_2C_1 = 28\,(F = 0; U = 67.9).$$

2. Samuelson (1)-Kaldor (2):

$$_1C_2 = 23\,(F = 0; U = 13.0),$$
$$_2C_1 = 10\,(F = 0; U = 70.0).$$

3. Solow (1)-Kaldor (2):

$$_1C_2 = 13\,(F = 0; U = 7.7),$$
$$_2C_1 = 5\,(F = 0; U = 60).$$

4. Solow (1)-Robinson(2):

$$_1C_2 = 7\,(F = 0; U = 42.9),$$
$$_2C_1 = 18\,(F = 0; U = 66.7).$$

5. Arrow (1)-Bergson (2) (not reciprocal):

$$_1C_2 = 16\,(F = 6.2; U = 0),$$
$$_2C_1 = 56\,(F = 0; U = 48.2).$$

6. Arrow (1)-Little (2):

$$_1C_2 = 26\,(F = 11.5; U = 61.5),$$
$$_2C_1 = 30\,(F = 0; U = 50).$$

7. Kaldor (1)-Hicks (2):

$$_1C_2 = 10\,(F = 0; U = 50),$$
$$_2C_1 = 6\,(F = 16.7; U = 33.3).$$

8. Samuelson (1)-Robinson (2):

$$_1C_2 = 15\,(F = 0; U = 6.7),$$
$$_2C_1 = 7\,(F = 0; U = 42.9).$$

There are too few cross-citations to allow analysis of most other possible pairs.[27]

We emerge with two sets of allies. The Cambridge (U.S.) group of Arrow, Samuelson, and Solow are consistently together and are consistently opposed by the Cambridge (England) group of Kaldor and Robinson. Hicks comes much closer to the American Cambridge. In addition, if we analyze pairs for which there are considerable cross-citations but less than the number (four each way) required above, we can distinguish several additional groups of allies:

1. The monopolistic competition school, including Bain, Chamberlin, Modigliani, and Steiner.[28]

2. An input-output (and related branches) group, containing Dorfman, Leontief, Solow.[29]

3. A vague hint of what others call the Chicago school (although Stigler is classified as Columbia): Becker, Friedman, and Stigler.[30]

In addition, a few clear antagonisms are revealed.[31]

We may combine citations of doctorates to the various groups we have distinguished in price theory, and this is done in table 19. It becomes apparent that the input-output area received chief attention from Berkeley and Harvard, and little elsewhere; and the exclusive appeal of monopolistic competition to Harvard is even more striking. The polarity of citations for Harvard and M.I.T. on the one hand and Chicago on the other is conspicuous, with Columbia in an ambiguous position between them.

27. The Solow (1)-Hicks (2) pairing is essentially neutral ($_1C_2 = 3$, $_2C_1 = 5$, all but one of eight citations neutral); and similarly for Arrow (1)-Baumol (2) ($_1C_2 = 4$, $_2C_1 = 5$, on balance favorable); and Samuelson (1)-Little (2) ($_1C_2 = 8$, $_2C_1 = 4$, favorable on average).

28. Letting Bain, Chamberlin, Modigliani, and Steiner have respective numbers 1, 2, 3, and 4:

$$_1C_2 = 9\,(F = 77.8); _2C_1 = 1\,(F),$$
$$_2C_4 = 12\,(F = 33.3; U = 8.3); _4C_2 = 1\,(F),$$
$$_3C_1 = 30\,(F = 33.3; U = 13.3).$$

29. Letting Dorfman = 1, Leontief = 2, and Solow = 3:

$$_1C_2 = 35\,(F = 8.6; U = 5.7),$$
$$_3C_1 = 9\,(F = 33.3),$$
$$_3C_2 = 20\,(F = 5; U = 5).$$

30. Letting Becker = 1, Friedman = 2, and Stigler = 3:

$$_1C_3 = 9\,(F = 22.2),$$
$$_2C_3 = 3\,(F = 66.7).$$

31. Bain-Stigler: $_1C_2 = 8\,(F = 0; U = 50)$,
Chamberlin-Kaldor: $_1C_2 = 10\,(F = 10; U = 80)$,
Samuelson-Scitovsky: $_1C_2 = 27\,(F = 7.4; U = 59.3)$,
Hirshleifer-Friedman: $_1C_2 = 18\,(F = 0; U = 50)$.

Table 19. *Citations to Groups of Allied Economists in Price Theory: Favorable and Unfavorable (Percentage Distribution)*

Cited Group	Doctorate					
	Berkeley	Chicago	Columbia	Harvard	M.I.T.	Total
Cambridge (U.S.) (Arrow, Samuelson, Solow)	(19)	(77)	(74)	(133)	(35)	(338)
Favorable	0.0	5.2	9.5	21.1	2.9	11.8
Unfavorable	0.0	11.7	1.4	0.8	5.7	3.8
Cambridge (England) (Kaldor, Robinson)................	(10)	(48)	(4)	(46)	(3)	(111)
Favorable	0.0	0.0	0.0	2.2	0.0	0.9
Unfavorable	0.0	0.0	0.0	8.7	0.0	3.6
Monopolistic competition (Bain, Chamberlin, Modigliani, Steiner)	(8)	(38)	(35)	(151)	(4)	(236)
Favorable	12.5	7.9	2.9	13.2	0.0	10.6
Unfavorable	0.0	21.1	2.9	21.9	0.0	17.4
Input-output (Dorfman), Leontief, Solow)	(50)	(13)	(17)	(90)	(4)	(174)
Favorable	10.0	15.4	11.8	21.1	0.0	16.1
Unfavorable	2.0	0.0	0.0	6.7	0.0	4.0
Chicago-Columbia (Becker, Friedman, Stigler)..........	(2)	(48)	(85)	(49)	(19)	(203)
Favorable	0.0	12.5	4.7	6.1	10.5	7.4
Unfavorable	0.0	2.1	15.3	12.2	36.8	13.3

NOTE.—Number of citations in parentheses.

The monetary authorities seldom fall into well-defined groups. We can distinguish only a few allies:

1. Metzler-Haberler:

$$_1C_2 = 13\,(F = 0; \quad U = 7.7),$$
$$_2C_1 = 10\,(F = 40; U = 0).$$

2. Hicks-Johnson:

$$_1C_2 = 3\,(F = 0; \quad U = 0),$$
$$_2C_1 = 9\,(F = 22.2; U = 0).$$

3. Hansen-Samuelson:

$$_1C_2 = 3\,(F = 33.3; U = 0),$$
$$_2C_1 = 8\,(F = 37.5; U = 0).$$

If we do not require reciprocal citation,[32] we may tally the allies and opponents of Keynes as shown in table 20. The list illustrates a limitation

32. In the preceding pairs we require at least three citations in each direction.

Table 20. *Citations of Keynes by Authorities*

Citer	N	Favorable (%)	Unfavorable (%)
Lerner	33	6.1	0
Hicks	28	17.9	0
Tobin	20	10.0	0
Harrod	14	21.4	0
Robertson	16	12.5	6.2
Hansen	44	9.1	6.8
Metzler	18	0	0
Smith, W.	12	0	0
Bronfenbrenner	18	5.6	11.1
Friedman	26	11.5	15.4
Johnson	51	3.9	19.6

of citations. The great dispute between Keynes and Robertson was conducted primarily outside the journals.

A comparable tabulation for Friedman (table 21), the leading monetarist, forms an interesting companion. The Keynes and Friedman lists clearly classify Lerner and Tobin, and probably Klein (no citations of Keynes) and Harrod (no citations of Friedman) as Keynesians and non-monetarists. The monetarists, non-Keynesians are Bronfenbrenner, Brunner, Friedman, Johnson, and Selden. We combine the citations of the doctorates to these two groups in table 22.

The Chicagoans pay great, and only moderately unfavorable, attention to the Keynesians, but all other schools are predominantly favorable. The monetarists are accorded somewhat less attention, but only two schools (Columbia and Harvard) are on balance modestly unfavorable to these authorities. (It is apparent from our tabulations that the English economists in our sample were strongly favorable to Keynes and largely ignored the monetarists.)

Comparison of Citations by Authorities and Doctorates

The citations of the 30-odd leading authorities on price theory and monetary and fiscal theory are available (in reference tables 6 and 7). These tables, which necessarily exclude economists not writing after 1950[33] and also self-citations, are the bases for the present section.

The citation practices of the authorities display the same heavy influence of propinquity that we find among the doctorates. If we compare

33. In price theory this includes Marshall, Keynes, Walras, Knight, Pareto, and Schumpeter. In monetary and fiscal economics the exclusions are Clark, Fisher, Hamilton, Keynes, Lange, and Marshall.

Table 21. *Citations of Friedman by Authorities*

Citer	N	Favorable (%)	Unfavorable (%)
Bronfenbrenner.....	20	15	0
Selden	45	17.8	4.4
Johnson............	23	43.5	13.0
Duesenberry........	9	33.3	22.2
Brunner............	98	11.2	25.5
Tobin..............	54	14.8	35.2
Lerner	8	12.5	37.5
Klein	16	0	56.2

the citation of American and English economists by American and English authorities in price theory we find:

	Citation by	
Citation of	American (%)	English (%)
American.........	71.5	48.9
English	28.5	51.1

An equal measure of chauvinism is found also in the monetary citations.[34] The only question, which we are not presently equipped to answer, is: Which country is chauvinistic? It is a plausible conjecture that the larger the relative size of a group, the more relatively (to size) that group cites itself, but we do not test that hypothesis.

There is, of course, a family resemblance between the citations of the authorities and the doctorates. The simple rank correlation coefficients are .346 for price theory and .625 for monetary and fiscal theory (based on reference tables 6 and 7).[35] The living authorities are considerably older: in 1950 they were about 45 years old on average, the doctorates' average age was 30 years. We find that with the single exception of Irving Fisher the authorities cite the older economists relatively more frequently than the doctorates do. We were inclined to explain some differences

34. The corresponding tabulation is

	Citation By	
Citation of	American (%)	English (%)
American	52.4	26.2
English	47.6	73.8

35. The rank correlation for price theory is slightly lowered by the omission of citations by eight authorities also in the doctorates group; the adjustment would be negligible for monetary theory.

Table 22. *Citations by Doctorates to Groups of Allied Economists in Monetary and Fiscal Economics: Favorable and Unfavorable (Percentage Distribution)*

Cited Group	Doctorate					
	Berkeley	Chicago	Columbia	Harvard	Wisconsin	Total
Keynesians (Keynes, Lerner, Tobin, Klein) ..	(66)	(127)	(53)	(93)	(5)	(344)
Favorable...........	22.7	12.6	20.8	12.9	20.0	16.0
Unfavorable.........	7.6	19.7	1.9	8.6	0.0	11.3
Monetarists (Friedman, Bronfenbrenner, Brunner, Johnson and Selden) ...	(15)	(66)	(105)	(39)	(12)	(235)
Favorable...........	23.1	21.2	17.1	15.4	16.7	18.7
Unfavorable.........	7.7	6.1	17.1	20.5	16.7	14.0

NOTE.—Number of citations in parentheses.

between the two rankings by the fact that one-third of the authorities were non-American whereas relatively few doctorates are non-American, but this proved not to be influential.[36]

V. Conclusion

Our foregoing analysis takes the citation as an acceptable statistical measure of influence or attitude, and we believe that this measure deserves deeper and more critical examination than it has so far received. But given its at least approximate validity in this role, citation analysis leads to the conclusion that there are genuine differences among the universities in the attention and respect paid to various scholars. Local faculty receive a perhaps inevitable preference in the students' work,[37] and the ideological preferences of the professors are communicated in some degree to the students.

The main fact, however, is that these influences are not of great strength. Especially in value theory the differences among schools are small compared with the authorities they share in common. We conjecture that larger differences would be found in the teaching of the other social sciences but presumably even smaller differences in fields such as mathematics. We know of no other studies with which such comparisons can be made, but suggest that this is a method of establishing the uniqueness and strength of a paradigm in a science.

36. The price and monetary and fiscal correlations for American authorities versus doctorates are .462 and .750, respectively.

37. We are reminded of the English mathematician G. H. Hardy, who said that to justify his existence a man had to believe in the importance of his work, and of his own capacities in this work (1957, p. 66). These beliefs are calculated to reach the student.

References

American Economic Association. *Index of Economic Articles.* Vols. 1 (1886–1924)–10 (1968). Homewood, Ill.: Irwin, 1961–71.

American Economic Association and Royal Economic Society. *Surveys of Economic Theory.* London: Macmillan; New York: St. Martin's, 1965–66.

Cole, J. R., and Cole, Stephen. *Social Stratification in Science.* Chicago: Univ. Chicago Press, 1973.

Eckstein, O., and Wilson, T. A. "The Determination of Money Wages in American Industry." *Q.J.E.* 76 (August 1962): 379–414.

Ellis, H. S., ed. *A Survey of Contemporary Economics.* Vol. 1. Homewood, Ill.: Irwin, 1948.

Haley, B. F., ed. *A Survey of Contemporary Economics.* Vol. 2. Homewood, Ill.: Irwin, 1952.

Hardy, G. H. *A Mathematician's Apology.* New York: Cambridge Univ. Press, 1957.

Hicks, J. R. "A Rehabilitation of 'Classical' Economics?" *Econ. J.*67 (1957): 279–89.

Merton, R. *The Sociology of Science.* Chicago: Univ. Chicago Press, 1973.

Tsiang, S. C. "Liquidity Preference and Loanable Funds Theories, Multiplier and Velocity Analyses: A Synthesis." *A.E.R.* 46 (1956): 539–64.

18

The Literature of Economics: The Case of the Kinked Oligopoly Demand Curve

The literature of economics is the accumulated product of innumerable economists. In a recent year nearly 6000 different economists published articles or books in English, and another (overlapping) group, possibly as large, published book reviews, pamphlets and other papers. The former group produced perhaps 800 books and 5000 articles, and the addition to the existing stock of literature in a year is on the order of 5 percent.

It is a literature that no one person could possibly read—the limits imposed by sanity are stricter than those imposed by time. Indeed it is a literature that perhaps is read by a number of economists only moderately larger than the number of writers. The best of memories can accurately recall only a tiny fraction of this literature, and if the literature were irrevocably destroyed, most of it would utterly perish from human knowledge.

Most of us, I suspect, have two very different views of this literature, views suited to different portions of the literature we have studied. There is a sweeping historical survey, in which the main stages in the evolution of the ruling theory are contemplated. To take an example, we consider the evolution of utility theory through Jevons and Walras, Pareto, Fisher, Edgeworth, Slutsky-Hicks-Allen, to Samuelson, Houthakker, and the ultra-moderns. In that account—the standard fare of histories of economic thought—the literature is dominated by major figures and major advances. The backing and filling, the digressions and confusions, the sometimes acrimonious debates, recede from memory and the major advances form the stuff of economic literature. The scores of articles on integrability conditions, consumer surplus, and the like coalesce into a few widely accepted propositions to which, if any name is attached, it is almost an adventitious christening.

There is, second, the view we hold today of the literature in which we are now actively engaged. Here if controversy is active almost every proposition seems open to debate, and the course of controversy shifts as rapidly as the situs of a fox hunt—indeed, a series of simultaneous and intersecting fox hunts. The participants are numerous, so the debate

Reprinted from *Economic Inquiry* 16 (April 1978).

I wish to express my debt to Claire Friedland for indispensable assistance. I also have benefitted from comments by Gary Becker and Robert K. Merton. An oral version of this paper was presented in April 1977 at a UCLA symposium in honor of Armen Alchian.

takes place simultaneously in many journals and a large number of economists enter the discussion. Occasionally the whole literature may have proved to be unfruitful—the theory of monopolistic competition is a truly major example—in which case the episode will never coalesce into a new example of scientific evolution described in the first view of the literature.

Of course most economic literature falls in neither category. It is not lively and rapidly shifting, because there are only a few topics which at any time capture the interest of a considerable number of active economists. It is not historical and masterly, because only a few topics achieve such scope, persistent importance, and breadth of professional acceptance and use as to dominate a generation or more of our literature. Most literature deals with the experimental, the temporarily relevant, the special (in scope) application of general knowledge, the idiosyncratic interests of writers and the whimsies of editors.

It is to this routine literature that this essay is devoted. I seek to determine why it exists,—that is, why that subject is being discussed— who is interested in the literature, how, if at all, it changes over time, and what finally terminates its course. The goal is to understand the nature of "normal" literature.

To this end, a reasonably full canvass has been taken of the literature of the kinked oligopoly demand curve. It is a literature to which I made one contribution in 1947 and then put aside as of no further interest to me. I have returned to it now with the wholly different purpose of examining the course of normal scientific literature in dealing with a particular topic. There is no way of knowing whether it is an atypical literature, since I know of no other similarly intensive study of economic literature.[1] The choice was commended to me by these attributes:

1. The literature began at a definite time—1939—and any precursor work was unknown. At least one partial anticipation was found.[2]
2. The theory of the kinked demand curve has attracted the attention of a substantial fraction of the leading economists for nearly 40 years, as we shall see. But the literature was not monopolized by prominent economists.

1. I have since been introduced by Stephen Stigler to Kenneth O. May's history of the literature of determinants, partly reported in "Growth and Quality of the Mathematical Literature," (1968–69) with additional material in "Who Killed Determinants?" (n.d.)

2. Joseph Spengler (1965) has found earlier kinked demand curves, but none has the economic content of asymmetrical oligopolistic behavior studied here. R. F. (Lord) Kahn (1937, pp. 8–9) sketched the essentials of the kinked demand theory without drawing the demand curve. But he did not accept the lower branch of the demand curve, for it violated (for him) the assumption, "the backbone of the theory of duopoly," that "no firm has any trust whatever in its competitors." A discontinuous oligopoly demand curve based upon different prices being charged by the rivals was used in R. H. Coase (1935, p. 139) "The Problem of Duopoly Reconsidered."

3. The literature is both theoretical and empirical.
4. The theory has run its course and is dying, so it is possible to treat it in a disengaged manner.

The last attribute proved, in fact, to be wholly mistaken, but I am prepared to derive some useful information about economic literature from this very fact.

I. The Genesis of the Kinked Demand Curve

This is a study of economic literature, not of references to the literature (citations), so we must concern ourselves with the scientific content as well as the literary pedigree of the work on the subject. So first a brief restatement of the kinked demand theory.

Paul Sweezy (1939) proposed the theory in a brief, wholly theoretical paper in 1939.[3] He proposed a demand curve for an oligopolist which takes account of the expected behavior of his rivals at each price he sets (which he termed an "imagined" demand curve, although he believed that it would be confirmed by experience). The typical rival responses will be to match price decreases (to prevent the loss of business) but not to follow a price increase (because a gain of business "is a pleasurable feeling"). The kink thus produced in the oligopolist's demand curve at the ruling price produces a discontinuity in the corresponding marginal revenue curve. The sharpness of the kink, and as a result the length of the gap in marginal revenue, was less when demand for the oligopolistic industry was strong; the converse was expected with a decrease in market demand. As a result, price reductions would be most uncommon in periods of low demand, price increases would become more common in periods of increasing demand. The rigidity of prices in oligopolistic markets appeared to be nicely explained by this construct. Sweezy explicitly rejected the hope that a theory of oligopoly could explain the level of prices; it could only seek to explain the process of price change.

Nearly simultaneously, Robert Hall and Charles Hitch (1939) presented another, related kinked demand curve under oligopoly. The Oxford version of the theory departs in one major respect from that of Sweezy. Hall and Hitch believe that the level of prices will be set at "full cost"; the average cost (including a "conventional allowance for profit") of producing at a normal rate of output. This full-cost price becomes the ruling price under oligopoly, apparently as a result of diverse influences such as collusion, long run tenability of price, moral notions of fairness, and ignorance of demand elasticities. It is enforced, so to speak, by the belief of oligopolists that rivals will not follow price increases but would match price decreases, thus producing a kink in each firm's demand

---

3. It is interesting to notice that Sweezy (1938, pp. 113 ff) drew an *industry* demand curve with a kink the preceding year.

curve. The main difference from Sweezy is the element of full cost pricing: "any circumstance which lowers or raises the average cost curves of all firms by similar amounts . . . is likely to lead to a re-evaluation of the full cost price." (ibid. p. 25).

The Oxford version thus has the advantage over Sweezy's version of explaining the level of prices, but this advantage is dearly bought: a fundamental conflict exists between a kinked demand curve and full cost pricing. If the kink does not exist so far as industry-wide cost changes are concerned, this means that firms succeed in acting jointly and harmoniously, and are not prevented from adjusting to the new cost level by kinks in their individual demand curves. Similarly, then, the kink should not exist so far as response to any other industry-wide change in circumstances is concerned. One of these industry-wide circumstances is that all firms will have larger profits by varying prices when industry demand changes—but the very purpose of the kink is to explain why such price changes do not occur. There are elements of slack in the Oxford version (e.g., the desire of firms to maintain large outputs, and irrational behavior leading to price reductions in deeply depressed times), and the subsequent literature shows a clear and correct preference for Sweezy's version.

The existence of a literal kink, it should be observed, was not necessary to either version of the theory. Even in a fully deterministic world there would presumably be some buyers who would obtain homogeneous goods from an oligopolist who charged slightly more than his rivals (perhaps because of costs of buyer search). With a probabilistic (or empirically determined) demand curve, continuity of slope would be all the more probable. The effects would be minor, however, if a literal kink were replaced by a very sharp bend in the demand curve at the ruling price.

II. The Scientific Evolution of the Theory

The theoretical evolution of the kinked demand curve has been remarkably meager, and despite the wide attention to the theory, the empirical testing has been almost equally meager. The main stages in the scientific evolution of the theory are quickly summarized.

1. *Bronfenbrenner (1940) and Efroymson (1943)*. Bronfenbrenner, in the first article devoted to the kink after it appeared, developed more explicitly its implications: (i) that prices under imperfect competition will be rigid; (ii) that open price agreements (advance notification of price changes to rivals) accentuate the inelasticity of demand with respect to price reductions, (iii) cutthroat competition is an exaggerated form of behavior leading to kinks, and (iv) kinks will appear in supply curves with oligopsony. The internal logic of the theory and the possibility of (or necessity for) testing it empirically are not considered.

C. W. Efroymson became perhaps the leading supporter of the theory. The already conventional kinked demand curve is given priority over the full-cost principle, I think correctly, even in the Hall and Hitch version. The main contribution consists of a cyclical analysis of oligopoly demand curves. When sales volume is cyclically low, an oligopolist will realize that his rivals are extremely loathe to lose volume, and hence will match price decreases but not price increases. But when volume is cyclically high and capacity is approached, the situation is reversed. Now a price rise will not lead customers to shift to a rival, for that rival will also be operating at a high rate of output and be unable to accommodate many more custom- ers, and similarly be unwilling to follow a price reduction. A "reflex" demand curve, elastic for price reductions and inelastic for price in- creases, will emerge.[4] The shift from one state of demand to the other is usually "sudden and decisive." With the reflex demand curve, profits are minimized at the kink, and prices change—how much, and in what direction, are questions left unexplored. Equilibrium is possible only after the conventional ("obtuse") kink is restored in the oligopolist's demand curve.

2. *Stigler's Critique.* My appraisal of the theory in 1947 was stimulated more by a growing interest in the empirical testing of theories than by the intrinsic interest in the kinked demand curve.

On the formal side, my chief criticism was that if price rises were indicated by the theory, they would contradict the existence of the kink. Hence the kink could, perhaps, explain the persistence of a given price, but not the reappearance of a kink. In retrospect I should have empha- sized (and not merely mentioned) instead the arbitrary asymmetry of the behavioral pattern attributed to each firm. Price decreases were promptly matched to preserve market share, whereas the rivals would not follow price increases in hope of increasing their share of the market. But surely the price increaser would usually promptly restore the former price if he was not followed, so that non-following rivals would in fact not get appreciable sales increases if they did not follow the price increase.

The main task of the article, however, was a test of the empirical fruitfulness of the theory. A modest direct test was first applied: price histories in seven industries were examined to see whether in fact price increases were not followed and price decreases promptly followed. The vast majority of the recorded price episodes were not in keeping with the assumption of the theory.

The larger test, however, was a study of BLS wholesale prices from June 1929 to May 1937. The following implications of the theory were tested:

1. Monopolies had no kink, so these prices should be more flexible than those of oligopolistic industries. (Here and later the impact of

---

4. A reverse kink had already been suggested by E. T. Grether (1939, p. 231n).

demand fluctuations was measured by the coefficient of variation of output, and used as a control.) The reverse was the case.

2. The fewer the number of firms, the less probable the kink, because of the realization that price increases that were not followed would quickly be rescinded. The facts were the reverse: price changed more often and more widely, the larger the number of firms.

3. Price leaders who were dominant firms (I proposed also a "barometric" price leader whose function was to adjust price to changing market conditions) should have no kinks and hence have more flexible prices. The reverse was true.

4. The kink is sharper, the more elastic the upper branch, so prices should be more flexible with oligopoly with differentiated products than those with homogeneous products. This prediction was also contradicted.

5. The kink disappears when the firms collude. Prices proved to be more rigid in periods of known collusion.

3. *The Rejoinders.* A considerable number of economists have objected to some or all of the tests I made. The objections will be inventoried, but first a comment should be made on one characteristic these defenders of the theory of kinked demand curves all share: the belief that they need not provide evidence to support the theory. If my criticisms could be rejected, apparently there has been a presumption that the theory is acceptable: theories, like other citizens, are presumed innocent until shown to be guilty.

The main lines of criticism of my tests have been:

1. Since the kink is based upon *expected* responses of rivals, and expectations may be independent of previous experience, and possibly geared to future experience, or even irrational, therefore actual experience cannot be used to prove the non-existence (or existence?) of the kink (Smith 1948, pp. 204–06). As Paul Streeten (1951, p. 109n.) put it,

As long as oligopolists believe in the kink, prices will not be altered. Only when they abandon this belief will they change prices, but these changes are no evidence of their disbelief in the kink at other times.[5]

I would like to think that this type of criticism is no longer publishable.

2. When a cost increase is common to all firms in the industry, they may reasonably assume that the rivals will follow a price increase. This is the single most popular criticism of my tests: they failed to include changes in variable costs (Smith 1948, p. 207 and Shepherd

5. The same point is made with more restraint by J. M. Clark (1961, p. 287) who then asks for an independent determination of when the kink exists.

1962, p. 423n). Needless to say, no one actually introduced this variable to rerun the tests. The response is remarkably ad hoc: if industry-wide phenomena are responded to jointly by all firms, then there *is no kink*. Industry-wide phenomena include changes in demand, and what, besides changes in industry supply and demand, could influence market price appreciably?

3. The reflex demand curve explains the price changes, so a different kink explains price increases (Efroymson 1955, pp. 119–22, 128 ff).

4. The seven price histories were too few in number to support a criticism (Shepherd 1962, p. 423n). Individual circumstances—collusion, memory of a previous episode, price leadership—had smoothed out the kink (Efroymson 1955, p. 127).

5. The tests relied on BLS list prices, which are notoriously inflexible relative to transaction prices (ibid., pp. 130ff). One would think that the denial of the phenomenon the kink theory was designed to explain was an unhappy defense.[6]

6. Collusion may be incomplete, and fail to remove the kink (ibid., p. 132). It is not explained how collusion makes for a sharper kink.

7. The lesser price flexibility of monopolies than of oligopolies, and of heterogeneous than of homogenous product oligopolies, shows only that other forces in addition to the kink explain price behavior (ibid., pp. 133–35; Clark 1961, p. 288).

8. One needs objective standards of competitive price behavior in order to judge patterns of oligopolistic price behavior (Shepherd 1962, p. 423n).

4. *Later Empirical Tests.* A second empirical test of the kinked demand curve was made by Julian Simon in 1969. The advertising rates in business magazines are compared for "groups" (journals serving the same markets), and the rates of monopolists are found to change less often than those groups with two or more magazines. This is of course contrary to the prediction of the theory.

A third empirical test, by W. J. Primeaux Jr., and M. R. Bomball (1974), examines electrical rates in cities with one and two independent electric utilities. Again monopolists changed rates less often than duopolists, and duopolists more commonly followed rate increases (with or without a lag) than rate decreases. W. J. Primeaux Jr. and M. C. Smith (1976) made a similar test of the price movements of prescription drugs of monopolists and oligopolists, and also found that the predictions of the kinked demand curve theory were contradicted. Both studies are weakened by the use of annual data on prices.

---

6. Efroymson (1955) finds discrepancies from list price most likely under oligopoly because of secret price cutting with ostensible collusion—which surely is inconsistent with the assumption that price reductions will be matched.

Although no other quantitative studies have been made, there are many assertions in the literature of the existence of a kink in the demand curve of a particular industry, perhaps at a particular time. Two examples are:[7]

1. Rayon. Markham (1952) found weak evidence of a kink (weak because price leadership was well established): the average delay of firms in following a price increase was 10 days, a price decrease 7 days.[8]

2. Steel. The cited passage states that U.S. Steel will not (cannot?) increase its market share by "undercutting" prices (Kaplan et al. 1958, p. 174). Yet the company led price moves frequently (ibid., p. 167).

These examples are not cited to show that there are no price episodes consistent with kinked demand curve theorizing: of course there are many episodes where a price increase by one firm has not been followed by others, or where price decreases have been followed. The examples suggest only that no extensive, careful search for supporting evidence has been made by anyone.

5. *Elaborations of the Theory.* The paucity of additional theoretical work on the kinked demand curve has been remarked. Only two suggested extensions seem worthy of note here. The first suggestion, by Cohen and Cyert (1965, pp. 251ff), is that until a firm has learned the behavioral pattern of its rivals, a kink is quite likely, so rigid prices are more likely to be found in (1) young industries, and (2) industries experiencing new entry.[9] An illustrative episode from the potash industry is given.

The second extension, this time by Cyert and DeGroot (1971)[10] can be

7. These were cited by F. M. Scherer (1970, p. 147n); repeated by A. A. Thompson (1973, p. 400n).

8. Markham (1952, pp. 88, 143, 199). The significance of the difference could not be calculated but since the reports carried a 15 to 30 day uncertainty of date (ibid., p. 86), it is improbable that a significance test would be passed.

9. It is instructive to set against this conjecture the contrary one of the National Bureau of Economic Research, Committee on Price Determination (1943), in a report which bears the imprint of the Committee's chairman, E. S. Mason:

"There is no doubt that this (the kinked demand curve) is a realistic picture of the demand situation as envisaged by individual firms in a great number of industrial markets a large part of the time. It goes a long way toward explaining some important aspects of industrial price behavior. There is rather strong reason for believing that leading firms in the automobile, steel, agricultural implement, and many other industries act upon approximately this view of the situation. As a working hypothesis, however, it is probably limited to industrial markets which have attained something like long run stability in the sense that demand is mainly for replacement and the entry of new firms is unimportant." (ibid, p. 278).

Characteristically, the remainder of the paragraph restricts the claims for the kink.

10. A later article suggests by its silence on the kink that it played only a temporary role in their work; see "An Analysis of Cooperation and Learning in a Duopoly Context." (Cyert and DeGroot 1973, 24–37).

viewed as an extension of the previous proposal: the learning behavior of the firm is allowed to produce kinks under certain conditions. For example, firm A believes that B will match price increases up to a certain level Θ, which is not known precisely, so it experiments with price increases to learn Θ. The extension is potentially interesting, but the behavior of the oligopolists is not related to ordinary profit maximizing parameters so in its present form this extension has no empirically graspable handles.

6. *The Extension to Limit Pricing.* The theory of limit pricing—the setting of oligopoly or monopoly prices that will make entry into the industry unattractive to prospective rivals—has an ancient history in economics.[11] The modern formulation, especially that of Paolo Sylos-Labini (1962),[12] bears a close affinity to kinked demand curve theory. In the more precise statement by Modigliani (1958) a definite price exists above which rivals will be attracted. The limit price is so chosen by the existing firms that after entry of a new firm, if the existing firms maintain their output and the new entrant enters at the smallest remunerative output, his average costs will equal the after-entry price. Hence the existing demand curve of the combined oligopolists has a kink (or at least sharply increased elasticity for price increases) at the limit price. This kink price should closely follow long run costs of production of entrants.

The similarities between the two kinds of kink are evident, as is also the crucial absence of oligopolistic uncertainty in the limit price version. There is no direct evidence that limit price theory was influenced by the kinked demand curve literature.[13] Neither Bain nor Sylos-Labini was an enthusiastic supporter of the kinked demand curve theory.[14] We have noticed, however, that Sweezy presented a limit price kink before he published the kinked oligopolistic demand curve.[15]

7. *Other Kinks.* Any asymmetry in the response of rivals to increases and decreases of a variable may lead to a kink in the relevant function. Hence one could readily have extended the theory to other dimensions of rivalry in addition to price. This was not done.[16]

Some economists have apparently been led to attribute kinks to quite different demand phenomena. L. Fouraker and W. Lee (1956) in an under-appreciated performance, managed to find a kink in the demand curve of individual Pennsylvania apple growers. Other variants have been proposed by H. R. Edwards (1952), Hieser (1953), M. Farrell

11. One classic exposition is J. B. Clark's in (e.g.) *The Control of Trusts* (1901, Ch. IV).
12. J. S. Bain (1956) offers a similar theory.
13. Joan Robinson (1933, p.81) used the situation of a monopolist who faced entry of rivals above a certain price as a possible source of kinks.
14. Sylos-Labini (1962, pp.98–99) rejected the theory; Bain (1960, p. 203) gave it little scope.
15. See above note 3.
16. Doyle (1968) attributes an advertising kink to Kaldor, but I have not been able to find it.

(1954), Grossack (1966), Hawkins (1954), McManus (1962), Greenhut (1967), Levitan and Shubik (1971), and Douglas (1973). Of course Edgeworth's theory of duopoly (1925, I, p. 118ff) which rested on capacity constraints on the rivals, produces a kinked demand curve which has often been reproduced.

8. *Dynamics of Individual Firm Prices.* An important potential service of the kinked oligopoly demand curve literature would have been to advance, or at least to arouse economic theorists' interest in, the problem of how the prices of individual firms change when market price changes. The kinked demand curve theory indeed contains a rudimentary, if unprepossessing, version of such a theory. No such catalytic role was served: the rapidly growing modern literature of the dynamics of price movements is intimately related to the economics of information but the kinked demand curve literature had no apparent influence.

III. The Reception of the Kink

The year 1939 was inauspicious for the launching of a new economic theory, but even a World War did not prevent a fairly wide acceptance of a plausible explanation for the existence of the pervasively inflexible ("administered") industrial prices for which Gardner Means had successfully argued.[17] Already by 1940 Bronfenbrenner had spelled out various implications of Sweezy's note, and in 1942 there were no less than 9 articles mentioning the theory (4 by Sidney Weintraub).

There is a measure of paradox in this marriage of the literatures of oligopoly and price inflexibility, because there was a serious incompatibility between the partners. The phenomenon that Means emphasized in the 1930's was the *downward* rigidity of prices. (In the late 1950's Means shifted his emphasis, indeed, to the upward aggressiveness of the price policies of oligopolies.) But the kink argues primarily against *upward* price changes: the kinked demand curve of an oligopolist for price reductions is the same as that with full collusion, so if a price were at the (industry) profit-maximizing level, it would be fully responsive to a large class of subsequent downward movements of cost and demand, and the upper branch of the firm's demand curve and the kink would be irrelevant. This was apparently seldom remarked.[18]

A statistical history of the references to the kinked demand curve is given in Table 3.1. This canvass of the literature underlies our discussion of its nature, so it is necessary to describe how it was compiled. An extensive search was made of all articles in the *Index of Economic Journals* under appropriate headings in microeconomic theory, price and

17. Beginning with the celebrated monograph, *Industrial Prices and their Relative Inflexibility* (Means, 1935).

18. See, however, D. H. Whitehead (1963, pp. 187–95) and W. Hamburger (1967, p. 268).

Table 3.1. *References to the Kinked Demand Curve, 1939–76*

Year	Total Number of Articles	Articles Primarily on Kink[a]	Number of Books (1st ed. only)
1939	2	2: Sweezy; Hall & Hitch	—
1940	3	2: Bronfenbrenner; Mikesell	—
1941	2		1
1942	9		—
1943	2	1: Efroymson	1
1944	—		1
1945	—		—
1946	1		—
1947	6	1: Stigler	4
1948	4	1: V. Smith	4
1949	—		3
1950	1		—
1951	4	1: Streeten	4
1952	3		2
1953	3	1: Hieser	—
1954	8		—
1955	7	1: Efroymson	4
1956	1		—
1957	1		2
1958	1		2
1959	1		2
1960	2		4
1961	2		4
1962	2	1: Shepherd	3
1963	1		3
1964	1		5
1965	2	1: Spengler	5
1966	1		4
1967	5		2
1968	5		5
1969	2	1: Simon	3
1970	6		7
1971	3	2: Smith & Neale; Cyert & DeGroot	2
1972	3	1: Peel	2
1973	4		4
1974	3	2: Primeaux & Bomball; Murphy & Ng	—
1975	3	1: Coyne	1
1976	1	1: Primeaux & Smith	2
1940's	27		14
1950's	30		16
1960's	23		38
1970's	23		18

[a]See starred items in list of references.

233

market theory of firm and industry, and public policy towards monopoly and competition. Undoubtedly there are other articles in which the kink appeared: anyone using oligopoly price theory in fields such as international trade, labor markets or public finance would be overlooked by this procedure. The foreign-language literature is omitted. Our search of books was even more narrowly confined to textbooks in principles and theory and works in industrial organization and price behavior.[19]

The canvass reported in Table 3.1 yields a respectable total of 103 articles in which the kinked demand curve is at least mentioned, 18 articles (not including those of Sweezy and Hall and Hitch) of which it was the main subject, and some 86 books. The latter count pertains only to the first (post-1939) edition in which the theory appeared (thus Samuelson's text is counted only in the 6th edition, 1964, when the kink was introduced, although it persists in all later editions). In terms of individual specimens of economic literature displaying a kinked demand curve, in recent years the *annual* count has probably been on the order of 300,000 or more (in many of the leading textbooks on principles or price theory) plus another 15,000 specimens in the two or three articles in journals. There is little evidence of abatement of the number of references; in fact the theory seems to have reached a steady state.

Unless an author explicitly sets out to refute a theory, one should characterize his attitude toward that theory as favorable, or at worst neutral, if he actually refers to the theory. For he is reviving its currency and advertising its existence. In classifying the attitudes in references to the kinked demand curve I have therefore leaned in the direction of classifying discussions as favorable unless they were fairly explicitly otherwise. Of the 189 references to the kink, 143 were favorable, 29 neutral, and 17 unfavorable (see Table 3.2). The favorable and neutral references have dominated throughout the period since 1939, but recently the unfavorable references have become moderately more common.[20] The theory has received no systematic empirical support and virtually no theoretical elaboration in these decades, but these lacks have been no handicap in maintaining its currency.

The *uses* made of the kink by various economists are difficult to classify in a reproducible fashion. Most references are simple "mentions" of the theory, for example.

> The commonest market situation is one of oligopoly with
> product differentiation, in which case the demand curve must
> be regarded as kinked (and the marginal revenue curve as
> discontinuous) at the existing price. In this case one cannot

---

19. I am indebted especially to Maurice Schiff and Herminio Blanco for compiling the basic canvass of the literature. *The Journal of Economic Literature* was used for years in which the *Index* was unavailable.

20. This article can be so classified!

Table 3.2. *Classification of Attitude Toward and Use Made of Kinked Demand Curve*

Year	Attitude			Use Made of Theory		
	Favorable	Neutral	Unfavorable	Economic Analysis	Mention	Exposition
1940	3	—	—	3	—	—
1941	3	—	—	—	3	—
1942	9	—	—	2	7	—
1943	3	—	—	2	1	—
1944	1	—	—	1	—	—
1945	—	—	—	—	—	—
1946	1	—	—	—	1	—
1947	9	—	1	2	6	2
1948	7	—	1	1	3	4
1949	2	—	1	1	2	—
1950	1	—	—	—	1	—
1951	5	1	2	1	5	2
1952	2	3	—	—	4	1
1953	1	—	2	1	2	—
1954	7	1	—	3	5	—
1955	6	4	1	1	8	2
1956	1	—	—	1	—	—
1957	2	1	—	—	2	1
1958	2	1	—	—	1	2
1959	1	2	—	—	3	—
1960	5	1	—	—	2	4
1961	5	1	—	1	2	3
1962	3	2	—	2	1	2
1963	4	—	—	1	—	3
1964	4	2	—	—	2	4
1965	7	—	—	2	1	4
1966	4	1	—	—	2	3
1967	6	—	1	2	3	2
1968	9	1	—	1	5	4
1969	3	1	1	1	1	3
1970	10	2	1	1	8	4
1971	3	2	—	2	2	1
1972	4	—	1	2	2	1
1973	6	—	2	1	4	3
1974	1	—	2	2	1	—
1975	1	3	—	1	2	1
1976	2	—	1	1	—	2
1940's	38	0	3	12	23	6
1950's	28	13	5	7	31	8
1960's	50	9	2	10	19	32
1970's	27	7	7	10	19	12
	143	29	17	39	92	58

really say that output and employment are determined by the intersection of the (horizontal) marginal cost curve and the (discontinuous) marginal revenue curve. The causal sequence starts rather with the determination of a price for the product. . . . (Reynolds 1948, p. 297).

The difficulty arises in setting a level of elaboration or application of the theory that involves some element of novelty, a category of use I label "analysis." It contains all (20) full-length articles devoted to the kinked demand curve, whatever their contribution, since surely analysis (professional development of the subject) was their purpose. In addition there are a large number of references of this type:

A rise in costs "justifies" a price increase in the sense that, if profit margins are left unchanged as a result of the cost-price alterations, no encouragement is given to potential competitors, suppliers, purchasers, the Government, trade unions, or anyone else to vary the incipient or actual pressures they are exerting in their various ways. However this does not fully explain why price changes would occur. Would it not be possible for the first firm raising its prices to be forced into an embarrassing and costly re-shuffle as a result of other firms failing to move? In most cases it is easy to see that the answer is in the negative. If the cost increase is large, any satisfaction over the embarrassment of a competitor would ring hollow in the face of substantially reduced profit margins in the other firms that failed to increase prices; also a dangerous precedence would have been created. Moreover, in many industries some minimal degree of collusion on such matters exists. Where the cost change is small the chances of its being absorbed are increased because uncertainty about the reaction of other firms is multiplied and in any case there are often costs attached to price changes. . . .
The analysis suggests that there is even more chance that a fall in costs will be quickly translated into price cuts. This is because there is no fear on the part of the first mover that he may not be followed—if he is not followed, so much the better! . . . It seems paradoxical in the extreme that economists have suggested that prices are more likely to be "sticky" downwards than upwards in the face of cost variations (Whitehead 1963)."

This discussion of the kink is fuller than most, but it does not constitute a new formulation nor does it introduce new variables, new relationships, or new kinds of facts. I have consistently labelled such discussions "analysis," nevertheless, because they represent at least a conscious rethinking of the theory.

Table 3.3. *Frequency of Appearance of the Kinked Demand Curve in Textbooks on Principles and Price Theory in Print*[a]

Period	No Kink	Kink	Total in Print	Percent with Kink
1947–49 (incl.)	12	4	16	25.0%
1950–52 "	13	6	19	31.6
1953–55 "	14	6	20	30.0
1956–58 "	15	7	22	31.8
1959–61 "	16	10	26	38.5
1962–64 "	19	15	34	44.1
1965–67 "	17	23	40	57.5
1968–70 "	13	25	38	65.8
1971–73 "	14	24	38	63.2
1974–76 "	13	22	35	62.9

[a]We exclude instances in which a text does not contain a kinked demand curve but the later known edition is unavailable, and those in which a kinked demand curve is present but an earlier edition is not available. If no revisions appear, a book is assumed to be out of print seven years after its publication.

Even with this undemanding criterion only 39 of the 189 references could be labelled analytical: all the remainder of the uses were mentions or textbook expositions. The kinked demand curve has not been part of the arsenal of the working economist.

The final category of use I have labelled "exposition" and it is restricted to textbooks plus one expository statement by B. F. Haley (1948). The treatment here is essentially didactic. As the count in Table 3.3 indicates, a steadily rising number of textbooks have devoted their 2 or 3 pages to the subject, and I have encountered no case in which the kinked demand curve, once introduced, is deleted.[21] At the present time two-thirds of the textbooks in print in principles and price theory that we examined contain a more or less routine exposition (see Table 3.3).

The geometrical implications of kinks are the chief subject of these textbook discussions: hardly ever do they even go so far as to compare the expected price behavior of monopolists and oligopolists under the theory. Yet if the instruction of students on the implication for marginal curves of kinks in curves of average quantities is the *raison d'etre* of the discussion of the kinked demand curve, the textbook writers could do that at least as well with the analyses of legal maximum and minimum prices. Nevertheless one must concede that the spread of textbook presentations is strong evidence of (kinky?) market demand.

21. The textbook collection of the Regenstein Library of the University of Chicago was supplemented to some degree by the library of Northwestern University, but the survey is far from complete.

In fact, the failure to use the theory as a source of hypotheses on the differential behavior of firms in different market structures and associations is the very hallmark of the kinked demand curve literature. One would expect the theory to explain phenomena such as:
—the nature of the industries in which periods of price rigidity are observed.
—the lengths of the periods of price rigidity.
—the conditions under which frequent price changes occur under oligopoly.
—the price rigidity observed in industries with numerous producers, or a single producer.

Instead the theory is a piece of scripture: it is to be taught and it is to be quoted in suitable contexts, but it is not to be tampered with.

IV. Some Hypotheses on Professional Literature

This review of the literature of the kinked demand curve suggests several hypotheses on the nature of scientific discourse.

The first and most fundamental hypothesis is that a theory need not be used in order to remain current. The fundamental "use" of the kinked demand curve in the literature is to suggest a reason for the observed fact that many prices do not appear to change frequently. But of course this is not a real use, since the theory is not related to the prices to be explained. No one, with almost no exceptions, uses the pattern of differences in price change frequency which the theory contains to explain differences in observed price changes. There is then no particular need for a special theory for so limited an explanation: literally *no* scientific function is now performed by the kinked demand curve theory that would not equally well be supplied by the simple argument that price changes cannot be made without cost.

A second hypothesis is that the textbooks of a discipline play a powerfully conservative role in the transmission of doctrine. The kinked demand curve is a meager theory and yet there surely cannot have been a new Ph.D. in economics in America in the last ten years who has not been exposed to it. Some textbook writers are scarcely authorities on any branch of economics, but economists of the stature of Samuelson, Lipsey and Steiner, Baumol, Henderson and Quandt, Cyert, Kuenne, Hirshleifer, Mansfield, and Ferguson and Gould repeat the scripture in each edition; the young economist must naturally consider it a necessary part of the mystery of the craft. The writing of textbooks is apparently not a thought-intensive activity: the modal number of changes of *any* sort between editions of a textbook in its discussion of the kinked demand curve is zero.

The third and most general hypothesis is that theories never perish. There is a belief, widespread but implicit, that one theory "supplants" another. Of course ruling theories undergo change, but the supplanted theory never vanishes completely.

It is seldom and perhaps never the case that two theories are in exact rivalry, so that the acceptance of one implies the complete rejection of the other. Consider a famous example in the history of economics. The theory of value of Ricardo and Mill asserted that for freely producible goods their relative prices were determined by their relative costs of production. Jevons, Menger, Wieser and Böhm-Bawerk asserted that the foundation of relative value was in the relative marginal utilities of the goods. The latter theory was more general, for it embraced goods that were not freely producible, but it was also less informative, for it did not even explain why a house sells for more than a banana or even why two pounds of bananas sell for twice as much as one pound. One can combine the two theories, and indeed Marshall and Walras did so, but that is hardly displacing one theory by another.

Even when one theory *includes* the second as a special case, it is not inevitable that the acceptance of the former leads to the abandonment of the latter. A simple example from oligopoly theory will suffice. The revenue of a duopolist, I, is

$$(1) \qquad q_1 f(q_1 + q_2)$$

where f is the demand function and q_i the output of firm i, and Cournot wrote the marginal revenue of firm I as

$$(2) \qquad q_1 f'(q_1 + q_2) + f(q_1 + q_2),$$

treating q_2 as a constant. The output of II, q_2, may however be treated as a function of q_1 and then I's marginal revenue becomes

$$(3) \qquad q_1 f'(q_1 + q_2)(1 + (dq_2/dq_1)) + f(q_1 + q_2),$$

and dq_2/dq_1 (sometimes called the conjectural variation) is not necessarily zero. The predictions of the Cournot model are much more definite, so many modern economists still use this model: the more general theory has not driven out the less general theory.

There is no obvious method by which a science can wholly rid itself of once popular theories, logical error aside (and even this may not be a true exception). This is not to deny that theories decline in currency: the fraction of scientists working on the subject to which the theory pertains who *know* a theory will decline with time, and eventually the fraction will become so small that the theory is no longer a part of the working knowledge of the science. The fraction of scientists working on a subject to which a theory applies who actually *use* the theory will of course decline sooner, and is near zero for the kinked demand curve. If at this stage a theory is revived, it is much more likely to be rediscovered than refurbished from the past.

The study of a single theory, which has not yet entered the long decline in currency, does not equip us to understand the rate of decline of a theory. The literature surveyed here suggests that adverse empirical evidence is not a decisive factor. It is a plausible conjecture that when a theory is actively and frequently used, its susceptibility to displacement is much greater than when it performs essentially ceremonial functions.

A final, and rather morbid, observation is that there is a simply enormous amount of unprogressive publication: articles which certainly add nothing to the accumulation of rigorous theory or tested findings. Of the hundred-odd articles which I have had occasion to read in part or whole in preparing this paper, it is a conservative estimate that two-thirds *at a minimum* made no positive contribution to received knowledge on oligopoly behavior: they contain neither a new idea nor a new fact.[22] In the case of the kinked demand curve this judgment is not based upon hindsight since scarce any progress has been made in the theory in thirty years. Do the articles serve as a poll of the views of the more communicative branch of a profession? Or can it be that ordinary scientific discourse is like ordinary social discourse: simply practice in communication, so that, when an important message needs to be communicated, the faculties for communication will not be impaired by atrophy?

22. Kenneth May (1968–69, p.367), in the history of determinants referred to (note 1), classified 1995 titles (sometimes into several categories) as follows:

New ideas and results	14%
Applications	12
Systematization and history	12
Tests and education	15
Duplications	21
Trivia	43
Total	117%

References

Bain, Joe S., *Barriers to New Competition*, Harvard University Press, 1956.
———, "Price Leaders, Barometers, and Kinks," *Journal of Business* July 1960. 33, 193–203.
*Bronfenbrenner, Martin, "Applications of the Discontinuous Oligopoly Demand Curve," *Journal of Political Economy*, June 1940, 48, 420–27.
Clark, J. B., *The Control of Trusts*, New York: Macmillan, 1901. Ch. IV.
Clark, J. M.; *Competition as a Dynamic Process*, Brookings, 1961.
Coase, Ronald H., "The Problem of Duopoly Reconsidered," *Review of Economic Studies*, February 1935, 2, 137–43.

*Starred items are those referred to in Table 3.1.

Cohen, K. J. and Cyert, R. M., *Theory of the Firm*, Prentice Hall, 1965.

*Coyne, John, "Kinked Supply Curves and the Labour Market," *Journal of Economic Studies*, November 1975, 2, 139–51.

*Cyert, Richard M. and DeGroot, M., "Interfirm Learning and the Kinked Demand Curve," *Journal of Economic Theory*, September 1971, 3, 272–87.

———, "An Analysis of Cooperation and Learning in a Duopoly Context," *Amerian Economic Review*, 1973, 63, 24–37.

Douglas, Evan J., "Price Strategy Duopoly with Product Variation—A Comment," *Kyklos*, 1973, 26, 608–11.

Doyle, Peter, "Advertising Expenditure and Consumer Demand," *Oxford Economic Papers*, N.S. 20, November 1968, 394–416.

Edgeworth, F. Y., *Papers Relating to Political Economy*, London: Macmillan, 1925, I.

Edwards, Harold R., "Goodwill and the Normal Cost Theory of Price," *Economic Record*, May 1952, 28, 52–74.

*Efroymson, Clarence W., "A Note on Kinked Demand Curves," *American Economic Review*, March 1943, 33, 98–109.

*———, "The Kinked Oligopoly Curve Reconsidered," *Quarterly Journal of Economics*, February 1955, 69, 119–36.

Farrell, Michael J., "An Application of Activity Analysis to the Theory of the Firm," *Econometrica*, July 1954, 22, 291–302.

Fouraker, Lawrence E. and Lee, W. A., "Competition and Kinked Functions in the Marketing of Perishables," *Southern Economic Journal*, January 1956, 22, 367–70.

Greenhut, Melvin L., "A Theory of the Micro Equilibrium Path of the Firm in Economic Space," *South African Journal of Economics*, September 1967, 35, 230–43.

Grether, E. T., *Price Control under Fair Trade Legislation*, New York: Oxford University Press, 1939.

Grossack, Irvin M., "Duopoly, Defensive Strategies, and the Kinked Demand Curve," *Southern Economic Journal*, April 1966, 32, 406–16.

Haley, B. F., "Value and Distribution," in *A Survey of Contemporary Economics*, Howard S. Ellis, editor, Irwin, Homewood, Ill., Vol. I, 1948.

*Hall, Robert L. and Hitch, C. J., "Price Theory and Business Behavior," *Oxford Economic Papers*, No. 2, May 1939, 12–45.

Hamburger, William, "Conscious Parallelism and the Kinked Oligopoly Demand Curve," *American Economic Review Supplement*, May 1967, 57, 266–68.

Hawkins, Edward R., "Price Policies and Theory," *Journal of Marketing*, January 1954, 18, 233–40.

*Hieser, Ron, "A Kinked Demand Curve for Monopolistic Competition," *Economic Record*, May 1953, 29, 19–34.

Kahn, Richard F., "The Problem of Duopoly," *Economic Journal*, March 1937, 47, 1–20.

Kaplan, A. D. H., Dirlam, Joel B. and Lanzilotti, R. F., *Pricing in Big Business*, Brookings, 1958.

Levitan, Richard E. and Shubik, M., "Price Variation Duopoly with Differentiated Products and Random Demand," *Journal of Economic Theory*, March 1971, 3, 23–39.

McManus, Maurice, "Numbers and Size in Cournot Oligopoly," *Yorkshire Bulletin of Economic and Social Research*, May 1962, 14, 14–22.

Markham, Jesse W., *Competition in the Rayon Industry*, Harvard University Press, 1952.

May, Kenneth O., "Growth and Quality of the Mathematical Literature," *Isis*, 1968–69, 59, 363–71.

———, "Who Killed Determinants?" *The Mathematical Association of America*, Film Manual No. 4 (n.d.).

Means, Gardiner C., *Industrial Prices and Their Relative Inflexibility*, Senate Document 13, 74th Congress, 1st Session, January 17, 1935.

*Mikesell, Raymond F., "Oligopoly and the Short-Run Demand for Labor," *Quarterly Journal of Economics*, November 1940, 55, 161-66.

Modigliani, Franco, "New Developments on the Oligopoly Front," *Journal of Political Economy*, 1958, 66, 215–32.

*Murphy, T. A. and Ng, Y. K., "Oligopolistic Interdependence and the Revenue Maximization Hypothesis—Note," *Journal of Industrial Economics*, March 1974, 22, 227–33.

National Bureau of Economic Research, Committee on Price Determination, *Cost Behavior and Price Policy*, 1943.

*Peel, David A., "The Kinked Demand Curve—The Demand for Labour," *Recherches Economiques de Louvain*, September 1972, 3, 267–73.

*Primeaux, Walter J. Jr., and Bomball, Mark R., "A Reexamination of the Kinky Oligopoly Demand Curve," *Journal of Political Economy*, August 1974, 82, 851–62.

*Primeaux, Walter J. Jr., and Smith, Mickey C., "Pricing Patterns and the Kinky Demand Curve," *Journal of Law and Economics*, April 1976, 19, 189–99.

Reynolds, Lloyd G., "Toward a Short-Run Theory of Wages," *American Economic Review*, June 1948, 48, 289–308.

Robinson, Joan, *Economics of Imperfect Competition*, Macmillan, 1933.

Scherer, F. M., *Industrial Market Structure and Economic Performance*, Chicago: Rand McNally, 1970.

*Shepherd, William G., "On Sales-Maximising and Oligopoly Behaviour," *Economica*, N.S. 29, November 1962, 420–24.

*Simon, J. L., "A Further Test of the Kinky Oligopoly Demand Curve," *American Economic Review*, December 1969, 59, 971–75.

*Smith, D. Stanton and Neale, Walter C., "The Geometry of Kinky Oligopoly: Marginal Cost, the Gap, and Price Behavior," *Southern Economic Journal*, January 1971, 37, 276–82.

*Smith, Victor E., "Note on the Kinky Oligopoly Demand Curve," *Southern Economic Journal*, October 1948, 15, 205–10.

*Spengler, Joseph J., "Kinked Demand Curves: By Whom First Used?" *Southern Economic Journal*, July 1965, 32, 81–84.

*Stigler, George J., "The Kinky Oligopoly Demand Curve and Rigid Prices," *Journal of Political Economy*, October 1947, 55, 432–49.

*Streeten, Paul, "Reserve Capacity and the Kinked Demand Curve," *Review of Economic Studies*, 1951, 18, 103–13.

Sweezy, Paul M., *Monopoly and Competition in the English Coal Trade, 1550–1880*, Harvard University Press, 1938.

*———, "Demand under Conditions of Oligopoly," *Journal of Political Economy*, August 1939, 47, 563–73.

Sylos-Labini, Paolo, *Oligopoly and Technical Progress*, Harvard University Press, 1962.

Thompson, A. A., *Economics of the Firm*, Prentice Hall, 1973.

Whitehead, Donald H., "Price-Cutting and Wages Policy," *Economic Record*, June 1963, 39, 187–95.

Bibliography of Works by
George J. Stigler

Books and Pamphlets

1941. *Production and Distribution Theories.* New York: Macmillan.

1942. *The Theory of Competitive Price.* New York: Macmillan.

1946. *The Theory of Price.* New York: Macmillan.

1946. (With Milton Friedman) *Roofs or Ceilings?* Irvington-on-Hudson, N.Y.: Foundation for Economic Education.

1947. *Domestic Servants in the United States.* New York: National Bureau of Economic Research.

1947. *Trends in Output and Employment.* New York: National Bureau of Economic Research.

1949. *Five Lectures on Economic Problems.* New York: Longmans, Green Co.

1950. *Employment and Compensation in Education.* New York: National Bureau of Economic Research.

1952. *Theory of Price.* revised ed. New York: Macmillan.

1952. (With Kenneth Boulding) *Readings in Price Theory.* Homewood, Ill.: Richard D. Irwin.

1956. *Trends in Employment in the Service Industries.* National Bureau of Economic Research. Princeton, N.J.: Princeton University Press.

1957. (With David Blank) *Supply and Demand for Scientific Personnel.* National Bureau of Economic Research. Princeton, N.J.: Princeton University Press.

1957. (Editor) *Selections from "The Wealth of Nations."* New York: Appleton-Century-Crofts.

1961. (Chairman) *The Price Statistics of the Federal Government.* A report to the Office of Statistical Standards, Bureau of the Budget. General Series, no. 73. New York: National Bureau of Economic Research, Inc.

1962. *The Intellectual and the Marketplace.* Selected Papers, no. 3. Chicago: University of Chicago Graduate School of Business.

1963. *Capital and Rates of Return in Manufacturing Industries.* National Bureau of Economic Research. Princeton, N.J.: Princeton University Press.

1963. *The Intellectual and the Market Place and Other Essays.* Glencoe, Ill.: Free Press.

1963. *An Invitation to Controversy.* Printed privately.

1963. (With Paul Samuelson) *A Dialogue on the Proper Economic Role of the State.* Selected Papers, no. 7. Chicago: University of Chicago Graduate School of Business.

1964. *The Tactics of Economic Reform.* Selected Papers, no. 13. Chicago: University of Chicago Graduate School of Business.

1965. *Essays in the History of Economics.* Chicago: University of Chicago Press.

1966. *The Theory of Price,* 3rd ed. New York: Macmillan.

1968. *The Organization of Industry*. Homewood, Ill.: Richard D. Irwin.

1970. (With J. K. Kindahl) *The Behavior of Industrial Prices*. National Bureau of Economic Research. New York: Columbia University Press.

1971. *Modern Man and His Corporation*. Selected Papers, no. 39. Chicago: University of Chicago Graduate School of Business.

1971. (With Manuel F. Cohen) *Can Regulatory Agencies Protect the Consumer?* Washington, D.C.: American Enterprise Institute.

1975. *The Citizen and the State*. Chicago: University of Chicago Press.

Articles

1937. "The Economics of Carl Menger." *Journal of Political Economy*, April.

1937. "Theory of Imperfect Competition." *Journal of Farm Economics*, August.

1938. "Social Welfare and Differential Prices." *Journal of Political Economy*, August.

1939. "Production and Distribution in the Short Run." *Journal of Political Economy*, June.

1939. "Limitations of Statistical Demand Curves." *Journal of American Statistical Association*, September.

1940. "Notes on the Theory of Duopoly." *Journal of Political Economy*, August.

1942. "The Extent and Bases of Monopoly," *American Economic Review, Proceedings*, June.

1943. "The New Welfare Economics." *American Economic Review*, June.

1945. "The Cost of Subsistence." *Journal of Farm Economics*, May.

1946. "The Economics of Minimum Wage Legislation." *American Economic Review*, June.

1947. "Notes on the History of the Giffen Paradox." *Journal of Political Economy*, April.

1947. "Stuart Wood and the Marginal Productivity Theory." *Quarterly Journal of Economics*, August.

1947. "The Kinky Oligopoly Demand Curve and Rigid Prices." *Journal of Political Economy*, October.

1947. "An Academic Episode." *Bulletin of the American Association of University Professors*, Winter.

1949. "A Survey of Contemporary Economics." *Journal of Political Economy*, April.

1949. "A Theory of Delivered Price Systems." *American Economic Review*, December.

1950. Two statements on monopoly. In *Hearings before the Subcommittee on the Study of Monopoly Power*. Committee on the Judiciary, House of Representatives, April 17–May 11.

1950. "Monopoly and Oligopoly by Merger." *American Economic Review, Proceedings*, May.

1950. "The Development of Utility Theory," part 1. *Journal of Political Economy*, August.

1950. "The Development of Utility Theory," part 2. *Journal of Political Economy*, October.

1951. "The Division of Labor Is Limited by the Extent of the Market." *Journal of Political Economy*, June.

1952. "Specialism: A Dissenting Opinion." *Bulletin of the American Association of University Professors*, Winter.

1952. "The Ricardian Theory of Value and Distribution." *Journal of Political Economy*, June.

1953. "Sraffa's Ricardo." *American Economic Review*, September.

1954. "The Early History of Empirical Studies of Consumer Behavior." *Journal of Political Economy*, April.

1954. "The Economist Plays with Blocs." *American Economic Review, Proceedings*, May.

1954. "Schumpeter's History of Economic Analysis." *Journal of Political Economy*, August.

1955. "The Nature and Role of Originality in Scientific Progress." *Economica*, November.

1955. "Mergers and Preventive Anti-Trust Policy." *Pennsylvania Law Review*, November.

1956. "The Statistics of Monopoly and Merger." *Journal of Political Economy*, February.

1956. "Industrial Organization and Economic Progress." In *The State of the Social Sciences*, edited by L. D. White. Chicago: University of Chicago Press.

1957. "Perfect Competition, Historically Contemplated." *Journal of Political Economy*, February.

1957. "The Tenable Range of Functions of Local Government." In *Federal Expenditure Policy for Economic Growth and Stability*. Joint Economic Committee, Washington, D.C., November 5.

1958. "Ricardo and the 93% Labor Theory of Value." *American Economic Review*, June.

1958. "The Goals of Economic Policy." *Journal of Business*, July.

1958. "The Economies of Scale." *Journal of Law and Economics*, October.

1959. "Bernard Shaw, Sidney Webb, and the Theory of Fabian Socialism." *Transactions of the American Philosophical Society*, June.

1959. "The Politics of Political Economists." *Quarterly Journal of Economics*, November.

1960. "The Influence of Events and Policies on Economic Theory." *American Economic Review*, May.

1960. "Prometheus Incorporated: Conformity or Coercion?" In *Social Control in a Free Society*, edited by R. Spiller. Benjamin Franklin Lectures. Philadelphia: University of Pennsylvania Press.

1961. "The Economics of Information." *Journal of Political Economy*, June.

1961. "Private Vice and Public Virtue." *Journal of Law and Business*, October.

1961. "Economic Problems in Measuring Changes in Productivity." In *Output, Input, and Productivity Measurement*. Studies in Income and Wealth, vol. 25. Princeton, N.J.: Princeton University Press.

1962. "Administered Prices and Oligopolistic Inflation." *Journal of Business*, January.

1962. "Henry L. Moore and Statistical Economics." *Econometrica*, January.

1962. "Marshall's Principles after Guillebaud." *Journal of Political Economy*, June.

1962. "Information in the Labor Market." *Journal of Political Economy, Supplement*, October.

1962. (With Claire Friedland) "What Can Regulators Regulate? The Case of Electricity." *Journal of Law and Economics*, October.

1963. "Elementary Economic Education." *American Economic Review, Proceedings*, May.

1963. "United States v. Loew's Inc.: A Note on Block-Booking." *Supreme Court Review*. Chicago: University of Chicago Press.

1964. "A Theory of Oligopoly." *Journal of Political Economy*, February.

1964. "Public Regulation of the Securities Markets." *Journal of Business*, April

1964. Comment on "The S.E.C. through a Glass Darkly." by I. Friend and E. S. Herman. *Journal of Business*, October.

1965. "The Economist and the State." *American Economic Review*, March.

1965. "Textual Exegesis as a Scientific Problem." *Economica*, November.

1965. "The Dominant Firm and the Inverted Umbrella." *Journal of Law and Economics*, October.

1965. "The Formation of Economic Policy." In *Current Problems in Political Economy*. Greencastle, Ind.: Depauw University.

1966. "The Economic Effects of the Antitrust Laws." *Journal of Law and Economics*, October.

1967. "The Changing Problem of Oligopoly." *Il Politico*, June.

1967. "Imperfections in the Capital Market." *Journal of Political Economy*, June.

1967. "The Foundations and Economics." In *U.S. Philanthropic Foundations*, edited by Warren Weaver. New York: Harper and Row.

1968. "Price and Non-Price Competition." *Journal of Political Economy*, January/February.

1968. Review of *Essays on Economics and Society*, by John Stuart Mill. *University of Toronto Quarterly*, October.

1968. "Competition," "Henry L. Moore." *International Encyclopedia of the Social Sciences*. Vol. 3. Edited by David L. Sills. New York: Macmillan.

1969. (Chairman) "Task Force Report on Productivity and Competition." In *Hearings before the Special Subcommittee on Small Business and the Robinson-Patman Act*. Select Committee on Small Business, Washington, D.C., October 7–9.

1969. "Does Economics Have a Useful Past?" *History of Political Economy*, Fall.

1970. "Director's Law of Public Income Redistribution." *Journal of Law and Economics*, April.

1970. "The Optimum Enforcement of Laws." *Journal of Political Economy*, May/June.

1970. "The Case, if Any, for Economic Literacy." *Journal of Economic Education*, Spring.

1971. "The Theory of Economic Regulation." *Bell Journal of Economics and Management Science*, Spring.

1971. "Smith's Travels on the Ship of State." *History of Political Economy*, Fall.

1972. "The Law and Economics of Public Policy: A Plea to the Scholars." *Journal of Legal Studies*, January.

1972. "The Process of Economic Regulation." *Antitrust Bulletin*, Spring.
1972. "Economic Competition and Political Competition." *Public Choice*, Fall.
1972. "The Adoption of the Marginal Utility Theory." *History of Political Economy*, Fall.
1973. "General Economic Conditions and National Elections." *American Economic Review*, May.
1973. (With James K. Kindahl) "Industrial Prices, as Administered by Dr. Means." *American Economic Review*, September.
1973. "Regulation: The Confusion of Means and Ends." In *Regulating New Drugs*. Chicago: University of Chicago Press.
1974. (With Gary Becker) "Law Enforcement, Malfeasance, and Compensation of Enforcers." *Journal of Legal Studies*, January.
1973. "Free Riders and Collective Action." *Bell Journal of Economics and Management Science*, Autumn.
1974. "Price System." *Encyclopaedia Britannica*. 15th ed.
1975. (With Claire Friedland) "The Citation Practices of Doctorates in Economics." *Journal of Political Economy*, June.
1976. "Do Economists Matter?" *Southern Economic Journal*, January.
1976. "The Sizes of Legislatures." *Journal of Legal Studies*, January.
1976. "The Xistence of X-Efficiency." *American Economic Review*, March.
1976. "The Successes and Failures of Professor Smith." *Journal of Political Economy*, December.
1976. "The Scientific Uses of Scientific Biography, with Special Reference to J. S. Mill." In *James and John Stuart Mill: Papers of the Centenary Conference*, edited by J. M. Robson and M. Laine. Toronto: University of Toronto Press.
1977. (With Gary Becker) "De Gustibus Non Est Disputandum." *American Economic Review*, March.
1978. "The Literature of Economics: The Case of the Kinked Oligopoly Demand Curve." *Economic Inquiry*, April.
1978. "Wealth and Possibly Liberty." *Journal of Legal Studies*, June.
1979. (With Claire Friedland)" The Pattern of Citation Practices in Economics." *History of Political Economy*, Spring.
1980. "An Introduction to Privacy in Economics and Politics." *Journal of Legal Studies*, December.
1980. "Merton on Multiples, Denied and Affirmed." In *Science and Social Structure: A Festschrift for Robert K. Merton*. Transactions of the New York Academy of Sciences, series 2, vol. 39. New York: New York Academy of Sciences.
1981. "Economics or Ethics." In *The Tanner Lectures on Human Values*. Vol. 2. Salt Lake City: University of Utah Press.

Book Reviews
1939. *La Théorie des Besoins de Carl Menger*, by H. S. Block. *American Economic Review*, June.
1939. *Introduction to Economic Analyses*, by A. M. McIsaac and J. G. Smith. *Journal of Political Economy*, June.

1939. *Elements of Modern Economics*, by A. L. Meyers. *Journal of Political Economy*, June.

1940. *A Study on the Pure Theory of Production*, by S. Carlson. *American Economic Review*, June.

1940. *The Control of Competition in Canada*, by L. G. Reynolds. *Journal of Farm Economics*, November.

1941. *Anticipations, Uncertainty and Dynamic Planning*, by A. G. Hart. *American Economic Review*, June.

1941. Review of ten T.N.E.C. monographs. *American Economic Review*, September.

1941. *Economic Analysis*, by K. E. Boulding. *Journal of Political Economy*, December.

1943. *Fiscal Planning for Total War*, by W. L. Crum et al. *Journal of Political Economy*, February.

1943. *National Income and Its Composition 1919–1938, by S. Kuznets. Journal of Farm Economics*, May.

1943. *Entrepreneural Costs and Price*, by G. J. Cady. *Journal of Political Economy*, June.

1943. *Outlay and Income in the U.S.*, by H. Barger. *Journal of Farm Economics*, August.

1943. *Social Science Principles in the Light of Scientific Method*, by J. Mayer. *American Economic Review*, September.

1944. *The Economics of Price Determination*, by C. Clive Saxton. *Journal of Political Economy*, February.

1944. *Wage Determination under Trade Unions*, by J. Dunlop. *Journal of Political Economy*, December.

1945. *Economics of Control*, by A. Lerner. *Political Science Quarterly*, March.

1946. *The Economics of Peace*, by K. Boulding. *Journal of Political Economy*, August.

1946. *Lapses from Full Employment*, by A. C. Pigou. *American Economic Review*, December.

1947. *Large and Small Business*, by J. Steindl. *Journal of Political Economy*, February.

1948. *A National Policy for the Oil Industry*, by E. V. Rostow. *Yale Law Journal*, June.

1948. *Investment, Location, and Size of Plant*, by P. S. Florence. *Journal of Political Economy*, December.

1948. *Pricing, Distribution and Employment*, by J. S. Bain. *American Economic Review*, December.

1948. *The Foundations of Economic Analysis*, by P. A. Samuelson. *Journal of American Statistical Association*, December.

1949. *Labor Productivity Functions in Meat Packing*, by W. H. Nicholls. *Journal of Farm Economics*, February.

1950. *Competition among the Few*, by W. Fellner. *American Economic Review*, September.

1951. *The Dynamic Economy*, by H. Moulton. *Journal of Political Economy*, February.

1951. *The American Cigarette Industry*, by R. Tennant. *Yale Law Journal*, May.

1951. *Divergence between Plant and Company Concentration*, F.T.C. *Journal of American Statistical Association*, September.

1952. *The Theory of Investment of the Firm*, by F. Lutz and V. Lutz. *American Economic Review*, March.

1952. *The Malthusian Controversy*, by K. Smith. *Journal of American Statistical Association*, June.

1952. *The Works and Correspondence of David Ricardo*, edited by P. Sraffa. *Econometrica*, July.

1952. *The Economics of the International Patent System*, by E. Penrose. *Journal of Political Economy*, August.

1953. *The Development of Economic Thought*, edited by H. W. Spiegel. *Kyklos* 6, no. 87.

1954. *Thorstein Veblen: A Critical Interpretation*, by D. Riesman. *The Freeman*, February 8.

1955. *The Logic of British and American Industry*, by P. S. Florence. *Journal of Political Economy*, February.

1956. *The Hard-Surface Floor-Covering Industry*, by R. Lanzilotti. *Journal of Political Economy*, October.

1956. *The Alphabet of Economic Science*, by P. H. Wicksteed. *Econometrica*, October.

1957. *The Meaning and Validity of Economic Theory*, by L. Rogin. *American Economic Review*, March.

1957. *A Revision of Demand Theory*, by J. R. Hicks. *Journal of Political Economy*, April.

1958. *High-Talent Manpower for Science and Industry*, by J. D. Brown and F. Harbison. *Southern Economic Journal*, July.

1959. *Ricardian Economics* by M. Blaug. *Journal of Political Economy*, December.

1961. *The Manchester School of Economics*, by W. D. Grampp. *Economica*, August.

1961. *A History of Economic Thought*, by O. H. Taylor. *American Economic Review*, June.

1963. *Economic Philosophy*, by J. Robinson. *Journal of Political Economy*, April.

1963. *Fabian Socialism and English Politics, 1884–1918*, by A. M. McBriar, *The Story of Fabian Socialism,* by M. Cole. *Victorian Studies*, June.

1965. *Free Trade in Books: A Study of the London Book Trade since 1800*, by James J. Barnes. *Explorations in Entrepreneurial History*, Winter.

1965. *The Business Establishment*, edited by Earl F. Cheit, and *The U.S. Economy*, by John Davenport. *New York Herald Tribune Book Week*, January 31.

1965. *The Great Discount Delusion*, by Walter H. Nelson. *Chicago Tribune*, July 11.

1965. *John Rae: Political Economist*, by R. Warren James. *Journal of Political Economy*, December.

1966. *Principles of Political Economy*, by John Stuart Mill. *Journal of Political Economy*, February.

1966. *Modern Capitalism: The Changing Balance of Public and Private Power*, by Andrew Shonfield. *New York Herald Tribune Book Week*, April 10.

1966. *The Stationary Economy*, by J. E. Meade. *Economica*, November.

1966. *New Dimensions of Political Economy*, by Walter Heller. *New York Review of Books*, December 29.

1967. *Ambassador to the Industrial State*, by J. K. Galbraith. Reith Lectures. *New York Times*, January 28.

1967. *The Travel Diaries of T. R. Malthus*, by Patricia James. *Journal of Political Economy*, February.

1967. *The New Industrial State*, by J. K. Galbraith. *Wall Street Journal*, June 26.

1967. *The Doctor Shortage*, by Rashi Fein. *Science*, December 29.

1968. *The Rich and the Super Rich*, by F. Lundberg. *New York Times*, July 28.

1968. *The Guaranteed Society*, by L. Baker. *Washington Post Book World*, September 8.

1969. *Events, Ideology, and Economic Theory*, by Robert V. Eagly. *Journal of Economic History*, June.

1969. *Think: A Biography of the Watsons and IBM*, by William Rodgers. *Science*, December 12.

1970. *The Evolution of Modern Economic Theory*. by L. Robbins. *Economica*, November.

1977. *Wealth of Nations*, by Adam Smith. *Journal of Political Economy*, February.

1977. *The Early Economic Writings of Alfred Marshall, 1867–1890*, by J. K. Whitaker. *Journal of Economic Literature*, March.

1977. *The Age of Uncertainty* (book and BBC television series), by J. K. Galbraith. *National Review*, May 27.

1978. *On Revolutions and Progress in Economic Knowledge*, by Terence W. Hutchison. *Minerva*, Winter.

1980. *The Politics of Regulation*, by James Q. Wilson. *Wall Street Journal*, August 1.

1981. *The Economics of David Ricardo*, by Samuel Hollander. *Journal of Economic Literature*, March.

Shorter Pieces

1940. Discussion of cost functions. *American Economic Review, Proceedings*, March.

1940. "A Note on Discontinuous Cost Curves." *American Economic Review*, December.

1942. "A Note on Price Discrimination in Steel." *American Economic Review*, June.

1946. "Labor Productivity and Size of Farm: A Statistical Pitfall." *Journal of Political Economy*, August.

1947. "Professor Lester and the Marginalists." *American Economic Review*, March.

1950. Discussion of oligopoly. *American Economic Review, Proceedings*, May.

1951. Discussion of methodology. *American Economic Review, Proceedings*, May.

1952. "The Case Against Big Business." *Fortune*, May.

1954. Introduction to *Business Concentration and Price Policy*. National Bureau of Economic Research. Princeton, N.J.: Princeton University Press.

1955. "Note on Mathematics in Economics." *Review of Economics and Statistics*, August.

1956. Discussion of antitrust policy. *American Economic Review, Proceedings*, May.

1959. Foreword to *Merger Movements in American Industry, 1895–1956*, by R. L. Nelson. National Bureau of Economic Research. Princeton, N.J.: Princeton University Press.

1961. "The Economic Role of the State." *Alumni Association Newsletter*. University of Chicago Graduate School of Business, Winter.

1962. "Archibald versus Chicago." *Review of Economic Studies*, October.

1962. Preface to *Diversification and Integration in American Industry*, by M. Gort. New York: National Bureau of Economic Research.

1962. Comment on "On the Chicago School of Economics," by H. Lawrence Miller, Jr. *Journal of Political Economy*, February.

1963. "Policies for Economic Growth." American Bankers' Association Symposium. Washington, D.C.

1964. "Financial Intermediaries and the Allocation of Capital." Conference of the U.S. Savings and Loan League, Chicago.

1964. "Competition and Concentration." *Challenge*, January.

1965. "The Problem of the Negro." *New Guard*, December.

1966. "Private Enterprise and Public Intelligence." American Bankers' Association Symposium. Washington, D.C.

1966. "The Unjoined Debate." *Chicago Today*, Winter.

1967. "The Economics of Conflict of Interest." *Journal of Political Economy*, February.

1967. "Alice in Fundland." *Barrons*, February 27.

1967. Comment on "The Application of an Entropy Theory of Concentration to the Clayton Act," by M. O. Finkelstein and R. M. Friedberg. *Yale Law Journal*, March.

1969. "Alfred Marshall's Lectures on Progress and Poverty." *Journal of Law and Economics*, April.

1970. Preface to *Risk, Uncertainty and Profit*, by F. H. Knight, Chicago: University of Chicago Press.

1971. (With Claire Friedland) "Profits of Defense Contractors." *American Economic Review*, September.

1972. Discussion on the *Report of the Commission on Financial Structure and Regulation. Journal of Finance*, May.

1973. "A Sketch of the History of Truth in Teaching." *Journal of Political Economy*, March/April.

1973. "In Memoriam: Frank Knight as Teacher." *Journal of Political Economy*, May/June.

1973. "Thought Control on the Campus." Commencement address, Carnegie Mellon University. *Chronicle of Higher Education*, August 13.

1973. "In Memoriam: F. H. Knight." *American Economic Review*, December.

1974. "Henry Calvert Simons." *Journal of Law and Economics*, April.

1975. "Buyer's Prices, Seller's Prices, and Price Flexibility: Reply." *American Economic Review*, June.

1975. Comment on "Determinants of Participation in Presidential Elections," by O. Ashenfelter and S. Kelley, Jr. *Journal of Law and Economics*, December.

1975. Comment on "The Effects of Economic Policies on Votes for the Presidency: Some Evidence from Recent Elections," by A. Meltzer and M. Vellrath. *Journal of Law and Economics*, December.

1977. "The Conference Handbook." *Journal of Political Economy*, February.

1979. "Babbage on Monopoly Price." *History of Economics Society Bulletin*, Winter.

1979. "Why Have the Socialists Been Winning?" *ORDO* 30.

1980. "Malthus on Gluts." *History of Economics Society Bulletin*, Winter.

1980. "Occupational Licensure for Economists?" In *Occupational Licensure and Regulation*, edited by S. Rottenberg. Washington, D.C.: American Enterprise Institute.

1981. "A Historical Note on the Short Run: Marshall and Friedman." *History of Economics Society Bulletin*, Winter.

Index

Abhorrence of Evidence, 86–87
Additive utility, 99
Addyston Pipe case, 45
Adoption of a theory, 76–83
Agricultural classes, 140
Agricultural nation, 9
Alchian, A., 223
Allen, R. G. D., 99
Altruism, 25
American Revolution, 141
Anderson, J., 101
Antitrust division, 47–49
Apprenticeship system, 143
Arnold, T., 47
Arrow, K., 215
Authorities, relationships among, 215–19
Auspitz and Lieben, 79
Austrian school, 116

Babbage, C., 76, 117, 156
Babbage's law, 118
Bain, J. S., 231
Barkai, H., 68–71
Barometric price leader, 228
Barone, E., 79, 99
Baxter, W., 38
Beatzoglou, T., 84
Becker, G., vii, 3, 21, 223
Ben-David, J., 92, 117
Bentham, J., 11, 72, 90, 122, 143
Bergson, A., 216
Bernoulli, D., 74
Black, J., 146
Black, J. D., 180
Blanco, H., 234
Blaug, M., 99, 160
Böhm-Bawerk, E., 79
Bomball, M. R., 229
Boring, E., 112
Bright, J., 64
Bronfenbrenner, M., 226
Buchanan, D., 151
Buchanan, D. H., 155
Buchanan, J., 9

Buffon, G. L., 75
Burns, M., 44

Cairnes, J. E., 15, 79, 131, 164
Cambridge group: England, 217; United States, 217
Campbell, Glenn, 3
Canard, N.-F., 76
Cannan, E., 79, 89–90, 109
Cantillon, R., 157
Capital, hierarchy of employments of, 152–53
Carlyle, T., 28
Cartels, 45, 167
Carter, K., 168
Carver, T. N., 17
Cassel, G., 79
Chamberlin, E. H., 99, 212
Chicago school of economics, 166, 170, 217
Citation practice(s), 173–91, 192–222; transitory nature of, 190
Citations: age of, 177; of articles and books, 175–79; chauvinism in, 220; counts of, 201; favorable and unfavorable, 203, 212–21; influence of schools on, 205–12, 217–18; language of, 189; in monetary and fiscal theory, 208–19; nature of, 173–78, 200; and output, 185–88; in value theory, 202, 206–20
Citees, 181–86, 204–9
Clapham, J., 182
Clark, J. B., 17, 42, 45, 46, 49, 79, 99, 184, 231
Clark, J. D., 42
Clark, J. M., 228
Clayton Act, 45
Coase, R. H., 25, 62, 156, 224
Cobden, R., 64
Coercion, 24
Cohen, K. J., 230
Cole, G. D. H., 176
Cole, J. R., 173
Cole, S., 173
Collins, R., 92

Combination Acts, 40
Comparative costs, theory of, 58, 99
Compensation principle, 96, 161
Competition: ethics of, 14–37; in the issue of bank notes, 94; monopolistic and imperfect, 99, 217, 224; workable, 51
Conjectural variation, 239
Consumer sovereignty, 60
Consumption, productive and unproductive, 94
Controversy, role of, 111
Corn: demand for, 68–71; laws, 64–65
Cossa, L., 87
Cournot, A.-A., 41, 75, 76, 157, 239
Crown lands, 144
Curates, pay of, 137
Currency debasement, 4, 153–54
Cyert, R. M., 230

Dalton, H., 203
Dantes, E., 7
DeGroot, M., 230
Dicey, A. V., 40
Diminishing returns, 101
Director, A., vii, 3, 38, 51, 168, 170
Discoveries, multiple, 98–103, 114–16
Distribution, laws of, 162
Doctorates: by academic affiliation, 196; by primary field, 195; publication by, 197–99; type of employer, 195; by undergraduate school, 194
Dorfman, J., 84
Douglas, P., 166, 185
Downs, A., 9
Dumont, E., 74
Dupuit, J., 41

East India Company, 5–6, 90, 145
Eckstein, O., 203
Economic classes and their political behavior, 138
Economic phenomena, 59
Economic relationships, empirical estimation of, 134
Economic theory of politics, 10
Economic theory of public regulation, 66
Economics: as academic discipline, 76–85; German, 81–82; history of, defined, 107–8; Keynesian, 100, 106; language of, 188–89; monetary and fiscal, 192; teaching of, 61
Economies: external, 135, 156; of scale, 45
Economist as Preacher, 3–13, 119–35

Economists: academic status of, 80–81, 84–85; and growth of state, 126–35; influence of, 46–49, 57–67; most frequently cited, 1886–1925, 182; most frequently cited, 1925–1969, 183; and the problem of monopoly, 38–54
Edgeworth, F. Y., 12, 19, 41, 79, 99, 109, 184
Edgeworth's taxation paradox, 131
Edwards, C., 47
Efficiency, 6–10
Efroymson, C. W., 226–27, 229
Ellert, J., 44
Ely, R. T., 42
Exchange, voluntary, ethical attractiveness of, 22
Ethics, 35–36; inductive, 21
Everett, C. W., 73
Exports, bounty on, 137

Fabian socialists, 13
Fame: and energy, 180; mortality of, 181
Fay, C. R., 64
Federal Trade Commission, 47–49, 169
Fisher, I., 38, 78, 79, 99, 108, 184
Fogel, R., 63
Foreign languages, decline of, 189
Forestallers and engrossers, 137
Fourier, C., 12
Fourier, J. B. J., 75
Fraud, 23–24
Free trade, 7, 130
Friedland, C., vii, 50, 61, 84, 173, 192, 223
Friedman, M., vii, 6, 64, 90, 110, 111, 168, 170, 182, 200, 204, 219
Full cost pricing, 226
Full employment policies, 65

Galbraith, J. K., 43, 57
Gambling, 6
George, H., 33, 117
Gide, C. 84
Gilchrist, G., 203
Godwin, W., 9
Gossen, H., 102, 157
Grampp, W., 40
Gray, A., 108
Grether, E. T., 227

Haberler, G., 218
Hadley, A. T., 43
Hall, R., 99, 225
Hand-picked example, 86

Hand-picked quotation, 69
Hansen, A., 170, 218
Hardy, G. H., 221
Harris, S., 176
Hawtrey, R., 80
Henderson, G. C., 48
Herbst, J., 85
Hicks, J., 99, 203, 204, 216, 218
Hilton, G., 139
Hitch, C., 99, 225
Hobson, J. A., 109
Honesty, 24–25
Howey, R., 79
Human capital, 148
Hume, D., 146, 154
Hutchison, T., 65
Hutton, J., 146
Hyndman, H. M., 79

Ideology, 34–35
"Imagined" demand curve, 225
Implicit Absurdity, 86–87
Income: averaging, 169; distribution, 11–13, 169; redistribution, 63
Inflation, quantity of money theory of, 70
Ingram, J. K., 82
Input-output group, 217
Intellectuals, 32–35
Interlocking directorates, 44
International factor equalization theorem, 99
Ippolito, R., 203

Jaffé, W., 92
Jenks, J. W., 42
Jevons, W. S., 4, 15, 72, 79, 99, 126–27
Johnson, H. G., 168, 218

Kahn, P., 84
Kahn, R. F. (Lord), 224
Kaldor, N., 216
Kalecki, M., 100
Katzman, R. A., 48
Keynes, J. M. (Lord), 65, 170, 204; citations of, 218–19
Keynes, J. N., 15
Keynesian economics, *see* Economics, Keynesian
Kinked oligopoly demand curve, 99, 223–43; empirical tests, 226–30; genesis, 225–26; uses made of, 234–38
Knight, F., 6, 18–19, 66, 166, 167, 170, 212
Knowledge, value-free, 61–62

Kuenne, R. E., 202
Kuhn, T. S., 86, 112, 112–14
Kuznets, S., 185

Labor: division of, 156; productive and unproductive, 150–51
Labor theory of value, 70, 94
Laissez-faire, 15, 125
Lange, O., 109
Laplace, P. S., 75
Lardner, D., 39
Launhardt, W., 81, 99
Leontief, W., 185
Lerner, A., 99, 203, 216
Leslie, T. E. C., 82, 158
Levi, E., 51, 168
Levinson, H. M., 203
Limit pricing, 231
Little, I. M. D., 216
Lloyd, W. F., 76
Local price cutting, 43
Longe, F., 99
Longfield, M., 21, 76, 102, 123
Lovell, M. C., 177
Lower classes, attitudes of, 30–32

Macaulay, T. B., 29, 123
Macgregor, D. H., 42
Malthus, T. R., 6, 9, 14, 76, 88, 99, 152, 155; wage theory of, 88, 157
Margin requirements, 134
Marginal productivity: ethics, 17–19; theory, 17, 99, 109, 163
Marginal utility theory, 99, 150; adoption of, 72–85
Markham, J., 230
Market definition, 51
Market system, 14–19
Marshall, A., 4, 6, 15, 19, 22–23, 41, 43, 65, 68, 79, 87–88, 99, 125, 132, 148, 155, 156, 182, 184, 200, 202; demand curve of, 107; value theory of, 134
Marshallian school, 116
Marx, G., 31
Marx, K., 5, 19, 116
Mason, E. S., 230
May, K., 224, 240
McCulloch, J. R., 40, 64, 122, 126, 151, 152; on post office, 126n
McGee, J. S., 47
McPherson, M., 36
Means, G., 232
Medawar, P., 107

Meek, R., 109
Menger, C., 72, 79, 81, 99, 108
Mercantilism, 10, 148–49; money in, 8
Merton, R. K., 76, 86, 92, 98–103, 112, 114–16, 214, 223; on "Matthew effect," 214
Methodenstreit, 82
Methodology, sermons on, 97
Metzler, L., 218
Middle classes, 31–32
Mill, J., 64, 122
Mill, J. S., 4, 6, 8, 11–12, 14–15, 39, 64, 66, 74, 86–97, 124, 125n, 147, 151, 152, 155; creativity of, 96–97; *Essays on Economics and Society*, 160–65; indocrination of, 93–97
Minimum sacrifice, 12
Minimum wage laws, 7, 15–16, 31
Mints, L., 170
Mistakes, 10, 36
Mitch, D. F., 173
Mixed agricultural-commercial system, 9
Modigliani, F., 231
Monopoly, 7, 24, 145; defined, 40; policy, influence of on economics, 49–52
Moral expectation, 74–76
Muth, J., 182
Myint, Hla, 151

Natural liberty, 7
Navigation Acts, 120
Newton, I., 147
Noncompeting groups, 197

Occupational choice, 34
Oligopoly, 41; theory of, 239
Optimum properties of a price system, 130
Owen, R., 12, 14

Pantaleoni, M., 79
Pareto, V., 78, 79, 117
Parochial loyalty, 209–12
Parrish, J. B., 85
Patinkin, D., 168, 203, 204
Peel, R., 64
Personal exegesis, principle of, 69
Peterman, J., 38
Physiocrats, 101
Pigou, A. C., 12, 18, 19, 108, 127–28, 184, 204
Pinto, J. V., 99
Place, F., 40

Playfair, W., 151
Posner, R., 3, 49
Powell, M., 167
Preaching: definition of, 3–5; equity, 10–13
Predatory competition, 47, 52
Prices: administered, 51; rigidity of, 225–40 passim
Price levels, regional, 94n
Primeaux, W. J., Jr., 229
Primogeniture, 137
Production, laws of, 162
Prosopography, 92
Public good, 145

Quantification, 134–35
Quételet, L. A. J., 75

Rae, J., 146
Rawls, J., 21, 36
Reciprocal demand, 96
"Reflex" demand curve, 227
Rent, theory of, 11–12, 99, 155
Ricardo, D., 4, 7, 11, 14, 39, 58, 64, 68, 77, 94–97, 99, 109, 110, 147, 160
Rist, C., 84
Robbins, L. (Lord), 160
Robertson, D., 60
Robinson, J., 99, 216
Robson, J., 165
Roll, E., 160
"Rotten kid theorem," 21
Ruskin, J., 28

Samuelson, P., 67, 99, 110, 180, 200, 215, 216, 218
Savage, J., 6
Say, J. B., 76, 93
Say's law, 95
Schiff, M., 234
Science: nature of, 98; sociology of, 92, 112–18
Scientific anomalies, 112–13
Scientific discourse, nature of, 238
Scientific exegesis, principle of, 69
Scientific literature, reading of, 108–12
Scientific schools, 116–17
Scientific societies, 117–18
Scientific biography, scientific uses of, 86–97
Schmoller, G., 81
Schumpeter, J., 24, 29, 33–34, 107, 157, 160
Self-citation, 186–88

Self-interest, 136–45, 147; failures of, 144–45
Senior, N., 25, 76, 108, 124, 151, 152
Sharfman, L., 169
Shaw, G. B., 79
Sherman Act, 38–45 passim; attitudes toward, 41–46; success of, 44–46
Shopkeepers, nation of, 148
Sidgwick, H., 15, 19, 41, 41n, 79
Simon, J., 229
Simons, H. C., 43, 166–70
Singlētons, 98
Slavery, 137, 145
Slutsky, E. E., 99
Smith, A., 4–6, 7, 11, 21, 22–23, 25, 33, 38, 63, 108, 119; canons of taxation of, 142; on economic policy, 120–22, 136–45; monetary theory of, 154; on taxation, 139
Smith, M. C., 229
Snapp, B., 38
Solow, R. M., 215
Southey, R., 27–28
Spengler, J., 224
St. Petersburg paradox, 74–76
Stalin, J., 109
Stamp, J. (Lord), 80
State: economic role of, 132–35; and higher education, 32–33
Statute of Labourers, 137
Stephen, L., 87
Stigler, G. J., 9, 76, 93, 114, 173, 212, 227–28
Stigler, S., 3, 38, 224
Stone, L., 92
Streeten, P., 228
Stubbs, B., 111
Sweezy, P., 99, 225–26
Sylos-Labini, P., 231

Taussig, F. W., 79, 88, 150, 180
Tawney, R. H., 170
Taxation: of future increments in land rents, 95; of land, 162; of property incomes, 95
Tax system, just, 65
Taylor, H., 90
Taylor, O. H., 88
Telser, L. G., 47
Tenancy, 144
Ten-hour day, 123
Textbooks, conservative role of, 238

Textual exegesis, 68–71
Theories: adoption of, 76–83; never perish, 239; and policy, 130–35
"Three questions," 146
Thompson, T. P., 64
Thorelli, H., 42
Thornton, W. T., 99, 163
Thünen, J. H. von, 76, 102, 157
Tobin, J., 168
Tocqueville, Alexis de, 161
Torrens, R., 64, 99, 147
Trevou, F., 88
Trust, 148
Tsiang, S. C., 203
Tullock, G., 9
Turgot, A.-R.-J., 101
Turner, D., 48

Usury laws, 57, 122, 145
Utilitarian ethic, 25
Utilitarianism, 19–22
Utility: interpersonal comparisons of, 13; theory of, 12, 36, 72–76, 82–83

Value: measure of, 153–54; paradox of, 150
Value theory, 192
Viner, J., 50, 90, 96, 102, 121, 161, 168, 170

Wages: differentials in rates of, 148; subsistence, theory of, 154–55; truck, 139
Wages-fund theory, 131, 149–50, 162–65; refutation of, 88n, 99
Walker, F. A., 79
Walras, M. E. L., 72, 79, 99, 116, 202
Weaver, S., 48
Weisbrod, S. R., 173
Welfare economics, 62
West, E., 99
Whately, R., 24–25
Whewell, W., 76
Whitney, S., 44
Wicksell, K., 79
Wicksteed, P., 78, 79, 99
Wieser, F. von, 79
Williamson, O., 48
Winch, D. N., 88
Wood, S., 99

Young, A., 156

Zuckerman, H., 92